1001 Words You Need to Know and Use

An A–Z of Effective Vocabulary

Martin H. Manser

OXFORD
UNIVERSITY PRESS

OXFORD
UNIVERSITY PRESS

Great Clarendon Street, Oxford OX2 6DP

Oxford University Press is a department of the University of Oxford.
It furthers the University's objective of excellence in research, scholarship,
and education by publishing worldwide in

Oxford New York

Auckland Cape Town Dar es Salaam Hong Kong Karachi
Kuala Lumpur Madrid Melbourne Mexico City Nairobi
New Delhi Shanghai Taipei Toronto

With offices in

Argentina Austria Brazil Chile Czech Republic France Greece
Guatemala Hungary Italy Japan Poland Portugal Singapore
South Korea Switzerland Thailand Turkey Ukraine Vietnam

Oxford is a registered trade mark of Oxford University Press
in the UK and in certain other countries

Published in the United States
by Oxford University Press Inc., New York

British Library Cataloguing in Publication Data
Data available

Library of Congress Cataloging-in-Publication Data
Data available

Typeset by MPS Limited, A Macmillan Company
Printed in Great Britain
on acid-free paper by
Ashford Colour Press Ltd, Gosport, Hampshire
ISBN 978-0-19-956005-9

10 9 8 7 6 5 4 3 2

Contents

How to use this book

If you are a student writing an essay … if you are in business and need inspiration on how to express yourself in a report or want to persuade colleagues to adopt your proposal … if you are a team leader needing to motivate your staff … if you are a voluntary worker writing a fundraising bid … if you are applying for a job and are preparing your CV … if you are negotiating terms for a contract … if you are writing publicity material … then in each of these settings you need to use words convincingly. In such situations, you may find yourself:

- expressing your opinion
- writing clearly
- discussing a topic
- describing an event
- informing an audience
- talking about yourself
- evaluating a point of view
- speaking in an interview
- motivating personnel

but you may well also find yourself unable to think of words that would be positive and effective. This is the benefit of this book.

You can begin by turning to the **Index**. On the contents page are listed all the headings of the Index. For example, if you are *writing a report*, you can turn to page 162 and you will find a list of words you could use in your report, to help present your explanation or argument in a persuasive way. For example, you could choose *accurate, compelling, enterprise*, or *significant*. By then turning to the main A–Z sequence you will find guidance on the meaning and use of these words.

Each main entry word consists of the following:

headword, part of speech (word class), definition, and examples. The open square symbol '□' is used for clarity to separate multiple parts of speech and multiple example sentences. Where some words are used in particular contexts, e.g. *formal*, this is shown (see for example **propensity**). Many entries also include comments on **Usage** with advice on, for example, similar words, spelling tips, pitfalls to avoid, and words that combine with the headword in particular contexts. Under **Word family** are listed words that are related to the main headword.

important *adjective*
1 having a great effect on people or things; of great value: *Listening is an important part of the job.* **2** (of people or groups) having a lot of power or influence: *Some disabled people hold important jobs in industry.*

Usage **important** or **significant**? *Important* is the more general of these words. Things that are *significant* are important within a particular context or from a particular point of view. *Significant* is often used when someone wants to suggest that the level of importance of something has been measured in some way. Figures can be *statistically significant* but not *statistically important*. *Significant* but not *important* can mean 'great in degree': *a significant* (not: *important*) *proportion of the population*.

Word family **importance** noun: *The signing of the trade agreement was an event of immense importance.* **importantly** adverb: *More importantly, how much will it cost?*

significant *adjective*

large or important enough to have an effect or be noticed: *There are no significant differences between the two groups of students.* □ *The results of the experiment are not statistically significant.* □ *These views are held by a significant proportion of the population.*

Usage **significant** or **important**? See **important**.

Word family **significance** noun: *Tourism is of considerable significance in this area.* **significantly** adverb: *High calcium concentrations in drinking water have been correlated with a significantly reduced risk of developing breast cancer.*

Note that only a selection of the senses of a word that are relevant to this book are included, rather than an exhaustive list of all possible senses.

Note too that in some cases a word relevant to a particular use in the Index may be listed under the **Word family** part of an entry.

Key to pronunciation

A few words show the pronunciation where this might cause difficulty. Foreign pronunciations are shown in the way an English speaker would say them. For example:

penchant *noun*

a strong or habitual liking for something or tendency to do something: *He has a penchant for adopting stray dogs.* □ *the company's penchant for system integration.*

Usage The word *penchant* is pronounced **pon**-shon.

Pronunciations are divided into syllables by means of hyphens. The main stress is shown in **bold** type.

List of respelling symbols

Vowels	Examples	Vowels	Examples
a	as in **cat**	oh	as in **most**
ah	as in **calm**	oi	as in **join**
air	as in **hair**	oo	as in **soon**
ar	as in **bar**	oor	as in **poor**
aw	as in **law**	or	as in **corn**
ay	as in **say**	ow	as in **cow**
e	as in **bed**	oy	as in **boy**
ee	as in **meet**	u	as in **cup**
eer	as in **beer**	uh	as in the 'a' in **along**
er	as in **her**	uu	as in **book**
ew	as in **few**	y	as in **cry**
i	as in **pin**	yoo	as in **unit**
I	as in **eye**	yoor	as in **Europe**
o	as in **top**		

Consonants	Examples	Consonants	Examples
b	as in **bat**	p	as in **pram**
ch	as in **chin**	r	as in **red**
d	as in **day**	s	as in **sit**
f	as in **fat**	sh	as in **shop**
g	as in **get**	t	as in **top**
h	as in **hat**	th	as in **thin**
j	as in **jam**	th	as in **this**
k	as in **king**	v	as in **van**
kh	as in **loch**	w	as in **will**
l	as in **leg**	y	as in **yes**
m	as in **man**	z	as in **zebra**
ng	as in **sing**, **finger**	zh	as in **vision**
nk	as in **thank**		

The author's website: www.martinmanser.com

Acknowledgements

The author wishes to thank Gloria Wren for her meticulous typing of the text and Ben Harris at Oxford University Press for his encouragement at every stage of the book's production.

Aa

able *adjective*
1 with the power, skill, or means to do something: *He was able to read Greek at the age of eight.* **2** having considerable skill, proficiency, or intelligence: *a very able public speaker.*
Usage **able**, **capable**, or **competent**? If you describe someone as *able,* you emphasize the intellectual capacity: *The university attracts able students from across the world.* Describing someone as *capable* conveys a sense of confidence that a task entrusted to them will be done well: *She delegated management tasks to her highly capable deputy.* Someone described as *competent* has the necessary skills or knowledge to perform a certain task: *a team of competent trainers.*
Word family **ability** noun **ably** adverb

abundant *adjective*
1 existing or available in large quantities; plentiful: *There was abundant evidence to support the theory.* **2** (**abundant in**) having plenty of: *riverbanks abundant in beautiful wild plants.*
Word family **abundance** noun: *The tropical island boasts an abundance of wildlife.* **abundantly** adverb extremely: *She made her wishes abundantly clear.*

accelerate *verb*
1 to start to go faster: *The car accelerated to overtake me.* **2** to make something happen faster or sooner than expected: *The key question is whether stress accelerates ageing.*
Usage The opposite, *decelerate,* is used in more formal, especially written, contexts than *accelerate*: *Economic growth decelerated sharply in January.*
Word family **acceleration** noun: *a car with good acceleration.* □ *an acceleration in the rate of growth.*

accentuate *verb*
to make more noticeable or prominent; to emphasize: *A deep tan accentuated his blue eyes.*
Word family **accentuation** noun: *The conflict led to an accentuation of social divisions.*

access *noun, verb*
noun **1** the way or means of approaching or entering a place: *The staircase gives access to the top floor.* **2** the right or opportunity to use something or to see something: *We grant awards to help people gain access to good training.* □ *verb* **1** to enter a place: *Single rooms have private facilities accessed via the balcony.* **2** to obtain data stored in a computer: *the program used to access the data.*
Usage The verb *access* is standard and common in computing and related terminology. But its use outside computing contexts, although well established, is sometimes criticized as being 'jargon': *You must use a password to access the account.* If you want an alternative, you could use a word or phrase such as *enter* or *gain access to*: *to gain access to the information.*

accessible *adjective*
1 able to be reached or used: *The building has been made accessible to disabled people.* **2** friendly and easy to talk to; approachable: *He is more accessible than most tycoons.* **3** easily understood or enjoyed; clear: *The programme tries to make science more accessible to young people.*
Word family **accessibility** noun: *Internet accessibility is available.* □ *to monitor the accessibility of information.*

acclaim *verb, noun*
verb to praise enthusiastically and publicly: *The car was acclaimed as the best in its class.* □ *noun* enthusiastic public praise: *She has won international acclaim for her commitment to democracy.*

a

Word family *acclaimed* adjective: *a widely acclaimed novelist.*

accolade *noun*
something given as a special honour or as a reward for excellence: *He was finally awarded the ultimate accolade—British Hairdresser of the Year, 2007.*

accomplish *verb*
to succeed in doing or completing something: *The first part of the plan has been safely accomplished.*

Word family *accomplished* adjective having become very good at something through training or experience; expert: *He was an accomplished linguist, fluent in six languages.*

accomplishment *noun*
something impressive that has been done or achieved after a lot of work: *The reduction of inflation was a remarkable accomplishment.*

Usage *accomplishment* or *achievement*? *Accomplishment* is often used to describe a great success which has benefited others, especially in politics, and in contexts in which important intentions or discoveries are described: *the technical accomplishment of modern medicine. Achievement* is usually used to describe a person's academic, professional, artistic, or sporting success: *It was an extraordinary achievement for such a young player.*

accountability *noun*
the fact of being responsible for your decisions and expected to explain them when asked: *There have been proposals for greater police accountability.*

Word family *accountable* adjective: *Ministers were held accountable to parliament for the food shortage.*

accredited *adjective*
officially recognized or approved; working with official permission: *The former business school is now a fully accredited university.*

Word family *accreditation* noun: *the accreditation of engineering qualifications.*

accurate *adjective*
correct in every detail: *Accurate records must be kept at all times.*

Usage *accurate*, *exact*, or *precise*? An *accurate* statement has been put together with great care and corresponds to the facts:

an accurate and intelligible technical drawing. Exact emphasizes that something has been definitely identified, with no margin for vagueness or error: *We may never know the exact number of deaths. Precise* refers to minute attention to detail and implies that something can be measured or quantified: *We have no precise details of job losses yet.*

Word family *accuracy* noun: *They questioned the accuracy of the information. accurately* adverb: *The article accurately reflects public opinion.*

achieve *verb*
to succeed in bringing about or reaching a desired object or result by effort, skill, or courage: *He achieved his ambition to become a press photographer.*

Usage *achievement* or *accomplishment*? See **accomplishment**.

active *adjective*
1 always busy doing things, especially physical activities: *Although he's nearly 80, he is still very active.* **2** giving a lot of time or attention to something; making a determined effort and not leaving something to happen by itself: *They take an active part in school life.* **3** doing something regularly; functioning: *sexually active teenagers.*

Usage The opposites of *active* in sense **2** are *inactive* and *passive*: *The area has a large, but politically inactive population.* □ *He played a passive role in the relationship.*

activist *noun*
a person who works to achieve political or social change, especially as a member of an organization with particular aims: *Gay activists marched in London today to protest against the new law.*

Usage *activist* or *campaigner*? In many cases, you can use either word: *a human-rights/pro-democracy activist/campaigner.* An *activist* is likely to belong to an organization with particular aims, especially representing a particular group of people: *union activists.* A *campaigner* may belong to an organization or may work as an individual, sometimes for a specific aim: *He has long been a campaigner for better communication between doctors and patients.*

adapt *verb*
to change something in order to make it suitable for a new use or situation: *Most of*

these tools have been specially adapted for use by disabled people. □ These styles can be adapted to suit individual tastes.
Usage **adaptable** or **flexible**? Adaptable is used more to describe how people, animals, etc. manage when conditions change in the longer term, e.g. if the climate becomes much colder or warmer: The spider plant is perhaps the most adaptable of houseplants. Flexible is used especially to describe working situations in which people and systems need to be able to change frequently to suit conditions such as customer requirements or financial restrictions: job sharing and other flexible working arrangements.
Word family **adaptability** noun **adaptable** adjective able to change or be changed in order to deal successfully with new situations: Older workers can be as adaptable and quick to learn as anyone else.

adjust verb

to change something slightly to make it more suitable for a new set of conditions or to make it work better: This button is for adjusting the volume.
Usage **adjust** or **modify**? The word adjust is used especially to talk about changing the setting on a piece of equipment: to adjust the speed. It is often a continuous process, in response to changing conditions: to adjust the settings constantly. Modify is used especially to talk about making a more permanent change to a piece of equipment in order to make it perform a new function. You can also either adjust or modify your language or behaviour according to the situation you find yourself in.
Word family **adjustable** adjective: fully adjustable seat belts. **adjustment** noun: I've made a few adjustments to the design.

admire verb

1 to respect someone for what they are or for what they have done: I admire your courage. 2 to look at something that is attractive and/ or impressive: He stood back to admire his handiwork.
Usage **admire** or **respect**? Admire expresses a stronger feeling than respect. If you admire someone, it usually means you agree with them and/or want to be like them: You have to admire the way he handled the situation. If you respect someone you might not agree

with them or want to be like them, but you still recognize their good qualities: These academics may be respected as experts in their field, but they can also be quite arrogant.
Word family **admirable** adjective: She made her point with admirable clarity. **admiration** noun: I have great admiration for her as a writer. **admiring** adjective: She was used to receiving admiring glances from men.

advance noun, verb

noun progress or development in a particular activity or area of understanding: We live in an age of rapid technological advance. □ verb 1 (of knowledge or technology) to develop and improve: Our knowledge of the disease has advanced considerably in recent years. 2 to help something to succeed; to further: They worked together to advance the cause of democracy. 3 to suggest an idea, a theory, or a plan for other people to discuss: The article advances a new theory to explain changes in climate.
Usage The noun advance or advances is used especially to refer to scientific, technological, and medical achievements.
Word family **advanced** adjective 1 using the most recent technology, methods, or designs: Even in advanced technological societies, poverty persists. 2 (of a course of study) at a high or difficult level: There were only three of us on the advanced course. **advancement** noun (formal) the process of helping something to make progress or succeed; progress, e.g. in a job or social class: There are good opportunities for advancement if you have the right skills.

advantage noun

a condition or factor that puts someone or something in a more favourable position: Our technology will give you a competitive advantage.
Word family **advantaged** adjective being in a good social or financial position: We aim to improve opportunities for the less advantaged in society. **advantageous** adjective good or useful for a particular person or group: An agreement would be advantageous to both sides. **take advantage of** 1 to make unfair use of something for your own benefit: You mustn't let them take advantage of your generosity. 2 to make good use of the opportunities offered by something: He took advantage of his colleague's absence and tidied his office.

a

adventure *noun*
1 an unusual, exciting, and daring experience: *his recent adventures in Italy.* **2** excitement arising from this: *She travelled the world in search of adventure.*
Word family **adventurer** *noun* a person who enjoys exciting new experiences, especially going to unusual places: *He's a born adventurer.* **adventurous** *adjective* **1** (of a person) willing to try new things or enjoying being in exciting new situations: *For the most adventurous tourists, there are trips into the mountains with a local guide.* **2** (of a thing) new and exciting or unusual and sometimes dangerous: *The menu contained traditional favourites as well as more adventurous dishes.*

advice *noun*
an opinion or a suggestion about what someone should do in a particular situation: *Can you give me some advice on where to buy good maps?*
Usage *Advice* is usually given by someone with greater experience or authority than the person they are advising. If you say *take my advice* to someone who is older or more experienced than you, they may be offended.
Usage **advise** or **recommend**? See **recommend**.
Word family **advisable** *adjective* sensible and a good idea to achieve something: *Early booking is advisable.* **advise** *verb* to tell someone what they should do in a particular situation: *I'd advise you not to go out on your own.* **adviser** *noun* a person who gives advice, especially someone who knows a lot about a particular subject: *As your legal adviser, it is my duty to warn you against it.* **advisory** *adjective* having the role of giving professional advice: *He acted in a purely advisory capacity.*

advocate *verb, noun*
verb to request or recommend something publicly: *The group does not advocate the use of violence.* □ *noun* **1** a person who supports a speaker in favour of someone or a public plan or action: *a staunch advocate of free speech.* **2** a person who defends someone in court: *Those charged should be represented by trained, qualified legal advocates.*

affinity *noun*
1 (*formal*) a strong feeling that you understand and like someone or something: *He has a natural affinity with animals and birds.*
2 a close relationship between two people or things that have similar qualities, structures, or features: *There is a close affinity between Spanish and Italian.*

affirm *verb*
1 to state emphatically or publicly: *He affirmed the country's commitment to peace.* **2** to declare your support for; to uphold or defend: *The charter affirmed the rights of national minorities.* **3** to value someone highly; to recognize: *Children need to be affirmed by their parents.*
Usage **affirm** or **assert**? You *affirm* something in order to reassure people that it is true. You *assert* something when you want other people to believe and support you: *I can affirm no one will lose their job.* □ *He asserted he had no intention of resigning.*
Word family **affirmation** *noun*: *an affirmation of basic human values.*

agenda *noun*
a list of items to be discussed at a meeting: *The next item on the agenda is the publicity budget.*
Usage The phrase *hidden agenda* is used with disapproval to refer to the secret intentions behind what someone says or does: *There may be a hidden agenda behind this new proposal.*

agree *verb*
1 to have the same opinion as another person or people: *I agree with your analysis.* **2** to be willing to accept or do something suggested by another person: *Do you think they'll agree to my proposal?* **3** (of two or more people) to decide on something: *Can we agree a price?* **4** (**agree with**) to be consistent with: *Your body language doesn't agree with what you are saying.*
Usage **agree** or **approve**? To *agree* is to say that you will do what someone wants or that you will allow something to happen: *He agreed to let me go early.* To *approve* is to officially agree a plan, suggestion, or request: *The committee unanimously approved the plan.*
Word family **agreeable** *adjective*
1 enjoyable and pleasant. **2** willing to agree to do something: *Do you think they will be agreeable to our proposal?* **3** able to be agreed on; acceptable: *a compromise which is agreeable to both employers and unions.*

agreement *noun*: *An agreement was finally reached between management and employees.*

aim *noun, verb*
noun what someone is trying to achieve; what something is supposed to achieve: *Our main aim is to increase sales.* □ *verb* **1** to try or plan to achieve a particular goal: *The government is aiming at a 50% reduction in unemployment.* **2** to direct someone at something as an aim: *These measures are aimed at preventing violent crime.* **3** (of a product, service, or remark) to direct at a particular person or group; to intend for: *The book is aimed at young children.*
Usage **aim** or **purpose**? Your *aim* is what you want to achieve. Your *purpose* for doing something is your reason for doing it. *She set out the company's aims in her speech.* □ *The main purpose of the campaign is to raise money.*

alive *adjective*
1 continuing in existence or use: *Fortunately the old recipes are still very much alive.* **2** alert and active; animated: *Ken comes alive when he hears his music played.* **3** having interest and meaning: *We hope we will make history come alive for the children.* **4** (**alive to**) aware of and interested in; responsive to: *She was always alive to new ideas.*
Usage The word *alive* is not used in front of a noun.

all-purpose *adjective*
that can be used for several different purposes: *Cheddar is an all-purpose cheese for cooking and eating.*
Usage **all-purpose** or **multi-purpose**? Both words are used only before nouns. *Multi-purpose* is a more positive word than *all-purpose* and emphasizes how useful and versatile a thing is: *The concert hall is actually a multi-purpose building that serves as a theatre, exhibition hall, and community centre.* An *all-purpose* thing is more likely to be something quite ordinary that you just use for everything because you cannot afford or cannot be bothered to make or get something different for each purpose: *Each child had one pair of all-purpose shoes. All-purpose* is used more in American English.

all-round *adjective*
1 having very many abilities or uses; versatile: *an all-round artist.* **2** in many or all respects: *his all-round excellence.* **3** on or from every side

or in every direction: *The car's large glass area provides excellent all-round vision.*
Usage The word *all-round* is only used before a noun. In American English, the equivalent is *all-around.*
Word family **all-rounder** *noun* a person with a wide range of skills and abilities.

alter *verb*
1 to make different: *This development will alter the character of the town.* **2** to become different: *He had not altered greatly in the last ten years.*
Usage **alter** or **change**? *Change* is used more widely and frequently than *alter. Change* often suggests a complete change, whereas *alter* can suggest a smaller change: *The law needs to be altered* (= changed slightly to improve it). □ *The law needs to be changed* (= changed completely). *Alter* is also used when something does not change: *It doesn't alter the way I feel.*
Word family **alteration** *noun*: *The dress will not need much alteration.*

alternative *noun, adjective*
noun something that you can choose to have or do out of two or more possibilities: *There is a vegetarian alternative on the menu every day.* □ *adjective* **1** that can be used instead of something else: *Do you have an alternative solution?* **2** different from the usual or traditional way of doing something: *people attracted to alternative lifestyles.*
Usage **alternative**, **choice**, or **option**? *Alternative* is slightly more formal than *option; choice* is slightly less formal than *choice. Choice* is most often used for 'the freedom to choose', although you can sometimes use *option* (but not *alternative*): *She doesn't have much option but to learn.*
Word family **alternatively** *adverb*

amaze *verb*
to surprise very much: *What amazes me is how long she managed to hide it from us.*
Usage **amaze** or **astonish**? In most cases, you can use either word. If you are talking about something that both surprises you and makes you feel ashamed, you should use *astonish*: *He was astonished by his own stupidity.*
Word family **amazed** *adjective*: *She was amazed how little he had changed.* **amazement** *noun*: *To my amazement, he was able to recite the whole poem from memory.* **amazing**

adjective very surprising, especially in a way that makes you feel pleasure or admiration: *An amazing number of people registered.*

ambition *noun*
1 a strong desire to do or achieve something: *Her ambition was to become a model.* **2** desire and determination to achieve success: *young men and women with ambition.*
Usage **ambition** or **aspiration**? An *ambition* is usually a particular thing, often connected with success in your career. *Aspirations* are more general than *ambitions*: *aspirations* are all the things you hope to achieve in life, considered especially in terms of material possessions and social and career success.
Word family **ambitious** *adjective*
1 determined to achieve success: *a ruthlessly ambitious business executive.* **2** requiring a great deal of effort, time, or money to succeed: *an ambitious six-year development plan.*

amenable *adjective*
1 willing to cooperate or be influenced to do something; easy to control: *The manager was very amenable: nothing was too much trouble.* **2** (**amenable to**) able to be affected by: *conditions that are amenable to medical intervention.*
Usage The word *amenable* is used in rather formal, especially written, contexts, and is used showing that you feel approval or admiration for this quality.
Word family **amenability** *noun*

amend *verb*
to change a law, document, or statement slightly in order to correct a mistake or improve it: *He asked to see the amended version.*
Word family **amendment** *noun*: *Parliament passed the bill without further amendment.*

amenity *noun*
1 a feature that makes a place pleasant, comfortable, or easy to live in: *The property is situated in a convenient location, close to all local amenities.* **2** the pleasantness or attractiveness of a place: *Gravel working means lorries, dust, noise, and a general loss of amenity.*

analogy *noun*
a comparison of one thing or another that has similar features, especially in order to explain

it: *The teacher drew an analogy between the human heart and a pump.*
Word family **analogous** *adjective* comparable in certain respects: *Sleep has often been thought of as being in some way analogous to death.*

analyse *verb*
to examine the nature of something, especially by separating it into its parts, in order to understand or explain it: *The job involves gathering and analysing data.*
Word family **analysis** *noun*: *an analysis of popular culture.* **analyst** *noun* a person whose job is to watch and consider events and situations in a particular area such as finance or politics so that they can give an opinion on them: *City analysts forecast pre-tax profits of £40 billion this year.* **analytical** *adjective*: *an analytical mind/approach.*

animated *adjective*
1 full of life or excitement: *an animated conversation.* **2** (of a film) made to look as if pictures are moving: *an animated version of a classic fairy tale.*
Word family **animation** *noun*: *They started talking with animation.*

announce *verb*
to tell people officially about a decision or plans: *They haven't formally announced their engagement yet.*
Usage **announce** or **declare**? *Announce* is used more for giving facts; *declare* is used more for giving judgements: *The company's financial results were announced this afternoon.* □ *The painting was declared to be a forgery.*
Word family **announcement** *noun*: *An announcement by the minister is expected this afternoon.*

anticipate *verb*
1 to believe that something will happen or that someone will do something: *We don't anticipate any major problems.* **2** to see what might happen in the future and try to take action to prepare for it: *We need someone who can anticipate and respond to changes in the fashion industry.*
Usage Some people prefer to limit the use of *anticipate* to sense **2** as there is a risk of ambiguity in certain contexts, e.g. *I anticipated his resignation,* which could mean 'I expected it' or 'I expected and took action to prepare for it'.

Word family **anticipation** noun: People are buying extra groceries in anticipation of heavy snowstorms.

apparent *adjective*
1 clearly seen or understood; obvious: She laughed for no apparent reason. 2 seeming real, but not necessarily so: his apparent lack of concern.
Word family **apparently** adverb as far as you know or can see: The child nodded, apparently content with the promise.

appeal *verb, noun*
verb 1 to make a serious or heartfelt request: Police are appealing for information about the incident. 2 to be attractive or interesting: It's a book that appeals to people of all ages.
□ noun 1 a serious or heartfelt request: His mother made an appeal for the return of the ring. 2 the quality of being attractive or interesting: the popular appeal of football.
Word family **appealing** adjective attractive or interesting: Village life is somehow more appealing.

applaud *verb*
to express praise for someone or something because you strongly approve of them: We applaud his decision not to resign.
Usage This verb is not usually used in progressive tenses: I applaud her [not: I am applauding her] for having the courage to refuse.

applicable *adjective*
directly connected with someone or something; likely to be true of someone or something: The same considerations are equally applicable to accident claims.
Word family **applicability** noun

applied *adjective*
(especially of a subject or study) used in a practical way: applied mathematics.
Usage The word applied is usually used before a noun. The opposites are theoretical and pure, which are used to describe subjects that people study to increase their knowledge of the subject rather than to use that knowledge in a practical way: to study technology as opposed to pure science.

apply *verb*
1 to make a formal request, usually in writing, for something such as a job or a place at a

college or university: You can apply for the position by letter or online. 2 to be relevant: The regulations apply to all member states.
3 (**apply yourself**) to put all your effort into a task: If he applied himself, he could be the best in the world.
Word family **applicant** noun a person who is applying for something such as a job or a place at a college or university: There were over 500 applicants for the job. **application** noun 1 a formal, often written request for something, such as a job, permission to do something, or a place at a college or university: We put in our planning application over six weeks ago.
2 the practical use of something, especially a theory, discovery, or invention: This essay examines the application of new technology to teaching.

appoint *verb*
to choose someone for a job, especially an important one, or for a position of responsibility: They have appointed a new principal at my son's school.
Word family **appointment** noun: She took up an appointment as head of communications.

appraisal *noun*
an assessment of the quality, performance, or nature of something: She carried out a thorough appraisal of the work.
Usage Appraisal is also the usual term in British English for a performance review, a meeting in which an employee discusses with their manager how well they have been doing their job: I've got my appraisal tomorrow.
Word family **appraise** verb 1 to assess the quality or nature of: There is a need to appraise existing techniques. 2 to give an employee an appraisal.

appreciate *verb*
1 to recognize the full worth of: She feels that he doesn't appreciate her. 2 to be grateful for; to welcome: I'd appreciate any information you can give me. 3 to understand a situation fully; to grasp the full implications of: I don't think you appreciate the difficulties we are facing.
Word family **appreciation** noun: Candidates should have a broad appreciation of contemporary issues. **appreciative** adjective feeling or sharing gratitude or pleasure: They were the most appreciative audience we'd played to.

a

approach *verb, noun*

verb to start to deal with in a particular way; to tackle: *you must approach the matter with caution.* □ *noun* **1** a way of dealing with something: *the traditional British approach to controlling air pollution.* **2** an initial proposal or request: *Doctors are considering an approach to the High Court.*

Word family **approachable** *adjective* friendly and easy to talk to: *Most students said they found the staff approachable.*

appropriate *adjective*

acceptable or correct for a particular situation or person: *Jeans are not appropriate for a formal interview.*

Usage The word *appropriate* may convey pleasure or satisfaction at the particular relevance of something: *It is appropriate that healing should still be considered important in the village where the Red Cross was born.* It can also be used to persuade others, sometimes by slight subterfuge, to agree with you that something is desirable: *We consider it is now appropriate to consult interested individuals and agencies.*

Usage **appropriate** or **suitable**? See **suitable**.
Word family **appropriately** *adverb*

approve *verb*

1 to agree officially to or accept as satisfactory: *The budget was approved by parliament.* **2** (**approve of**) to think that someone or something is good, acceptable, or suitable: *His boss doesn't approve of his party-boy lifestyle.*

Usage **approve** or **agree**? See **agree**.
Word family **approval** *noun*: *Proposals for the new licensing system will now go forward to the ministry for approval.* **approving** *adjective* showing that you think someone or something is good or acceptable: *He gave me an approving nod.*

apt *adjective*

suitable for a particular situation: *The theme could not be more apt.*
Word family **aptly** *adverb*: *the aptly named Grand Hotel.*

aptitude *noun*

a natural ability to do something well: *children with an aptitude for painting and drawing.*
Usage The word is used in rather formal, especially written, contexts.

Word family **aptitude test** *noun* a test designed to show whether someone has the natural ability for a particular job or educational course.

arbitrate *verb*

to officially settle an argument or disagreement between two people or groups: *The board has the power to arbitrate in disputes.*
Word family **arbitration** *noun*: *Both sides in the dispute agreed to go to arbitration.*
arbitrator *noun* a person who is chosen to settle a dispute: *When no agreement can be reached, the matter will be referred to an independent arbitrator.*

archetype *noun*

the most typical or perfect example of a particular kind of person or thing: *She is the archetype of an American movie star.*
Usage *Archetype* is not usually used with words that describe qualities such as *kindness* or *style*. It is more often used with concrete nouns to refer to how people and things match what we expect from someone or something of a particular class, profession, or type.
Word family **archetypal** *adjective*: *Blackpool is the archetypal British seaside resort.*

ardent *adjective*

very enthusiastic; passionate: *an ardent supporter of organic agriculture.*
Usage The word *ardent* is used in rather formal, especially written, contexts.
Word family **ardently** *adverb* **ardour** *noun*: *The rebuff did little to dampen his ardour.*

arena *noun*

a place or scene of activity, debate, or conflict: *He has re-entered the political arena.*
Usage The word *arena* is more commonly used in written than spoken contexts and especially where there is opposition between different groups or countries: *Space became an arena for global competition between the United States and the Soviet Union.*

argue *verb*

1 to give reasons or evidence in support of something: *Sociologists argue that inequalities in industrial societies are being reduced.* **2** to speak angrily to someone because you disagree with them: *We're always arguing with each other about money.*
Word family **arguable** *adjective* **1** able to be argued or asserted: *It is arguable that the*

company was already experiencing problems.
2 open to disagreement: *a highly arguable
assumption.* **argument** noun **1** a reason or set
of reasons that someone uses to show that
something is true or correct: *There are strong
arguments for and against childhood
vaccinations.* **2** an angry disagreement.

aroma *noun*
a pleasant, fairly strong smell, especially of
food or drinks such as coffee: *the tantalizing
aroma of fresh coffee.*
Usage **aroma**, **fragrance**, or **scent**? All three
words describe a pleasant smell. *Aroma* is a
fairly strong smell, especially of food, or drink
such as coffee: *The aroma of fresh coffee
wafted toward them.* *Fragrance* is a pleasant
smell, for example of flowers or fruit: *These
flowers were chosen for their delicate fragrance.*
Scent is a light, pleasant smell: *The air was
filled with the scent of wild herbs.*
Word family **aromatic** *adjective*: *aromatic
oils/herbs.*

arrange *verb*
1 to put tidily or in a particular order: *The
columns are arranged in rows.* **2** to organize or
plan something: *A news conference was hastily
arranged.*
Word family **arrangement** *noun*
1 (usually **arrangements**): *I made
arrangements for them to be met at the airport.*
2 an agreement to do something. **3** something
that has been arranged in a neat or
attractive way.

array *noun*
a group or collection of things or people,
often one that is large or impressive: *There is a
vast array of literature on the subject.*
Usage The word *array* is usually used with an
adjective that suggests that the large number
of things makes a strong impression on
someone: *faced with a bewildering array of
choices.*

arrest *verb*
to attract the attention of: *The church's
stillness arrested her.*
Word family **arresting** *adjective* striking; eye-
catching: *At 6 ft 6 in he was an arresting figure.*
□ *another arresting performance by the movie
star.* **arrestingly** *adverb*: *arrestingly beautiful.*

articulate *adjective, verb*
adjective **1** (of a person) good at expressing
ideas or feelings clearly in words: *He was
unusually articulate for a ten-year-old.* **2** (of
speech) clearly expressed or pronounced: *All
we could hear were loud sobs, but no articulate
words.* □ *verb* **1** to pronounce clearly and
distinctly: *He articulated each word with
precision.* **2** to express clearly in words: *The
president articulated the feelings of the majority.*
Word family **articulately** *adverb*

artistic *adjective*
1 having natural creative skill: *He applied his
artistic abilities to connect with his family's
cultural heritage.* **2** relating to or characteristic
of art or artists: *an artistic temperament.*
3 pleasing to look at: *artistic designs.*
Word family **artistically** *adverb* **artistry** *noun*
the skill of an artist: *I admired her exquisite
musical artistry.*

ascertain *verb*
to find out for certain the facts of a situation:
*an attempt to ascertain the cause of the
accident.*
Usage **ascertain** or **establish**? *Ascertain* is an
even more formal way of saying *establish*.
However, *establish* is usually only used in the
context of official or scientific investigations;
ascertain can also be used when you are trying
to find out about someone's intentions and
feelings, although it is still very formal: *Could
you ascertain whether she will be coming to the
meeting?* □ *The police have established that his
injuries were caused by a fall.*

aspect *noun*
1 a particular part or feature of something:
*a training course covering all aspects of the
business.* **2** a particular appearance or quality:
*The black eyepatch gave his face a sinister
aspect.* **3** the side of a building facing a
particular direction: *a summer house with a
southern aspect.*
Usage In grammar, *aspect* is also used to
show the form of a verb. There are three
aspects in English: the progressive or
continuous aspect (expressing duration,
typically using the auxiliary verb *be* with a
form in *–ing*, as in *I was reading a book*), the
perfect (expressing completed action,
typically using the auxiliary verb *have* with a
past participle, as in *I have read the book*), and
unmarked aspect (as in *He reads books*).

aspire *verb*
to have a strong desire to achieve or become
something: *She aspired to a scientific career.*
Word family **aspiration** *noun* (usually
aspirations) a strong desire to do or have
something: *He never had any aspirations to
enter politics.* **aspiring** *adjective*: *advice to
aspiring writers.*

assert *verb*
to state clearly and firmly that something is
true: *She continued to assert her innocence.*
Usage **assert** or **affirm**? See **affirm**.
Word family **assertion** *noun* a statement of
an opinion that you strongly believe to be
true, although it has not been proved:
*I questioned his assertion that the risk was
minimal.*

assertive *adjective*
expressing opinions or desires strongly and
with confidence, so that people take notice:
*You need to learn to be assertive and stand up
for your rights.*
Usage **assertive** or **forceful**? *Assertive*
emphasizes the confidence you have. *Forceful*
emphasizes that you are strongly trying to
persuade other people to believe the opinions
that you express clearly and firmly. Note that
both adjectives are used with approval in
contrast to the adjectives *aggressive* and
pushy. Those words are usually disapproving
in tone and are used to describe someone
who is trying too hard and may appear rude.
Word family **assertiveness** *noun*: *an
assertiveness training programme for women
managers.*

assess *verb*
1 to evaluate or estimate the nature, ability,
or quality of: *The committee must assess the
relative importance of the issues.* 2 to calculate
or estimate the price or value of: *The damage
was assessed at £5 billion.* 3 to test a student's
knowledge or ability by giving them written
work, examinations, or practical exercises:
*Students will be assessed on their use of these
skills.*
Word family **assessment** *noun*: *undertake a
detailed assessment of students' abilities.*

asset *noun*
a useful or valuable thing or person, especially
because they help you to be successful: *She'll
be a great asset to any company she works for.*

Usage The *assets* of a person or company are
the property owned by them. The opposite of
asset is *liability*. The *liabilities* of a person or
company are the amount of money they owe.
A *liability* is also a person or thing that causes
a lot of problems: *Since his injury, Jones has
become more of a liability than an asset to
the team.*

assiduous *adjective*
(*formal*) showing or done with great care and
thoroughness: *She was assiduous in pointing
out every feature.*
Word family **assiduity** *noun* **assiduously**
adverb

assign *verb*
1 to give someone something that they can
use, or to give them a task or responsibility:
*Work duties were assigned at the beginning of
the shift.*
Word family **assignment** *noun* a task that
someone is given to do, usually as part of
their job or studies: *You will be expected to
complete three written assessments.*

assist *verb*
to make it easier or possible for someone to
achieve something by doing something for
them: *I spend much of my time assisting
the chef.*
Usage The word *assist* is a more formal word
for *help*. It is used in rather formal, especially
written, contexts. It can also be used
specifically to show that someone plays a
subordinate role in a joint action: *A
subcommittee should be appointed to assist the
chairman.*
Word family **assistance** *noun*: *The work was
completed with the assistance of carpenters.*
assistant *noun* 1 a person who ranks below a
senior person. 2 a person who provides help
in a particular role or type of work: *an
administrative assistant.*

associate *verb, noun*
verb to connect in your mind: *I associated
wealth with freedom.* □ *noun* a work partner or
colleague: *The bank was run by his business
associate.*
Usage **associate** or **colleague**? See **colleague**.
Usage **associate**, **connect**, or **relate**? When
you *associate* two things in your mind, the
connection just happens, often because of
experiences you have already had. When you
relate or *connect* two things in your mind, it

requires more of an effort because the connection is not so obvious or natural to you: *I always associate the smell of baking with my childhood. □ I found it hard to relate/connect the two ideas in my mind. Relate* can also be used to talk about a deliberate decision to make two things dependent on each other: *Pay increases will be related to productivity. Connect* can also be used to talk about facts or evidence that provide a link between things: *There was nothing to connect him with the crime.*
Word family **associated** adjective connected with someone or something because the two things often happen or exist together or because one thing causes the other: *Young people need to be made aware of the risks associated with drugs.* **association** noun **1** a group of people organized for a joint purpose. **2** a connection or relationship: *his close association with the university.* **3** an idea, memory, or feeling that is connected to someone or something: *The name had unpleasant associations for him.*

assume *verb*
1 to accept as true without having any proof: *I think we can safely assume the situation will continue.* **2** (*formal*) to take or begin to have power or responsibility: *The court assumed responsibility for the girl's welfare.* **3** (*formal*) to begin to have: *Foreign trade has assumed greater importance in recent years.* **4** to pretend to have: *He assumed an air of indifference.*
Word family **assumed** adjective: that you believe to be true or to exist: *This report takes into account the assumed differences between the two states.* **assumption** noun a belief or feeling that something is true or that something will happen, although there is no proof: *They made certain assumptions about the market.*

assure *verb*
1 to tell someone that something is definitely true: *She's perfectly safe, I can assure you.* **2** to make something certain to happen: *Victory would assure her a place in the finals.*
Word family **assurance** noun: *They asked for assurance on the safety of the system.* **assured** adjective certain to happen: *The French team are now assured of a place in the next round.*

astonish *verb*
to surprise someone very much: *The news astonished everyone.*

Usage *amaze* or *astonish*? See amaze.
Word family **astonished** adjective: *He was astonished to learn he'd won the competition.* **astonishment** noun: *To my utter astonishment, she remembered my name.*

astound *verb*
to surprise or shock someone very much: *His arrogance astounded her.*
Word family **astounding** adjective surprisingly impressive or notable: *The summit offers astounding views.*

astute *adjective*
good at making accurate judgements about what to do in a particular situation: *An astute politician, he understood the need to get them on his side.*
Word family **astutely** adverb **astuteness** noun

atmosphere *noun*
the way that a particular place or situation feels to you; feeling between two people or in a group of people: *In this playgroup, your children will play with other children in a warm friendly atmosphere.*
Usage *atmosphere* or *mood*? An *atmosphere* belongs especially to a place, and may stay the same over a period of time; a *mood* belongs to a group of people at a particular time and may change as time passes: *The mood of the meeting was distinctly pessimistic.*

attention *noun*
the act of listening to, looking at, or thinking about someone or something carefully: *Now, please sit up and pay attention to what I am going to say.*
Word family **attentive** adjective listening or watching someone or something carefully and with interest: *Never before had she had such an attentive audience.*

attract *verb*
(of a thing) to have qualities that you notice and like; (of a person) to have qualities that make you like and admire them: *The tall trees are what first attracted me to the place.*
Word family **attraction** noun a feature, quality, or person that makes something seem interesting and enjoyable and worth having or doing: *The apartment's main attraction is the large pool.*

a

attractive *adjective*
1 pleasant to look at: *This is a big house with an attractive garden.* **2** having qualities that arouse interest: *an attractive investment proposition.*
Usage The word *attractive* is used when the speaker or writer does not want to give the impression of being influenced by strong personal feelings.
Word family *attractively* adverb

audacious *adjective*
showing a willingness to take surprisingly bold risks: *a series of audacious takeovers.*
Usage *audacious*, *bold*, or *daring*? See **bold**.
Word family *audaciously* adverb *audacity* noun: *The sheer audacity of the plan amazed everyone.*

audition *noun, verb*
noun an interview for an actor, singer, etc. in which they give a practical demonstration of their skills: *He went for an audition with the Royal Ballet.* □ *verb* to assess or be assessed by means of an audition: *I auditioned and was lucky enough to be given the part.*

augur *verb*
(**augur well/badly**) (*formal*) to be a sign of a good/bad outcome: *Conflicts among the various groups do not augur well for the future of the peace talks.*
Usage The word *augur* should not be confused with the noun *auger*, a tool for boring holes.

aura *noun*
a quality or feeling that is very noticeable and seems to surround a person or place: *There was a faint aura of mystery about him.*

auspicious *adjective*
(*formal*) showing signs that something is likely to be successful in the future: *It seemed an auspicious start to the new year.*
Usage The word *auspicious* usually describes a time or occasion; it is used with such nouns as *day, moment, occasion, start,* and *beginning.*
Usage *auspicious*, *opportune*, or *timely*? See *opportune*.

austere *adjective*
1 simple and plain, with no decoration, usually because that is what someone prefers: *the austere simplicity of the building.* **2** without

comforts or luxuries: *their austere living conditions.*
Usage When used to refer to a person to mean 'strict and serious in appearance and behaviour' (*My father was a distant austere man*) the word *austere* tends to be used with disapproval. This is in contrast to the more approving sense **1** above, which is used to refer to things. Sense **2** above is more neutral in tone.
Word family *austerely* adverb *austerity* noun

authentic *adjective*
1 known to be real, genuine, and not a copy: *I don't know if the painting is authentic.* **2** true and giving an accurate and realistic description of something: *an authentic account of life in the desert.* **3** made to be exactly the same as the original: *an authentic model of the ancient town.*
Word family *authentically* adverb
authenticate verb to prove or show something to be true, genuine, or valid: *He must produce evidence that will authenticate his claim.* *authenticity* noun

authoritative *adjective*
1 that you can trust and respect as true and correct: *He is credited with writing the most authoritative and up-to-date book on the subject.* **2** commanding and self-confident: *His voice was calm and authoritative.*
Word family *authoritatively* adverb
authoritativeness noun

authority *noun*
a person with special knowledge of a subject: *She is an authority on early musical instruments.*
Usage *authority* or *expert*? An *expert* is usually someone who is very skilled at something, and/or is able to give useful advice or training to someone else. An *authority* is usually someone who knows a lot about an academic subject, which may be very interesting, but may not be necessary or useful for other people to know about or be advised about.

authorization *noun*
1 official permission to do something: *Authorization to attend courses must be obtained from the education chairman.* **2** a document that gives someone official permission to do something: *Can I see your authorization please?*

Usage *authorization*, *permission*, or *consent*? Superiors within some institution or system give *authorization*, which often involves an actual delegation of authority: *Authorization of credit card transactions in the UK typically takes about 3 to 5 seconds.* Permission is generally given by someone with power because of their position, authority, or ownership who does not usually intend to participate in the activity for which it is sought: *They are seeking planning permission for a supermarket on the site.* Consent is typically used when what is at issue is not a difference in power, but rather whether someone is able or allowed to make a free choice that is informed by at least some knowledge of possible alternatives and consequences: *In English law, a woman may not be given in marriage without her consent.*

authorize *verb*
to give official permission for something, or for someone to do something: *I can authorize payments up to £5,000.*
Word family *authorized* adjective done with or having the permission of someone in authority; official: *The family agreed to an authorized biography of the artist.*

autonomy *noun*
1 the freedom to make decisions and do things without being controlled by anyone else: *Schools have gained greater autonomy from government control.* 2 freedom for a country or region to govern itself independently: *There has been a campaign for greater autonomy for the region.*
Usage In sense 1, the word *autonomy* is used especially about organizations or classes of people being free from official control; it is used less about individual people. In sense 2, *autonomy* is usually a degree of freedom that is less than complete independence.
Word family *autonomous* adjective: *The federation included 16 autonomous republics.*

available *adjective*
1 that you can get, buy, or find: *A few seats are still available.* 2 free to do something: *The nurse is only available in the mornings.*
Word family *availability* noun: *the availability of cheap flights.*

avant-garde *adjective, noun*
adjective (in the arts) new and experimental: *The theatre shows a lot of avant-garde work.*
□ *noun* (**the avant-garde**) new and experimental ideas or artists.
Word family *avant-gardism* noun *avant-gardist* noun

avid *adjective*
showing great enthusiasm for something such as a hobby: *I have always been an avid reader.*
Usage If you are *avid* for something, you want to get it very much: *She was avid for more information.* In British English, *avid* is a rather formal word and the word *keen* is usually used in its place in less formal contexts; in American English, *avid* is the usual word.
Word family *avidly* adverb

award *noun, verb*
noun something, such as money or a special title, given to someone for something they have done or achieved: *the company's annual award for high-quality service.* □ *verb* to give something officially as a prize, payment, or reward: *A 3.5% pay rise was awarded to staff.*

aware *adjective*
knowing or realizing something; noticing that something is present or that something is happening: *Most people are aware of the dangers of sunbathing.*
Word family *awareness* noun: *There is a growing awareness of the links between diet and health.*

awe *noun*
a feeling of great respect and slight fear because you are very impressed by someone or something: *They gazed in awe at the beauty of the scene.*
Word family *awe-inspiring* adjective: *awe-inspiring scenery.* *awesome* adjective very impressive or very difficult and perhaps rather frightening: *the awesome power of the atomic bomb.* The sense of *awesome* meaning 'very good' (*The show was just awesome!*) is informal and should not be used in formal contexts. *awestruck* adjective: *Caroline was too awestruck by her surroundings to reply.*

axiom *noun*
a statement regarded or accepted as obviously true: *the axiom that sport builds character.*
Word family *axiomatic* adjective: *It is axiomatic that dividends have to be financed.*

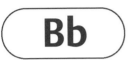

back verb

to give help or support to: *Her parents backed her in her choice of career.*

Usage The word *back* is often used when someone who is in an influential, powerful, or a more senior position is giving their support. The phrasal verb *back up* is used in rather informal contexts to say or do something in order to support an opinion, claim, or argument and to say that what someone has said is true: *As a writer, you should back up your arguments with examples.*

Word family *backer* noun: *The project receives its money from European backers.* ***backing*** noun: *Doctors gave the proposals their full backing.*

balance verb

1 to be equal in value, amount, or strength to something else that has the opposite effect: *this lack of experience was balanced by a willingness to learn.* **2** to establish an even degree of proportions or elements in: *She manages to balance work and family life.*

Usage To *balance* something against something else is used in rather formal contexts to compare the relative importance of two contrasting things: *The cost of obtaining legal advice needs to be balanced against its benefits.*

Word family *balanced* adjective in good proportions: *a balanced team.*

bargain noun, verb

noun **1** something bought for less than the usual price: *I picked up a few good bargains in the sale.* **2** an agreement between two or more people or groups to do something for each other: *Finally, the two sides struck a bargain.* □ *verb* to discuss prices, conditions, etc. with someone in order to reach an agreement: *He bargained with the council to rent the stadium.*

Usage The phrasal verb *bargain for/on*, meaning 'to expect something to happen and be prepared for it', is usually used in negative sentences and in fairly informal contexts: *When he agreed to answer your questions, he obviously got more than he bargained for.*

base noun, verb

noun **1** an idea, or fact, or situation from which something is developed: *His arguments have a sound economic base.* **2** the main place where a business works from or where a person lives or stays: *The company has its base in Berlin and branch offices throughout the world.* □ *verb* to use a particular city, country, or region as the main place for something such as a business; to stay in a particular area in order to be able to do something such as work or travel there: *She works for a company based in Chicago.*

basic adjective, noun

adjective **1** concerning the most central and important parts of something from which other things develop: *During the first term, we will concentrate on the basic principles of law.* **2** necessary and important to all people: *Food and shelter are basic human rights.* □ *noun* (**the basics**) the most important, necessary, and often practical facts, skills, or ideas from which other things develop: *I need to learn the basics of computer programming.*

Usage *basic* or ***fundamental?*** Something described as *basic* is seen as a necessary minimum, to which further elaborations may be added. The *basic* design of something is the essential core of what may be a more complex design. *To teach basic camera skills* refers to a necessary minimum that can be improved upon for further proficiency. Something that is *fundamental* to something else is essential to it, determining its nature. So physics might be called a *fundamental* aspect of the curriculum if it influences and shapes some or all of the other topics taught, but *basic* if it simply provides an elementary educational grounding.

basis *noun*
1 a principle, idea, or fact that supports something and that it can develop from: *This article will form the basis of our discussion.*
2 the reason why people take a particular action: *On what basis will this decision be made?*
Usage **basis** or **foundation**? *Foundation is often used to talk about larger or more important things than basis: These figures form the basis of their pay claim.* □ *He laid the foundation of Japan's modern economy.*

bask *verb*
1 to lie exposed to warmth and sunlight for pleasure: *I sat on the bank, basking in the warm sunshine.* 2 (**bask in**) to take great pleasure in: *They were still basking in the glory of success.*

beautiful *adjective*
1 (especially of a woman or girl) very pleasant to look at: *She looked stunningly beautiful that night.* 2 (of a place or something pleasant to look at) pleasing to the eyes, to the other senses, or to the mind: *If I look out of the window, I can see all this beautiful countryside.*
Usage **beautiful** or **lovely**? *Lovely is slightly more informal than beautiful and is used more in spoken English than in written English. Something that is lovely always has a warm quality that appeals not only to the eyes but also to the heart; lovely does not just describe physical appearance: It was a lovely evening—calm and still. Beautiful things often have this quality too, but they can appeal to the eyes and mind rather than the heart: The designs were pure, austere, and coldly beautiful.*
Word family **beautifully** adverb: *She sings beautifully.* **beauty** *noun* 1 a person or thing that is beautiful: *The woods were designated an area of outstanding natural beauty.* 2 the best advantage: *The beauty of the system is that information can be called up instantaneously.*

benchmark *noun*
a standard or point of reference that other things can be compared with: *The German recycling system is seen as a benchmark for schemes throughout Europe.*
Usage The word *benchmark* is also found in occasional use as a verb meaning 'to evaluate something by comparison with a standard': *We are benchmarking our performance against external criteria.*

beneficial *adjective*
having a helpful or useful effect: *Relaxation classes can be beneficial to people of all ages.*
Usage **beneficial** or **good**? *Beneficial is much more formal than good. Good in this sense is used mostly in such phrases as good for someone or something, no good to someone.*

benefit *noun, verb*
noun 1 a good or useful effect of something: *She had the benefit of a good education.*
2 something given by your employer in addition to your pay: *Benefits include a company pension and free health insurance.*
□ *verb* 1 to get an advantage or benefit from something: *Most crime victims benefit greatly by talking about their experiences.* 2 to be useful or bring an advantage to someone or improve their way of life: *The new tax laws will clearly benefit those on low wages.*
Usage **benefit** or **gain**? *In many cases you can use either word: Who stands to benefit/gain from these changes? However, gain is used more often to talk about financial advantages, or having an advantage over other people: Who stands to gain from the deal? Benefit is used more often to talk about someone being in a better position than before, for example because they are happier, healthier, or better educated. Benefit is slightly more formal than gain: areas that would benefit from regeneration.*

bespoke *adjective*
written or adapted for a specific user or purpose: *a bespoke computer program.* □ *bespoke software packages.* □ *offer a bespoke service.* □ *bespoke training solutions.*
Usage This usage derives from the sense referring to goods, especially clothing, and meaning 'made to order': *a bespoke suit.*

best *adjective*
most suitable or appropriate: *What's the best way to cook steaks?*
Word family **best practice** noun used to refer to a way of doing something that is seen as a very good example of how it should be done and can be copied by other companies or organizations: *Their methods of recruitment and retention are currently considered best practice in the private sector.*

bijou *adjective*
(of a building or garden) small but attractive and fashionable: *The house was very small and*

cramped, but the agent described it as a bijou residence.

blend *noun, verb*

noun **1** a pleasant or useful combination of different things: *a blend of youth and experience.* **2** a mixture of different types of the same thing: *several different blends of freshly ground coffee.* □ *verb* **1** to combine with something in an attractive and effective way: *The old and new buildings blend together perfectly.* **2** to mix two or more substances or flavours together; (of substances or flavours) to be mixed together: *Blend the flour with the milk to make a smooth paste.*

Usage **blend** or **mix**? If you *blend* things when you are cooking, you usually combine them more completely than if you just *mix* them.

blessing *noun*

1 approval or support from a person or group: *This arrangement received the full blessing of the committee.* **2** something that makes a situation good or better: *It's a blessing no one was in the house when the fire started.*
Usage **blessing** or **good thing**? A *blessing* is something important or something that is good from any point of view (such as not getting burnt to death). A *good thing* can be important, but it is also used for less important things that you just happen to be pleased about (such as remembering your camera).

bliss *noun*

a feeling of great happiness and peacefulness: *The first six months of marriage were sheer bliss.*
Word family **blissful** adjective very happy: *We spent three blissful weeks away from work.*
blissfully adverb: *blissfully ignorant of the truth.*

bloom *verb*

to become or be healthy or become confident and successful: *The children had bloomed in the soft Devonshire air.*
Usage See **blossom**.

blossom *verb*

(of people) to become more healthy, confident, and successful; (of a relationship, career, or talent) to develop into something better or quickly become successful: *The idea has now blossomed into a successful business.*
Usage The words *bloom* and *blossom* are both commonly used in these figurative senses of developing in a healthy, promising way.

blue-chip *adjective*

1 (of a company or shares) considered to be a reliable investment: *When investing, look for blue-chip companies.* **2** of the highest quality: *blue-chip art.*
Usage This usage derives from the *blue chip* used in gambling games, which usually has a high value.

blueprint *noun*

a plan that shows what and how something can be achieved; a model showing how something should be done or made: *The government has recently unveiled a blueprint for an integrated transport system.*

boast *verb*

to have something that is impressive and that you can be proud of: *The hotel boasts two swimming pools and a golf course.*
Usage The word *boast* in this sense is not used in progressive tenses or in the passive. It is used especially in written contexts and is often used to advertise places, e.g. in information for tourists on a hotel or city.

bold *adjective*

1 (of people or their behaviour) brave and confident; not afraid to say what you feel or to take risks: *It was a bold move on their part to open a branch of the business in France.* **2** (of colours) strong, clear, and easy to see: *a coat with bold polka dots.*
Usage **bold**, **daring**, or **audacious**? A *bold* action typically does not involve physical danger and is more likely to be approved of than a *daring* or *audacious* one: *People are looking to their leaders to take bold decisions now.* A *daring* action involves adventurousness undeterred by physical danger and does not necessarily describe activities that are approved of: *one of the most daring crimes of the century.* *Daring* can also refer to a readiness to shock: *She smoked in the street, which was considered very daring in those days.* An *audacious* act is one that goes well beyond the normal boundaries in a readiness to take risks: *He hit the post with an audacious drop goal attempt.*
Word family **boldly** adverb **boldness** noun

bolster *verb*

to support or improve something or make it stronger: *Falling interest rates may help to bolster the economy.*

Usage The word *bolster* is used especially to talk about making someone or something stronger emotionally or financially or to make an argument or case for something stronger.

bonus *noun*
1 money that you receive from your employer in addition to your normal wages or salary, especially because you have done your job well: *Everyone in the company gets a 10% Christmas bonus.* **2** something extra that is more or better than you were expecting: *Good weather is a bonus but the real appeal is the scenery.*

boom *verb, noun*
verb (of a business or economy) to have a period of rapid growth; to become bigger or more successful: *Business is booming.* □ *noun* a period of rapid economic growth: *a boom in car sales.*
Usage The verb is used especially in the progressive tenses and in rather informal contexts, especially in journalism. The opposite of the noun is *slump*, a period when a country's economy or business is doing badly: *Housing sales are finally coming out of a six-month slump.*

boost *verb, noun*
verb to make something increase, or become better or more successful: *The new service helped to boost pre-tax profits by 10%.* □ *noun* an increase or improvement: *The cut in interest rates will give a further boost to the economy.*
Usage The word *boost* is used with approval, often in journalism. It is always used to describe a positive increase: *to boost productivity/sales/confidence/morale.*

bountiful *adjective*
1 large in quantity; abundant: *The ocean provides a bountiful supply of fresh food.* **2** giving generously: *This bountiful God has thought of everything.*
Usage The word *bountiful* is used in formal contexts. The noun *bounty* is more literary, and is used to refer to something given or occurring in generous amounts: *For millennia, people living along the Nile have depended on its bounty.*

boutique *noun*
a small shop selling fashionable clothes or accessories.
Usage In the extended sense, the word *boutique* is also applied to a business serving a sophisticated or specialized clientele: *The company has nine four-star boutique hotels in Asia and the United States.*

brand *noun, verb*
noun **1** a type of product mark by a particular company, especially a food or drink you might buy in a supermarket: *Which brand of toothpaste do you use?* **2** someone's particular way of doing or thinking about something: *She has her own unique brand of humour.*
□ *verb* to describe as being bad or unpleasant, especially unfairly: *The newspapers branded her a liar.*
Usage As a verb, in the sense shown, *brand* is often used with disapproval.
Word family of **brand new** *adjective* completely new: *We've just spent £1000 on a brand-new computer.*

brave *adjective*
1 (of a person) willing to do things which are difficult, dangerous, or painful. **2** (of an action) showing no fear of doing something difficult, dangerous, or painful: *I wasn't brave enough to tell her what I thought of her.*
Usage **brave** or **courageous**? *Courageous* is about facing opposition, for moral reasons, although this may involve the threat of physical punishment, as well as threats to your career or reputation: *her courageous human rights work. Brave* is more often a willingness to face physical danger or pain: *She died after a brave fight against cancer.*
Word family **bravely** *adverb* **bravery** *noun*

breathtaking *adjective*
very impressive or exciting, usually in a pleasant way; spectacular: *The scene was breathtaking in its beauty.*
Usage The word *breathtaking* derives from the idiom *take your breath away*, (of a sight, action, or performance) to surprise or impress someone very much, especially with its beauty or skill: *My first vision of the island from the air completely took my breath away.*
Word family **breathtakingly** *adverb*: *breathtakingly spectacular.*

brief *adjective*
1 lasting for only a short time: *The prime minister is due to make a brief visit to South Korea.* **2** using few words: *The author makes only a brief mention of the role of Japan in this period.*

Usage *brief* or *short*? In many cases, you can use either word: *a short/brief account/ description/answer*. *Short* is used more often than *brief* in informal and spoken English: *I'm going to Amsterdam for a short* (not: *brief*) *break*. *Short*, but not *brief*, is used to describe books, lists, etc. that take only a short time to read or deal with. *Brief* is often used when you are talking about speech rather than writing: *Please be brief.*
Word family *briefly* adverb *briefness* noun

bright *adjective*
1 full of light; shining strongly; (of colours) strong: *She stood blinking in the bright sunlight.* 2 cheerful and lively: *I was not feeling very bright after the party the night before.* 3 quick to learn; intelligent: *She's a very bright student and will go far.* 4 (especially in journalism or business) likely to be successful; promising: *Prospects for the coming year look bright.*
Word family *brightly* adverb *brightness* noun

brilliant *adjective*
1 very bright: *The sky was a brilliant blue.* 2 (*informal*) extremely good: '*How was the show?*' '*Brilliant!*'
Word family *brilliance* noun *brilliantly* adverb

broaden *verb*
to expand to take in more people or things: *He has to broaden Labour's appeal to the whole community.*
Usage The word *broaden* is also often used in the sense 'to increase your experience or knowledge': *Few would disagree that travel broadens the mind* (= helps you understand other people's beliefs, customs, etc.). Typical words used with *broaden* are: *horizons, outlook, understanding,* and *interests.*

budding *adjective*
1 (of a person) beginning and showing signs of promise in a particular sphere: *budding young actors.* 2 beginning and showing promising signs of continuing: *their budding friendship.*

budget *adjective, noun, verb*
adjective (especially in advertising) cheap because it offers only a basic level of service: *You can save pounds on budget flights to the sun.* □ *noun* the money that is available to an organization, government, or person and a plan of how it will be spent over a period of time: *The government is planning to increase* the education budget. □ *verb* to be careful about the amount of money you spend; to plan to spend an amount of money for a particular purpose: *If we budget carefully, we'll be able to afford the trip.*
Word family *budgetary* adjective connected with a budget: *The new accounting procedures will improve budgetary control.*

buffer *noun*
a thing or person that reduces shock or protects someone or something against difficulties: *Support from family and friends acts as a buffer against stress.*
Word family *buffer zone* noun a neutral area that serves to separate two hostile forces: *Peacekeepers have been sent in to establish a buffer zone between the rival sides.*

build *verb*
1 to create something, especially a way of life or an impression that you develop and improve over a period of time: *She's built a new career for herself.* 2 to become gradually stronger: *The tension and excitement built gradually all day.*
Word family *build in/into* verb to make something a permanent part of a structure, plan, or system: *A certain amount of flexibility needs to be built into the system.* *build up* verb 1 to become greater or more powerful: *All the pressure built up and he was off work for weeks with stress.* 2 to make stronger: *you need more protein to build you up.* 3 to give a very positive and enthusiastic description of someone or something, sometimes with exaggeration: *The play was built up to be a masterpiece but I found it very disappointing.*

bullish *adjective*
1 feeling confident and positive about the future: *He was in a bullish mood about the future of the company.* 2 (*finance*) causing, or connected with, an increase in the price of shares: *a bullish market.*
Usage The opposite of *bullish* in sense 2 is *bearish*: *American banks remain bearish.*

buoyant *adjective*
(*finance*) (of prices or business activity) tending to increase or stay at a high level, usually showing financial success: *Sales have remained buoyant even during the recession.*
Usage Words that are described as *buoyant* include: *market, economy, trading, sales,* and *demand.*

Word family *buoyancy* noun *buoyantly* adverb

business *noun*

1 a commercial organization such as a company, shop, or factory: *I've decided to start my own business.* **2** a particular kind of activity that includes producing, buying, selling, or providing goods or services for money: *She works in the computer business.* **3** the activity of providing, buying, selling, or providing goods or services for money; the rate or quality of their work: *It's been a pleasure to do business with you.* **4** the fact of a person or people buying goods or services at a shop, company, etc.: *We're losing business to our main rivals.*

Usage The word *business* places the emphasis more on the management activities involved in an industry or service than on the physical work involved. It is used especially to talk about the service industries: *the catering/hotel/entertainment/advertising/insurance business.* It is also used to talk about very large industries that produce or trade in very basic products or raw materials, where it is a slightly more informal choice than *industry*, used especially in journalism: *the energy/oil/food business.*

Usage *Businessman* or *businesswoman* is often used to describe someone who works for himself or herself rather than for an employer. It is also used to describe someone who is skilful in business and financial matters: *I should have got a better price for the car, but I'm not much of a businessman.* *Business people* is often used in the plural to talk about businessmen and businesswomen as a group; when you are talking about an individual person it is more usual to use *businessman* or *businesswoman.*

Word family *businesslike* adjective efficient; not wasting time: *He adopted a brisk, businesslike tone.* **businessman**, **businesswoman**, **business person** noun a person who works in business, especially at a high level: *For many years he was a successful businessman, running his own small business.*

Cc

calculate *verb*

1 to use numbers to find out a total number, amount, bill, distance, etc: *Use the formula to calculate the volume of the container.*
2 (**calculate on**) to include something as an essential element in your plans: *We had calculated on a quiet Sunday.*
Usage *calculate*, *work out*, or *compute*? *Calculate* is the most frequent of these words in written English, but *work out* is the most frequent in spoken English and is used especially to describe small, quick calculations done by people. *Compute* is used in formal written English, especially to describe calculations done by a machine.
Word family *calculation noun*

calibre *noun*

1 the quality of someone's character or the level of their ability: *They could ill afford to lose a man of his calibre.* **2** the standard reached by something: *educational facilities of a very high calibre.*
Usage In American English, this word is spelt *caliber.*

calm *adjective, noun, verb*

adjective **1** not excited, anxious, or upset: *In an emergency it is important to keep calm.* **2** (of the sea) without large waves; (of the weather) without wind; (of an atmosphere) without noise or without feeling: *The city is calm again* (= free from trouble or fighting) *after yesterday's riots.* □ *noun* **1** a quiet and relaxed manner in which you are in control of your feelings: *He spoke with studied calm.* **2** a situation in which there is no violence, anger, or argument: *The police appealed for calm.* **3** a quiet or peaceful time or situation: *We sat together in the calm of the evening.* □ *verb* **1** to make someone or something become quiet and more relaxed: *Have some brandy; it'll calm your nerves.* **2** (**calm down**) to make or become relaxed, especially in your behaviour: *Calm down! We'll find her.*

Usage *calm*, *cool*, or *relaxed*? *Relaxed* describes how you feel about something: you are genuinely not anxious or worried about it. *Cool* is used more to describe how someone behaves: whether or not they feel angry or emotional, they don't let it affect their behaviour but continue to think clearly and act sensibly. *Calm* can describe feelings or behaviour.
Word family *calming adjective* *calmly adverb* *calmness noun*

campaign *noun, verb*

noun a series of planned activities that are intended to achieve a particular social, commercial, or political aim: *She led the campaign for parliamentary reform.* □ *verb* to carry out a campaign: *We have campaigned against whaling for the last 15 years.*
Usage *campaign* or *fight*? *Campaigning* often involves such activities as making speeches, putting advertisements in newspapers, and writing to members of the government. The aim is often to persuade people that a political or social change is needed or a practice needs to be stopped. You can *fight* for social or political change too, but this word is also used to talk about achieving justice for yourself, for example gaining the right to do something. The emphasis with *fight* is on the determination someone shows to achieve something.
Word family *campaigner noun*. See **activist**.

candid *adjective*

saying what you think openly and honestly: *The ex-minister gave a candid interview about his reasons for resigning.*
Word family *candidly adverb* *candour noun*

capable *adjective*

having the ability to manage things well: *She's an extremely capable teacher.*
Usage *capable*, *competent*, or *able*? See **able**.

Word family **capability** noun: *Age affects the range of a person's capabilities.* **capably** adverb

capacity *noun*
1 the maximum amount that something can contain or produce: *When running at full capacity, the factory will employ 500 people.* **2** the ability to understand or do something: *She has an enormous capacity for hard work.* **3** a specified role or position: *I was engaged in a voluntary capacity.*
Usage In sense **2**, the word *capacity* is often used to refer to social, educational, and work-related life skills: *a capacity for learning languages/reflective thinking.*

captivate *verb*
to get and keep someone's close attention by being extremely interesting or attractive: *The children were captivated by her stories.*
Usage **captivate, entrance,** or **enthral**? You can be *captivated* by another person—their looks, charm, or what they say or do. You can be *entranced* by a person or by something that appeals to your senses, such as music, art, or beauty: *I was entranced by the bird's beauty.* You can be *enthralled* by something that you see or something that appeals to your imagination, such as a story: *This book will enthral readers of all ages.*
Word family **captivating** adjective **captivation** noun

care *noun, verb*
noun **1** the attention or thought that you give to something that you are doing so that you will do it well and avoid mistakes or damage: *She chose her words with care.* **2** the provision of what is necessary for the health, welfare, maintenance, and protection of someone or something: *The child is in the care of her grandmother.* □ verb to feel that something is important and worth worrying about; to worry about what happens to someone because you like or love them: *He cared passionately about environmental issues.*
Word family **take care of** to be responsible for or to deal with a situation or task: *Don't worry about the travel arrangements—they are being taken care of.*

careful *adjective*
giving a lot of attention to details when considering, studying, or explaining something: *After careful consideration, we have decided to offer you the job.*

Usage The opposite of *careful* is *careless*: *You've made a lot of careless mistakes in your work.*
Word family **carefully** adverb **carefulness** noun

cascade *verb, noun*
verb to pass something on to a succession of others: *teachers who are able to cascade their experience effectively.* □ noun a process by which something, e.g. information or knowledge, is successively passed on: *Normally, new developments filter down in a cascade system.*
Usage These figurative usages derive from *cascade* in the sense of a small waterfall, typically one of several that fall in stages down a steep, rocky slope.

catalyst *noun*
a person or thing that causes a change: *I see my role as being a catalyst for transformation in the company.*
Usage This figurative usage derives from the scientific use of *catalyst*, meaning 'a substance that increases the speed of a chemical reaction without itself undergoing any permanent chemical change'.

categorical *adjective*
expressed clearly and in a way that shows you are very sure about what you are saying: *The government has still to make a categorical statement on the issue.*
Word family **categorically** adverb: *They categorically rejected our offer.*

cater *verb*
1 (**cater for**) to give or offer the things that a particular person or situation needs or wants: *The class caters for all abilities.* **2** (**cater to**) to gain or offer the things that a particular kind of person wants: *They only publish novels which cater to the mass market.*
Usage **cater for** or **cater to**? If you *cater for* someone or something, you provide the things that they need; if you *cater to* someone or something you give them what they want. *Cater for* someone or something is used to talk about either the wide range of things that is offered or particular things that are offered: *to cater for individual preferences/children with special needs.* Organizations typically *cater to* the mass market, tourists, an elite, or local tastes; *cater to* sometimes has disapproving tones.

C

cause *noun, verb*

noun **1** a thing or person that makes something happen: *Unemployment is a major cause of poverty.* **2** a reason for behaving in a particular way or for having particular feelings: *There is no cause for alarm.* **3** an organization or idea that people support or fight for: *Animal welfare campaigners raised £70,000 for their cause last year.* □ *verb* to make something (especially something bad or unpleasant) happen: *Do they know what caused the fire?*
Word family **cause and effect** *noun* phrase the relationship between an action or event and the effect it produces: *Science would collapse if this law of cause and effect were denied.*

celebrate *verb*

1 to show that a day or event is important by doing something special on it: *We celebrated our 25th wedding anniversary in Florence.* **2** to publicly express admiration of someone or something, especially in a film, song, or work of art: *It was a movie celebrating the life and works of Martin Luther King.*
Usage **celebrated**, **famous**, **renowned**, or **well-known**? *Celebrated* suggests that someone or something is highly thought of: *a portrait of a celebrated actress.* A person, place, or thing that is *famous* is usually much admired: *He became a famous conductor,* but occasionally they may be widely recognized but little admired: *a famous landmark.* *Renowned* means widely known and respected; the word tends to be used more in written than spoken English: *Burgundy is renowned for its beef, poultry, and wine.* *Well-known* conveys the idea of being recognized by many people but generally does not have the glamorous connotations of *famous*: *Many well-known companies built ships.*
Word family **celebrated** *adjective* famous for having good qualities; often used to refer to people who are successful in the arts as well as their works: *He is one of France's most celebrated painters.* **celebration** *noun* (*often plural*) a special event that people organize to celebrate something: *They are already planning a celebration of the school's 50th birthday.* **celebrity** *noun* **1** the state of being a famous person, especially in the media: *His prestige and celebrity grew.* **2** a famous person, especially one who often appears on television: *The show's success made him a celebrity overnight.*

central *adjective*

most important; essential or principal: *Reducing inflation is central to the government's economic policy.*
Usage **central**, **key**, **major**, or **principal**? The word *key* is used most frequently in business and political contexts. It can be used to talk about ideas, or the part that someone plays in a situation, but not physical things. It is slightly more informal than *major*, especially when used after a noun and linking verb: *Speed is key at this point. Central* is used in a similar way to *key*, but is more formal. It is most frequently used in the phrase *something is central to something else* and is used with a slightly smaller range of nouns than *key*. These mostly relate to the part someone or something plays in something (*character, component, feature, figure, motif, part, role, theme, topic*), what someone is trying to achieve (*aim, focus, issue, preoccupation, problem, recommendation*), or ideas that someone has about something (*belief, concept, doctrine, truth*). *Principal* is mostly used for statements of fact about which there can be no argument: *My principal concern is to get the job done fast.* To state an opinion, or to try to persuade someone of the facts as you see them, it is more usual to use *key* or *central*: *The key/central issue here is... Major* is most often used after *a* with a singular noun or no article with a plural noun. When it is used with *the* or *my/your/his/her/our/their* it means 'the largest or most important': *Our major concern here is combating poverty.* In this meaning it is only used to talk about ideas or worries that people have, not physical things, and it is also more formal than *main*.

centre *noun, verb*

noun **1** the point towards which people direct their attention: *The prime minister is at the centre of a political row.* **2** the middle point or root of an area or thing: *There was a long table in the centre of the room.* **3** a building or place used for a particular purpose or activity: *A new leisure centre is being built on the outskirts of the city.* □ *verb* **1** (**centre in**) to occur mainly in or around: *The textile industry was centred in Lancashire and Yorkshire.* **2** (**centre around/ on**) to have as a major concern or theme: *The case centres around the couple's adopted children.*
Usage In American English, this word is spelt *center*.

certain *adjective*
1 that you can rely on to happen or be true: *She looks certain to win an Oscar.* **2** sure that you are right or that something is true: *Are you absolutely certain about this?* **3** used to refer to a particular thing, person, or group without giving any further detail about them: *They refused to release the hostages unless certain conditions were met.*
Usage certain or **sure**? *Certain* is slightly more formal than *sure*; *sure* is more frequent, especially in spoken English. In formal English, *certain* can be used when mentioning a person who has been named but who is not known: *A certain Dr Davis performed the operation.*
Word family certainly *adverb*: *This prestigious address certainly adds to the firm's appeal.*
certainty *noun* **1** an event that will definitely happen; an undoubted fact or situation: *He accepted defeat as a certainty.* **2** the state of having no doubt that something is true or correct: *She knew with absolute certainty that they were dead.*

certify *verb*
1 to confirm or state something in a formal document: *The profits for the year had been certified by the auditors.* **2** to officially recognize that someone or something meets certain standards: *Scenes of violence had to be cut before the film could be certified.*
Usage The word *certify* in the above senses should be distinguished from the meaning 'to officially declare someone insane': *Patients must be certified before they can be admitted to the hospital.*
Word family certificate *noun* an official document that may be used to prove that the facts it states are true: *Your marriage certificate is an important document and it should be kept in a safe place.*
certification *noun*

challenge *noun, verb*
noun a new or difficult task that tests someone's ability and skill: *The role will be the biggest challenge of his acting career.* □ *verb* **1** to raise doubt as to whether something is true or genuine: *This discovery challenges traditional beliefs.* **2** to invite someone to do something demanding: *The opposition leader challenged the prime minister to call an election.*
Usage Care should be taken with use of the adjective *challenged* when used with a

preceding adverb (e.g. *physically challenged*). Such usage was originally to give a more positive tone than terms such as *disabled* or *handicapped*. Despite the originally serious intention, the term rapidly became stalled by uses whose intention was to make fun of the attempts at euphemism and whose tone was usually clearly ironic: mocking examples include *cerebrally challenged* and *follicularly challenged*.
Word family challenging *adjective* difficult in an interesting way that tests your abilities: *the challenging and rewarding career of a teacher.*

champion *noun, verb*
noun **1** a person or team etc. that has won a competition, especially in sport: *He was the undisputed heavyweight champion of the world.* **2** a person who fights for, or speaks in support of, a group of people or a belief: *She was a champion of the poor all her life.* □ *verb* to fight for, or speak in support of, a group of people or a belief: *He has always championed the cause of gay rights.*
Word family championship *noun* **1** a competition to find the best player or team in a particular sport: *He won a silver medal at the European championship.* **2** the position of winning a competition to become champion: *They've held the championship for the past two years.*

character *noun*
1 the qualities and features that make a person or group of people different from others: *She revealed her true character when anyone disagreed with her.* **2** strong personal qualities such as the ability to deal with difficult situations: *He showed great character returning to the sport after the accident.* **3** the interesting or unusual quality that a place or person has: *The modern hotels here have no real character.* **4** the opinion that people have of you, especially whether you can be trusted or relied on; reputation: *He had been discharged without a strain on his character.*
Usage In senses **2** and **3** above, the word *character* is used with approval.
Usage characteristic, **distinctive**, or **typical**? See **distinctive**.
Word family characteristic *noun* a part of a person's character, appearance, or behaviour; something typical of a place or thing: *The need to communicate is a key characteristic of human society.* **characteristic** *adjective*

charisma *noun*
the powerful personal quality that some people have to attract, impress, and influence other people: *The President has great personal charisma.*
Usage The words *charisma* and *charismatic* are used with approval.
Word family **charismatic** adjective having a powerful personal quality that attracts and impresses other people: *a charismatic leader.*

charm *noun, verb*
noun **1** the power of pleasing and attracting other people and making them like you: *He was a man of great charm.* **2** the quality that a place or thing has of being pleasing or attractive, especially in a way that is slightly old-fashioned; a pleasing or attractive feature: *The hotel is full of charm and character.*
□ *verb* to please or attract in a way that makes other people like you or be willing to do what you want: *He charmed his mother into letting him have his own way.*
Word family **charming** adjective **1** (of a person) very polite, friendly, and attractive: *She's a charming person.* **2** (of a place) very pleasant or attractive, especially in a way that is slightly old-fashioned: *The cottage is tiny, but charming.*

cheerful *adjective*
1 happy and showing your happiness in your behaviour or expression: *She tried to sound cheerful and unconcerned.* **2** causing happiness by its nature or appearance: *The room was painted in cheerful colours.*
Word family **cheerfully** adverb: *He cheerfully admits to being the wrong side of 50.*
cheerfulness noun

cherish *verb*
1 to love someone or something very much and want to protect them: *Children need to be cherished.* **2** to keep a memory or pleasant feeling in your mind for a long time: *She had long cherished a secret fantasy about his future.*
Word family **cherished** adjective loved very much and looked after by someone: *her most cherished possession.*

chief *noun, adjective*
noun a person in a high position or the highest position in a company or organization: *the former CIA chief of European operations.* □ *adjective* **1** highest in rank: *He was appointed as the Chief Education Officer.*

2 most important: *Unemployment was the chief cause of poverty.*
Usage As a noun, *chief* is used as part of some official job titles especially in American English. In British English, especially in journalism, it is often rather informal: *Health chiefs say waiting times are down.* As an adjective, in sense **1** above, *chief* is mainly used in names of positions. In sense **2**, it is also often used to talk about people in various different roles: *someone's chief enemy/rival/opponent.*
Word family **chiefly** adverb: *He is remembered chiefly for his violin concertos.*

choice *noun, adjective*
noun **1** an act of choosing between two or more possibilities: *Many women are forced to make a choice between family and career.* **2** a person or thing that is chosen: *She's the obvious choice for the job.* **3** the freedom to choose what you do: *He's going to do it; he doesn't have much choice, does he?* **4** a number or range of different things to choose from: *a menu offering a wide choice of dishes.* □ *adjective* (especially of food) of very good quality: *He picked some choice early plums.*
Usage **choice**, **alternative**, or **option**? See **alternative**.
Word family **of choice** that is chosen by a particular group of people or for a particular purpose: *It's the software of choice for business use.*

choose *verb*
1 to make a decision about which thing or person you want out of the ones available: *There are plenty of restaurants to choose from.* **2** to prefer or decide to do something or behave in a particular way, after thinking about the different possibilities available: *Employees can retire at 60 if they choose.*

chronicle *noun, verb*
noun a written record of events (with little or no explanation) in the order in which they happened: *a chronicle of the turbulent years of the region's past.* □ *verb* to record events in the order in which they happened: *Her achievements are chronicled in a new biography.*
Word family **chronology** noun a list of events in order: *At the front of the book is a chronology of the artist's life.*

circumstance *noun*

1 (usually **circumstances**) the facts that are connected with and affect a situation, event, or action: *The company reserves the right to cancel their agreement in certain circumstances.* **2** (usually **circumstances**) the conditions of a person's life, especially the money they have: *Grants are awarded according to your financial circumstances.* **3** the set of situations and events that affect you and influence you and that are not in your control: *He was a victim of circumstance* (= suffered because of a situation that he could not control).
Word family **circumstantial** *adjective* **1** (of evidence) strongly supporting something, but not proving it conclusively. **2** (of a description) containing full details: *a circumstantial log of our travels.*

civil *adjective*

polite in a formal way, but sometimes rather reserved: *His replies were civil, but scarcely welcoming.*
Usage The word *civil* is also used in a wide range of other senses, including 'relating to ordinary citizens, as distinct from military or church matters' (*civil aviation*) and 'non-criminal' (*a civil court*).
Word family **civility** *noun* **1** polite behaviour: *Staff members are trained to treat customers with civility at all times.* **2** (**civilities**) remarks that are said only to be polite and to avoid being rude: *She didn't waste time on civilities.*
civilly *adverb*: *She greeted him civilly, but with no sign of affection.*

claim *noun, verb*

noun **1** a statement that something is true, although it has not been proved: *There are conflicting claims about the cause of the fire.* **2** a request for a sum of money that you believe you have a right to, especially from a company or the government: *You can make a claim on your insurance policy.* **3** a right that someone believes they have to something, e.g. property or land: *The court ruled that they had no claim on the land.* □ *verb* **1** to state something as a fact, but without giving proof: *He claims he wasn't given a fair hearing.* **2** to ask for something, especially money, from a company or the government because you believe you have a right to it: *He's not entitled to claim unemployment benefit.*

clarify *verb*

to make something clearer or easier for someone to understand: *The report succeeded in clarifying the government's position.*
Word family **clarification** *noun*: *I am seeking clarification of the regulations.* **clarity** *noun* the state or quality of being easy to understand, see, or hear: *She analyses the pros and cons with admirable clarity.*

class *noun*

(*informal*) an elegant quality or a high level of skill that is impressive; stylishness: *She has class all right—she looks like a model.*
Usage This sense is often found in the phrase *a touch of class*: *A real parquet floor will add a touch of class to the room.* The noun *class* is also found in a wide range of other senses, including 'a set of people or things with common characteristics' (*a new class of antibiotics*), 'a social division' (*the ruling class*), and 'a group of pupils or students taught together; a lesson'.
Word family **classy** *adjective* (*informal*): *The car was a classy German make.*

classic *adjective, noun*

adjective **1** elegant, but simple and traditional in style or design: *a classic navy blazer.* **2** judged over time to be of the highest quality: *the classic work on the subject.* **3** very typical as an example: *the classic symptoms of flu.* □ *noun* **1** a work of art that is recognized as being of high quality. **2** something which is an excellent example: *Tomorrow's game should be a classic.*
Usage The word *classic* should not be confused with *classical*. *Classical* generally means 'relating to Greek or Roman antiquity' or 'relating to serious or conventional music': *The museum was built in the classical style.* □ *He plays jazz as well as classical violin.* Often *classical* is mistakenly used when *classic* is more appropriate: *a classical example* would be one taken from Greek or Latin whereas *a classic example* is the most typical example of its kind.

classify *verb*

to arrange things in groups according to features that they have in common; to decide which group someone or something belongs to: *Soils can be classified under two main headings.*

Word family *classification* noun: the classification of disease according to symptoms.

clean *adjective*

1 having a simple, well-defined, and pleasing shape: *The various parts blended with the clean lines of the aircraft's design.* **2** (of a taste, sound, or smell) giving a clear and distinctive impression to the sense: *clean, fresh, natural flavours.*

Usage The word *clean* is also used in a wide range of other meanings including 'free from dirt, stains, etc.' (*Are your hands clean?*) and 'free from faults' (*a clean driving licence*).

clear *adjective, verb*

adjective **1** easy to see or understand; leaving no doubts: *It is clear from the graph that sales have dropped sharply.* **2** easy to understand; not causing any confusion: *She gave me clear and precise instructions.* **3** that you can see through: *The water was so clear we could see the bottom of the lake.* **4** free from obstruction or unwanted objects: *a clear road.* □ *verb* **1** to make or become clear. **2** to declare (someone) innocent: *He was cleared of a crime.* **3** to authorize: *I cleared him to return to his squadron.*

Word family *clearance* noun official permission: *It is safest to seek advance clearance from the tax office.* **clearly** adverb: *Clearly, there have been disasters and reversals here.*

clever *adjective*

quick at learning and understanding things: *She was a very clever and studious young woman.*

Usage People use *clever* in the phrase *Clever boy/girl!* to tell a young child that they have learnt or done something well. When used to or about an adult, *clever* can be disapproving (if someone or something is *too clever* or merely *clever*), ironic (= meaning that you think someone or something is not clever at all), or patronizing (= showing, in a way that can be insulting, that you find someone's cleverness surprising).

Word family *cleverly* adverb: *Beneath the postmodern gloss of its bright shiny surfaces lies a cleverly disguised core of rational modernity.* **cleverness** noun

close *adjective*

1 giving careful attention to detail when looking at or considering something: *Take a close look at this photograph.* **2** (of a race or contest) won by only a small amount or distance; concerning something that nearly happens, especially a dangerous or unpleasant situation: *It's a desperately close race; I can't see who is ahead.* **3** very similar to something else: *There's a close resemblance between them* (= they look very similar).

Word family *closely* adverb: *She closely resembled her mother at the same age.* **closeness** noun

closure *noun*

the feeling that a difficult or an unpleasant experience has come to an end or been dealt with in an acceptable way: *The conviction of their son's murderer helped to give them a sense of closure.*

Usage The word *closure* is also used in other senses including the act or process of closing (*hospitals that face closure*) or a device that closes something.

coach *verb, noun*

verb to train someone to play a sport or improve a skill: *She was coached for the Olympics team.* □ *noun* a person who trains a team or person in a sport.

Usage *coach* or *train*? Both these words are used to talk about preparing sportsmen and women for competition or preparing musicians etc. for performance. You can *train* but not *coach* people in skills for their job: *All members of the team have been trained* (not: *coached*) *in first aid.* You can *train* but not *coach* animals: *They train* (not: *coach*) *dogs to sniff out drugs.* You can *coach* a person or sport, but you can only *train* a person: *He coaches* (not: *trains*) *basketball.*

Word family *coaching* noun the process of giving a student extra teaching in a particular subject: *Extra coaching is available for students who need more help.*

coax *verb*

to persuade someone to do something by talking to them in a kind and gentle way; to make an animal or machine do something by treating it gently: *He was coaxed out of retirement to help the failing company.*

Usage the verb *coax* is usually used with an adverb or preposition: *She coaxed the horse into coming a little closer.*

Usage *coax* or *cajole*? In many cases you can use either word: *He was coaxed/cajoled out of* *retirement.* However, *coax* can suggest a kinder, gentler action than *cajole*: you *coax* someone to do something that is good for them as well as you: *Police managed to coax him down from the ledge. Cajole* can suggest that someone is only pretending to be nice to someone else in order to get them to do what they want. *Cajoling* is sometimes used along with other, less gentle methods, such as *bullying*, *threatening*, *menacing*, and *bribing*.

cocktail *noun*
a mixture of different substances, usually ones that do not mix together well: *a lethal cocktail of drugs.*
Usage The word *cocktail* is usually used to describe a dangerous or unpleasant combination (*a lethal cocktail of drugs*) but not always (*a strange cocktail of scents, coconut conditioner and fresh toast.*)

code *noun*
1 a set of rules or behaviour that are generally accepted by or forced on a group of society: *Young people unconsciously conform to a dress code but reject any kind of uniform.* **2** a system of laws or written rules that state how people in an organization or country should behave: *The company has drawn up a new disciplinary code.*

cogent *adjective*
(*formal*) (of an argument, a reason, or evidence) expressed firmly and clearly in a way that influences what people believe: *His criticisms still seem as cogent today as they did 20 years ago.*
Word family **cogency** noun **cogently** adverb

coherent *adjective*
1 (of an idea, system, or explanation) logical, well organized, and consistent; clear and easy to understand: *They have yet to come up with a coherent policy on this issue.* **2** (of a person) able to talk and express yourself clearly: *She was lucid and coherent and did not appear to be injured.*
Usage In sense **1**, the word *coherent* is used especially to describe plans and organization; typical nouns that are referred to as *coherent* include *approach*, *framework*, *pattern*, *plan*, *policy*, *scheme*, *system*, and *theory*.
Word family **coherence** noun **coherently** adverb

cohort *noun*
a group of people with a shared characteristic: *a cohort of students.*
Usage The earliest sense of *cohort* is 'a unit of men within the Roman army'. From this it developed the meanings of 'a group of people with a shared characteristic': *The Church in Ireland still has a vast cohort of weekly churchgoers.* From the 1950s onwards a new sense developed in the US, meaning 'a companion or colleague', as in *Young Jack arrived with three of his cohorts.* Although this meaning is well established, some people object to it on the grounds that *cohort* should only be used for groups of people (as in its extended sense), never for individuals.

collaborate *verb*
to work jointly on an activity or project: *He collaborated with her on numerous special projects.*
Usage The word *collaborate* is also used in a negative sense, 'to betray your country by cooperating with an enemy'.
Word family **collaboration** noun: *He wrote a book in collaboration with his son.*
collaborative adjective: *collaborative research.*
collaborator noun

colleague *noun*
a person that you work with, especially in a profession or business: *I'd like you to meet a colleague of mine from the office.*
Usage **colleague** or **associate**? *Colleague* is much more frequent than *associate* and is a general word for someone you work with, especially in an office, a school, in government, etc: *the Prime Minister and his Cabinet colleagues.* An *associate* is used more to describe someone you have a business connection with, for example because you have done or are doing business with them: *The company is called Landor Associates.*

colourful *adjective*
1 having many or varied colours; bright: *a colourful array of fruit.* **2** lively and exciting; full of interest: *a controversial and colourful character.*
Usage You should take care in using the adjective *colourful* because it can also be used to describe involvement with disreputable activities (*The financier had had a colourful career*) or rude or vulgar language: *She made it*

clear, in colourful language, that she did not want to talk to the police.

combine *verb*

1 to bring or come together to form a single thing or group; to join or put together two or more things or groups etc: *Several factors had combined to ruin our plans.* **2** to do two things at the same time: *This modem combines a phone and a fax machine.*
Word family combination noun: *Technology and good management: a winning combination (= one that will certainly be successful)!*

comfort *noun, verb*

noun **1** the state of being physically relaxed and free from pain; the state of having a pleasant life, with everything you need: *With DVDs you can watch the latest movies in the comfort of your own home.* **2** a feeling of being less unhappy or not suffering or worrying so much: *I tried to offer a few words of comfort.* □ *verb* to make someone who is worried or unhappy feel better by being kind and sympathetic towards them: *The victim's widow was today being comforted by family and friends.*
Word family comfortable adjective: *It's advisable to wear loose, comfortable clothing.* **comfortably** adverb: *All the rooms were comfortably furnished.* **comforting** adjective: *It's comforting to know you'll be there.* **comfortingly** adverb: *comfortingly familiar.*

command *noun, verb*

noun **1** an authoritative order: *He obeyed her commands without question.* **2** the power to give orders to a group of people, especially in the armed forces or police: *He has 1,200 officers under his command.* □ *verb* **1** to use your position to tell someone to do something: *He commanded the forces to retreat.* **2** to be in charge of a group of people in the army, navy, or air force: *He was the officer commanding the troops in the Western region.* **3** to be in a position that gives a good view or control of something: *a rocky outcrop commanding a good view of the valley.* **4** to be in a strong position to have or secure: *He commanded considerable personal loyalty.*

commemorate *verb*

to take action to honour the memory of: *The town held a silent march to commemorate the dead.*

Word family commemoration noun: *a statue in commemoration of a national hero.* **commemorative** adjective: *Veterans of the battle will attend commemorative services.*

commend *verb*

1 to praise, especially publicly or officially: *She was commended for her handling of the situation.* **2** to present as suitable for approval or acceptance; to recommend: *I commend them to you without reservation.*
Word family commendable adjective deserving praise: *He showed commendable restraint.* **commendation** noun: *The film deserves the highest commendation.*

commensurate *adjective*

corresponding in size or degree; in proportion: *Salaries will be commensurate with age and experience.*
Word family commensurately adverb: *If you have a larger project, you'll need a commensurately larger internal drive.*

comment *noun, verb*

noun something that you say or write that gives an opinion on something or is a response to a question: *She made helpful comments on my work.* □ *verb* to express an opinion or give facts about it: *We were just commenting on how well you look.*
Usage comment, **remark**, or **observation**? A comment can be official or private. A remark can be made in public or private but is always unofficial and the speaker may not have considered it carefully: *What exactly did you mean by that last remark?* An observation is unofficial but is usually more considered than a remark: *He began by making a few general observations about the report.*

commentary *noun*

a written explanation or discussion of something such as a book or play: *He wrote a commentary on Paul's letter to the Romans.*
Word family commentator noun a person whose job it is to watch and consider events and situations on a particular subject and talk or write about them on television or radio or in a magazine: *She's a political commentator for the BBC.*

commerce *noun*

trade, especially between countries: *Leaders of industry and commerce met at the summit in Paris.*

Word family *commercial* adjective
1 connected with the buying and selling of goods and services: *They have offices in the commercial heart of the city.* **2** making or intended to make a profit: *They are an educational charity, not a commercial publisher.* *commercially* adverb

commission *noun, verb*

noun **1** a formal request for something to be made; instruction, command, or duty: *One of his first commissions was to redesign the exhibition building.* **2** a group of people given official authority to do something: *A commission was appointed to investigate allegations of police violence.* **3** a sum of money paid to an agent for selling something: *Foreign banks may charge a commission.* **4** an officer's position in the armed forces. □ *verb* **1** to order or authorize the production of: *The council commissioned a study of the issue.* **2** to bring something newly produced into working order: *We had a few minor problems getting the new heating system commissioned.* **3** to appoint to the rank of officer in the armed forces.

commit *verb*

1 to allocate or dedicate time or money to a course of action: *The Government should commit more money to training judges.* **2** (**commit yourself**) to promise to do something: *Local business leaders committed themselves to community projects.* **3** (**commit to**) to put something somewhere to preserve it: *She committed each detail to memory.* Word family *committed* adjective (of a person) willing to work hard and give their time and energy to something; believing strongly in something: *We have a highly-motivated trained and committed staff.*

commitment *noun*

1 dedication to a cause or activity: *We are looking for candidates who will make a long-term commitment to the project.* **2** an obligation or engagement that restricts freedom of action: *He resigned because of the pressure of family commitments.*

communicate *verb*

to make information, ideas, or feelings known to other people; exchange information or ideas with someone: *He was eager to communicate his ideas to the group.*

Word family *communication* noun: *Doctors do not always have good communication skills.* *communicative* adjective willing or eager to talk or impart information: *communicative skills.* *communicator* noun a person who is able to describe their ideas and feelings clearly to others: *The local candidate will be an effective communicator.*

community *noun*

1 all the people who live in a particular local area when talked about as a group: *The local community was shocked by the murders.* **2** a group of people who share the same race, religion, job, or interests, especially when they live in the same place: *Representatives of the city's Asian community had a meeting with the mayor.* **3** the holding of certain attitudes and interests in common: *the sense of community that organized religion can provide.* Usage The word *community* is often used in front of another noun to refer to a resource designed to serve the people of a particular area: *community health services.* □ *community policing.*

compact *adjective*

1 (of a room or place) using only a small amount of space: *The kitchen was compact but well equipped.* **2** small and tiny to carry: *a compact camera.* Usage You can describe a place as *compact* if you think this is a good thing because the available space has been used as effectively as possible.

compare *verb*

1 to examine people or things in order to see how they are similar and how they are different: *Standards in health care have improved enormously compared with 40 years ago.* **2** to be as good as; to be similar to: *How do these results compare with last year's?* Usage *compare to* or *compare with*? There is a slight difference between *compare to* and *compare with*. It is usual to use *to* rather than *with* when describing the resemblance of two quite different things, as in *Shall I compare thee to a summer's day?* In the other sense, 'to make a detailed comparison of', it is traditionally held that *with* is more correct than *to*: *Schools compared their facilities with those of others in the area.* However, in practice the distinction is not clear-cut and both *compare with* and *compare to* are used in either context.

Word family **comparable** *adjective* similar to another thing, situation, or person and able to be compared with them: *The situation in Holland is comparable with that in England.* **comparison** *noun*: *The tallest buildings in London are small in comparison with New York's skyscrapers.*

compatible *adjective*

1 able to exist or be used together without problems or conflict: *We've selected a contemporary design theme that's compatible with any décor.* **2** (of two people) able to have a good relationship; well suited. **3** consistent or in keeping: *The bruising is compatible with his having had a fall.*

Word family **compatibility** *noun*: *The system's user-friendliness and compatibility with conventional video hardware opens up possibilities for education and training.*

compelling *adjective*

1 arousing strong interest or attention in a powerful and irresistible way; not able to be proved false; inspiring conviction: *a compelling argument for adopting the policy.* □ *There is compelling evidence that the recession is coming to an end.* **2** so exciting or interesting that it holds your attention and you cannot stop reading, watching, or looking at it: *Her latest book made compelling reading.* **3** (of a need or desire) so strong that you must do something about it: *He was a sad man with a compelling need to talk about his unhappiness.*

competent *adjective*

having enough skill or knowledge to do something well or to the necessary standard: *Make sure the builders are competent to carry out the work.*

Usage The word *competent* can mean either that someone can do something well, or that they can do it just well enough: *Ron was a competent player—more than that, he was good!*

Usage **competent**, **able**, or **capable**? See **able**.

Word family **competence** *noun*: *This area of research is beyond my technical competence.* **competently** *adverb*: *You must be able to perform the following tasks competently and efficiently.*

competitive *adjective*

(of prices, goods, or services) as cheap as or cheaper than those offered by other companies; able to offer goods or services at relatively cheap prices: *We need to work harder to remain competitive with other companies.*

Usage The word *competitive* can also mean 'strongly (sometimes aggressively) desiring to be more successful than others': *He has a strong competitive streak.*

Word family **competitively** *adverb* **competitiveness** *noun*

complement *noun, verb*

noun **1** a thing that contributes extra features to something else so as to improve it: *Local ales provide the perfect complement to the food.* **2** the number or quantity that makes something complete: *We have a full complement of staff.* □ *verb* to add extra features to someone or something in a way that improves: *This mouth-watering sauce complements the dessert beautifully.*

Usage This word should not be confused with **supplement.**

Usage The words *complement* and *compliment* are frequently confused. They are pronounced in the same way but have quite different meanings: as a verb *complement* means 'to add to something in a way that enhances or improves': *A classic blazer complements a look that's smart or casual. Compliment* means 'to admire and praise someone for something': *He complimented her on her appearance.* Mistakes are common, particularly where *complementary* is written but *complimentary* is meant, as in *Honeymooners receive complementary* [should be: *complimentary*] *fruit and flowers.*

Word family **complementary** *adjective* combining so as to form a whole or to improve each other: *They have different but complementary skills.*

complex *adjective*

made up of many different things or parts that are connected; difficult to understand: *She managed to communicate a complex argument in a brilliantly simple way.*

Usage **complex** or **complicated**? In many cases you can use either word: *a complex/complicated problem.* □ *complex/complicated instructions. Complicated* is used slightly more in conversation and to describe everyday situations: *I'll send you a map of how to get*

here: it's a bit too complicated to describe.
Complex is used slightly more in written
English to describe serious, academic,
scientific, or technical issues: *a complex*
mathematical equation/formula. Both words
can describe something that is difficult to
understand because of its nature or design.
Complicated is often used to describe a
situation that has become less simple, more
messy, and more difficult to understand or
deal with over time because of events,
changes, or problems.

compliment *noun, verb*
noun a polite expression of praise or
admiration: *She blushed at the unexpected*
compliment. □ *verb* to politely congratulate or
praise: *Critics complimented the orchestra's*
performance.
Usage *compliment* or *complement*? See
complement.
Word family **complimentary** *adjective*
1 praising or approving: *a complimentary*
remark. **2** given free of charge: *a*
complimentary breakfast.

comprehensive *adjective*
1 including all, or almost all, the items,
details, facts, or information that may be
concerned: *to compile a comprehensive list of*
addresses. **2** having a large content or scope: *a*
comprehensive collection of photographs.
Word family **comprehensively** *adverb*: *The*
matter has been comprehensively discussed.
comprehensiveness *noun*

concise *adjective*
giving only the information that is necessary
and important, using few words: *a concise*
account of the country's history.
Usage The word *concise* can also be used to
describe a book that is shorter than the
original work on which it is based: *a concise*
edition of the dictionary.
Word family **concisely** *adverb*: *He spoke*
clearly and concisely.

conclude *verb*
to arrive at a judgement or opinion on the
basis of the information you have: *The report*
concluded that the cheapest option was to close
the laboratory.
Word family **conclusion** *noun* a judgement or
decision reached by reasoning: *Each research*
group came to a similar conclusion. **conclusive**
adjective proving something and allowing no

doubt of uncertainty; decisive: *The transcripts*
provided conclusive evidence that the accounts
had been falsified. **conclusively** *adverb*: *He was*
able to state conclusively that the virus could be
passed to humans.

concomitant *adjective*
(*formal*) naturally accompanying or
associated; attendant: *the Gulf crisis and the*
concomitant rise in oil prices.
Word family **concomitantly** *adverb*:
Individualism prevailed concomitantly with
nationalism so that people felt proudly ethnic.

condition *noun*
1 the state of something or someone, with
regard to appearance, fitness, or working
order: *You should visually check the condition of*
your wiring. **2** (**conditions**) the circumstances
affecting something: *the health risks*
associated with poor living conditions. **3** a state
of affairs that must exist before something
else is possible: *For a country to borrow money,*
three conditions must be met.
Word family **conditional** *adjective* subject to
one or more conditions or requirements
being met: *The supporters' approval is*
conditional on success.

conducive *adjective*
(**conducive to**) making a certain situation or
outcome likely or possible: *an environment*
which is conducive to learning. □ *The harsh*
lights and cameras were hardly conducive to a
relaxed atmosphere.

confident *adjective*
1 feeling sure about your own ability to do
things and be successful: *She was a confident*
outgoing girl. **2** completely sure that
something will happen in the way you want or
expect: *The team feels confident of winning.*
Usage *confident* or *sure*? The word *confident*
is stronger and more definite than *sure* and is
more often used in positive statements, when
you feel no anxiety: *She was quietly confident*
that everything would go as planned.
Usage *confident* or *self-confident*? See **self-**
confident.
Word family **confidence** *noun*: *He's brimming*
over with confidence. □ *I have little confidence in*
these figures. **confidently** *adverb*

confirm *verb*
1 to state or show that something is true or
correct: *The Financial Services Authority*

confirmed that it was investigating the rumours.
2 to make something definite or formally valid: *Hotels often require a deposit to confirm a booking.* **3** (**confirm in**) to make someone feel or believe something more strongly: *The experience confirmed her in her decision not to employ a nanny.*
Word family **confirmation** noun: *There was no independent confirmation of the reported deaths.* □ *Confirmation of your appointment is dependent upon satisfactory references.*

congratulate *verb*
1 to express good wishes or praise at the happiness or success of someone:
I congratulated them on their exam results.
2 (**congratulate yourself**) to feel pleased and proud because you have achieved something: *You can congratulate yourself on having done an excellent job.*
Usage **congratulate** or **praise**? The object of the verb *praise* can be a person, or their qualities, abilities, or achievements, but the object of *congratulate* must be a person: *I praised/congratulated him.* □ *I praised* (not: *congratulated*) *his ability to stay calm under pressure.* You might praise a child, an employee, or someone else that you are responsible for or have authority over. You would not usually praise your friend, partner, boss, or someone who is older than you or who has authority over you: *He praised/ congratulated his son/class/team.* □ *He congratulated* (not: *praised*) *his colleague.* You congratulate someone on something they have achieved on a particular occasion, especially when there is an obvious result: *She congratulated me on passing my driving test.* □ *She praised me for the way I deal with difficult customers.*
Word family **congratulations** noun: *Congratulations on getting a first!*

connect *verb*
1 to join together so as to provide access and communication: *The buildings were connected by underground passages.* **2** to bring together so as to establish a link: *The electrodes are connected to the recording device.* **3** to be related in some way: *Bonuses are connected to the firm's financial performance.*
Usage **connect**, **associate**, or **relate**? See **associate**.
Word family **connection** noun: *a connection between smoking and cancer.*

connotation *noun*
an idea or attitude suggested by a word in addition to its main meaning: *The word 'professional' has connotations of skill and excellence.*

conscientious *adjective*
taking care to do things carefully and correctly: *He was thorough and conscientious, rather than brilliant.*
Usage A *conscientious objector* is a person who refuses to serve in the armed forces for moral reasons.
Word family **conscientiously** adverb: *She performed all her duties conscientiously.*

consensus *noun*
an opinion that all members of a group agree with: *There is a general consensus among teachers about the need for greater security in schools.* □ *There is a growing consensus of opinion on this issue.* □ *She is skilled at achieving consensus on sensitive issues.*

consent *noun, verb*
noun permission or agreement: *A change in the rules requires the consent of all members.* □ verb **1** to give permission for something: *He consented to a search by a detective.* **2** to agree to do something: *She consented to work as an external assessor on the panel.*
Usage **consent**, **authorization**, or **permission**? See **authorization**.

consequence *noun*
1 a result or effect: *Inflation is a consequence of rapid growth in the money supply.*
2 importance or relevance: *The past is of no consequence.*
Word family **consequent** adjective following as a result or effect of something: *the social problems of pupils and their consequent educational difficulties.* **consequently** adverb: *Flexible workers find themselves in great demand, and consequently gain higher salaries.*

consider *verb*
1 to think carefully about something: *She hesitated, considering her choices.* **2** to believe or think: *people considered to be at risk of contracting the disease.* **3** to take something into account when making a judgement: *His record is even more remarkable when you consider his age.*
Word family **considerable** adjective large in amount, degree, or importance: *a position of*

considerable influence. **consideration** *noun*
1 careful thought: *I will give the matter some consideration.* **2** a fact taken into account when making a decision: *Time is an important consideration.*

consistent *adjective*

1 unchanging over a period of time: *consistent growth in the economy.* **2** acting or being done in the same way over time, especially so as to be fair or accurate: *The parents are being consistent and firm in their reactions.* **3** (of an argument or set of ideas) not containing any logical contradictions: *a consistent explanation.* **4** (**consistent with**) compatible or in agreement with: *The injuries are consistent with falling from a great height.*
Word family **consistency** *noun*: *the consistency of measurement techniques.* **consistently** *adverb*: *Her work has been of a consistently high standard.*

consolidate *verb*

1 to reinforce or strengthen your position or power: *The company consolidated its position in the international market.* **2** to combine a number of things into a single more effective or coherent whole: *All manufacturing activities have been consolidated in new premises.* □ *You must consolidate the results of the audit into an action plan.* **3** to combine a number of financial accounts or funds into a single overall account or set of accounts: *All the debts have been consolidated.*
Word family **consolidation** *noun*: *the consolidation of Japan's banking industry.*

conspicuous *adjective*

1 clearly visible: *He was very thin, with a conspicuous Adam's apple.* **2** attracting notice; noticeable: *Bay windows are a conspicuous feature of his architecture.*
Usage If something is *conspicuous by its absence*, it is obviously not present when it should be: *Sadly, leadership was conspicuous by its absence in word or deed.*
Word family **conspicuously** *adverb*: *Women were conspicuously absent from the planning committee.*

constructive *adjective*

having a useful and helpful effect rather than being negative or with no purpose: *You should always welcome constructive criticism of your work.*

Usage The phrase *constructive dismissal* refers to the changing of an employee's job or working conditions with the aim of forcing their resignation.
Word family **constructively** *adverb*

consult *verb*

1 to seek information or advice from someone, especially an expert or professional: *If you consult a solicitor, making a will is a relatively simple procedure.* **2** to have discussions with someone, before undertaking a course of action: *Patients are entitled to be consulted about their treatment.* **3** to refer to something for information: *consult a dictionary.*
Word family **consultancy** *noun* a professional practice that gives expert advice in a particular area: *a management consultancy firm.*

consultant *noun*

a person who knows a lot about a particular subject and is paid by a company to give advice about it: *Consultants were brought in to sort out the mess.*
Word family **consultation** *noun*: *They improved standards in consultation with customer representatives.* **consultative** *adjective*: *Branch offices are embarking on a consultative process about the changes in the constitution.*

consummate *adjective*

(*formal*) **1** (of a person) extremely skilled at something: *a consummate performer/actor/politician.* **2** (of a skill or quality) very great: *He weaved his way past the England defenders with consummate ease.*
Usage As a verb, meaning 'to make a marriage or relationship complete by having sexual intercourse', *consummate* is pronounced **kon**-syuu-mayt: *The marriage was never consummated.* As an adjective, *consummate* is traditionally pronounced kuhn-**sum**-uht, with the stress on the second syllable, but the pronunciation **kon**-syuu-muht, with the stress on the first syllable, is equally correct.

contemporary *adjective*

1 belonging to or occurring in the present: *the tension and complexities of our contemporary society.* **2** following modern ideas in style or design: *an exhibition of contemporary ceramics by leading potters.*

Usage **contemporary** or **modern**? In many cases you can use either word, especially when talking about art, culture, or society: *modern/contemporary art/architecture/dance/ fiction/literature/music/painting/culture/society/ politics/history.* □ *the modern/contemporary world/scene. Modern* (but not *contemporary*) is also used to talk about science and technology: *modern technology/physics/ medicine/warfare/equipment/machinery/ techniques.*

contour noun, verb
noun the outer edges of something; an outline of its shape or form: *The road follows the natural contours of the coastline.* □ *Cooperation between the two groups is more likely if the contours of a final settlement are sketched out from the outset.* □ *The orchestra tends to smooth the music's contours.* □ *verb* to mould into a specific shape, typically one designed to fit into something else: *The compartment has been contoured with smooth rounded corners.*
Usage A *contour* or a *contour line* is a line on a map joining points of equal height above or below sea level.
Word family **contoured** adjective: *the contoured leather seats.*

contrast noun, verb
noun 1 the state of being noticeably different from something else when put or considered together: *In contrast to karate, tae kwon do is characterized by high kicks.* 2 a thing or person noticeably different from another: *The castle is quite a contrast to other places where the singer has performed.* □ *verb* 1 to differ noticeably: *This view contrasts significantly from his earlier opinion.* 2 to compare in such a way as to emphasize differences: *The poem contrasts youth and age.*
Word family **contrasting** adjective: *The book explores contrasting views of the composer's early work.*

convince verb
1 to make someone firmly believe that something is true: *They convinced me that I was wrong.* 2 to make someone do something by giving them good reasons for doing it: *I've been trying to convince him to see a doctor.*
Usage **convince**, **persuade**, or **induce**? All these words refer to causing someone to do something that you wish them to do.

Convince refers primarily to getting someone to believe something by presenting them with arguments or evidence: *He managed to convince the police that his story was true.* The word can also mean 'persuade': *She convinced my father to branch out on his own*, but this use is disapproved of by some people. *Persuade* refers primarily to getting someone to do something through reasoning or argument, possibly against their better judgement or personal preference: *He persuaded Tom to accompany him.* □ *She was persuaded to return to work. Persuade* can also be used of causing someone to accept a belief, but *persuading* someone that something is the case may take considerable argument: *He persuaded her that nothing was going on.* □ *We need to be persuaded of the case. Induce* is used only of getting someone to do something. It is a forceful word, suggesting a good deal of effort or sacrifice on the part of the inducer, and often the use of bribes or threats rather than argument: *We had to give the driver a huge tip to induce him to carry the luggage.*
Word family **convinced** adjective: *I'm totally convinced of her innocence.* **convincing** adjective: *This seemed to me to be a convincing argument.*

cooperative adjective
1 involving people or groups doing something together or working together towards a shared aim: *This is a cooperative venture with the University of Copenhagen.* 2 helpful by doing what you are asked to do: *Employees will generally be more cooperative if their views are taken seriously.*
Usage The noun *cooperative* is used to refer to an organization such as a farm that is owned and run jointly by its members, who share in its profits or benefits.
Word family **cooperatively** adverb **cooperativeness** noun

coordinate verb
1 to bring together the different elements of a complex activity or organization into a harmonious or efficient relationship: *He had responsibility for coordinating London's transport system.* 2 to negotiate with others in order to work together effectively: *You will coordinate with consultants and other departments on a variety of projects.* 3 (of colours, clothes, or fabrics) to look nice

together; match or harmonize attractively: *This shade coordinates with a wide range of other colours.*
Usage The word *coordinate* is often used in the clothing or textile industries, or by people whose job is to comment on or advertise these goods.
Word family **coordination** noun: *The pamphlet was produced in coordination with residents' groups.* □ *advice on colour coordination.*

core *noun, adjective*
noun the most important part of a problem, activity, or set of ideas: *This report goes to the core of the argument.* □ *The plan has the interests of children at its core.* □ *adjective* being the most important part of a problem, activity, etc.: *Managers can concentrate on their core activities.* □ *Maths, English, and science are the core subjects* (= subjects that all the students have to study). □ *What are the core activities of the job?*
Usage **core** or **heart**? *Heart* is used to talk about the most important part of a problem, especially when morality or emotions are involved; it is used especially in the phrase *the heart of the matter/problem*. *Core* is used when the problem is seen in more logical or intellectual terms; *core* is also used to talk about the most important subjects or activities in education or business, and can be used as an adjective before another noun: *the core subjects/curriculum/activities/business.*

correlate *verb*
(*formal or technical*) **1** to have a mutual relationship or connection, in which one thing affects or depends on another: *Success in the educational system correlates highly with class.* **2** to establish such a relationship or connection: *He should correlate general trends in public opinion with trends in the content of television news.*
Word family **correlation** noun: *Research showed a clear correlation between recession and levels of property crime.* **correlational** *adjective*

corroborate *verb*
(*formal*) to provide evidence that supports a claim or theory, especially when someone has been accused of doing something wrong: *The witness corroborated the boy's account of the attack.*

Word family **corroboration** noun: *The newspaper should not have included the article without corroboration.* **corroborative** *adjective*: *corroborative evidence.*

cosmopolitan *adjective*
1 (of a place) containing people of different kinds or from different countries, and influenced by their culture: *She liked the cosmopolitan atmosphere of the city.* **2** (of a person) having or showing a wide experience of people or things from many different countries: *people with a truly cosmopolitan outlook.*
Usage In an extended sense, the word *cosmopolitan* has come to mean 'having an exciting and glamorous character associated with travel and a mixture of cultures': *Their designs became a byword for cosmopolitan chic.*

cost-effective *adjective*
effective or productive in relation to its cost: *the most cost-effective way to invest in the stock market.*
Word family **cost-effectively** adverb: *This constant connectivity means companies can deliver urgent and time-sensitive information to customers quickly and cost-effectively.* **cost-effectiveness** noun: *This author is not aware of any data examining the cost-effectiveness of testing all patients.*

cosy *adjective*
1 giving a feeling of comfort, warmth, and relaxation: *We stopped in a cosy little café for a cup of tea.* □ *The flickering lamp gave the room a cosy lived-in air.* **2** not seeking or offering challenge or difficulty; complacent: *a cosy assumption among audit firms that they would never go bust.*
Usage You should take care in using *cosy* as it also has an informal derogatory sense of 'beneficial to all those involved and possibly somewhat corrupt': *a cosy business deal.* In American English, the word is spelt *cozy*.
Word family **cosily** adverb: *We were sitting cosily by the fire.* **cosiness** noun: *I wished I was back in the cosiness and warmth of the kitchen.*

courage *noun*
willingness to face danger, pain, or opposition, especially when doing something that you believe to be right: *She displayed remarkable courage in the face of danger.*
Usage **courageous** or **brave**? See **brave**.

Word family **have the courage of your convictions** to act on your beliefs despite danger or disapproval: *If you believe in something then have the courage of your convictions and act positively now.* **courageous** *adjective*: *They were courageous enough to speak out against injustice.* **courageously** *adverb* **courageousness** *noun*

creative *adjective*
involving the use of skill and the imagination to produce something new or a work of art; having or showing an ability to do this: *Change unleashes people's creative energy.* Usage The term may have a negative connotation in the expression *creative accounting* (or *creative accountancy*), the exploitation of loopholes in financial regulations to gain advantage or to present figures in a misleadingly favourable light. Word family **creatively** *adverb* **creativeness** *noun* **creativity** *noun*: *The theme of Vikings gives the class an opportunity to show their creativity.*

credential *noun*
(usually **credentials**) **1** a qualification, achievement, quality, or aspect of a person's background, especially when used to indicate their suitability for something: *Recruitment is based mainly on academic credentials.* **2** a document proving a person's identity or qualification: *Check the credentials of any unknown caller.*

credible *adjective*
that can be believed or trusted: *Few people found his story credible.*
Usage **credible** or **creditable**? Credible chiefly means 'convincing' (*Few people found his story credible*), while *creditable* means 'praiseworthy' (*Their 32nd placing was still a creditable performance, considering they had one of the smallest boats*).
Word family **credibility** *noun*: *The prosecution did its best to undermine the credibility of the witness.*

creditable *adjective*
of a fairly good standard, and deserving praise or approval: *The chairman welcomed the company's creditable performance in the previous years.*
Usage The word *creditable* is used more about achievements than efforts. It describes achievements that are of a fairly high standard but not excellent.
Usage **creditable** or **credible**? See **credible**.
Word family **creditably** *adverb*: *All three players performed creditably.*

criterion *noun*
a principle or level of quality by which something is judged or by the help of which a decision is made: *The listing in the guide is proof that the restaurant meets certain criteria.*
Usage Strictly speaking, the singular form (following the original Greek) is *criterion* and the plural form is *criteria*. It is a common mistake, however, to use *criteria* as if it were a singular, as in *A further criteria* (should be: *criterion*) *needs to be considered.*

critical *adjective*
1 expressing disapproving comments or judgements: *The press were very critical of him.* **2** expressing or involving an assessment or analysis of the merits and faults of a literary or artistic work: *She never won the critical acclaim she sought.* **3** having a decisive importance in the success or failure of something; crucial or essential: *Confidence has been a critical factor in their success.*
Word family **critically** *adverb*: *He spoke critically about the government.* □ *The next four days will be critically important for the president.* **criticism** *noun*: *criticism of the management.* □ *literary criticism.*

critique *noun, verb*
noun a detailed analysis and assessment of something, especially a literary, philosophical, or political theory: *She wrote a feminist critique of Freud's theories.* □ *verb* to analyse and assess a theory or practice in detail; evaluate or review: *The authors critique the methods and practices used in the research.*
Usage *Critique* is pronounced with stress on the second syllable: kri-**teek.** Although it may not be liked by some, *critique* is now also regularly used as a verb, especially in the arts world, in a general sense of 'to review' or even simply 'to criticize': *My writing has been critiqued as being too academic*, but you should avoid this usage in formal contexts.

crucial *adjective*
extremely important, because a particular situation or activity depends on it; decisive or critical, especially in the success or failure of

something: *Negotiations were at a crucial stage.* □ *This match is crucial to our survival.*
Word family *crucially* adverb: *These matters are all crucially important.*

crux *noun*
the most important part of a problem or an issue: *Now we come to the real crux of the matter.* □ *the crux of the problem/argument/issue.*

culture *noun*
1 the customs, beliefs, art, ways of life, and social organization of a particular country or group: *These ideas have always been central to Western culture.* **2** a country or group with its own customs, beliefs, etc.: *As young people started to have more money, a significant youth culture developed.* **3** the attitudes and behaviour characteristic of a particular social group: *We need a major culture change in our economic, social, and political life.*
Usage The word *multicultural* means 'relating to or containing several cultural or ethnic groups within a society': *multicultural education.* See also **ethnic**.

Word family *cultural* adjective: *Teachers need to be aware of cultural differences.* *culturally* adverb: *a culturally diverse society.* *cultured* adjective well educated and able to understand art, literature, etc.: *a sensitive, cultured man.*

custom *noun*
1 a traditional way of behaving or doing something that is specific to a particular society, place, or time: *the old English custom of dancing around the maypole.* **2** a thing that a person often does; a habit: *It is our custom to visit the Lake District in October.* **3** regular dealings with a shop or business by customers.
Word family *customary* adjective in accordance with custom; usual: *It is customary to mark an occasion like this with a toast.* *custom-built* adjective made to a particular customer's order: *a custom-built yacht.* *customize* verb to modify to suit a particular person or task: *Food manufacturers customize products for restaurant chains.* □ *It can be customized to the developing needs of your students.*

Dd

daring *adjective*
1 (of a person) brave and willing to do dangerous or unusual things: *the concept of the daring solo performer.* **2** (of a thing) involving danger and taking risks: *A torpedo bomber attempted a daring attack.*
Usage *daring*, *audacious*, or **bold**? See **bold**.
Word family *daringly* adverb: *This house would have looked daringly modern when it was first built.*

debate *noun*
1 a formal discussion on a particular matter in a public meeting, parliament, etc., in which opposing arguments are presented: *The prime minister opened the debate on prison reform.* **2** an argument or discussion expressing different opinions, especially when this is seen as good or necessary: *the national debate on education.*
Word family *debatable* adjective open to discussion or argument: *It is debatable whether the country is coming out of recession.*

decisive *adjective*
of the greatest importance in affecting the final result of a particular situation: *Morrison scored the decisive goal in the 75th minute of the game.*
Usage The word *decisive* is not used simply to mean 'extremely important'. It is used when you are making a judgement that someone or something was or will be the most important fact affecting the result of a particular past or future situation: *The archers played a decisive part in the victory.*
Word family *decisively* adverb: *The governing party is expected to win decisively in the elections.*

declare *verb*
to say something officially or publicly; to say firmly and clearly: *The court declared that strike action was illegal.*
Usage *declare* or *announce*? See **announce**.

Word family *declaration* noun: *We were asked to sign a declaration that we were UK citizens.*

dedicate *verb*
to give a lot of your time, effort, or resources to a particular activity or purpose because you think it is important: *He dedicated his life to helping the poor.*
Word family *dedicated* adjective **1** (of a person) working hard at something, because it is very important to you: *The ship was painstakingly rebuilt by a dedicated team of engineers.* **2** used or designed for one particular purpose only: *a dedicated high-speed rail link from the Channel Tunnel.*

definitive *adjective*
1 (of a conclusion or agreement) final; that cannot or need not be changed or added to: *a definitive decision.* **2** (of a book or other text) the most authoritative of its kind: *the definitive biography of the Queen.*
Usage *definitive* or *definite*? *Definitive* is often used, rather imprecisely, when *definite* is actually intended, to mean simply 'clearly decided'. Although *definitive* and *definite* have a clear overlap in meaning, *definitive* has the additional sense of 'having an authoritative basis'. Thus, a *definitive decision* is one which is not only conclusive but also carries the stamp of authority or is a benchmark for the future, while a *definite decision* is simply one which has been made clearly and is without doubt.

delegate *verb*
to give part of your work or authority to someone in a lower position than you: *Some managers find it difficult to delegate.*
Usage People typically *delegate responsibilities*, *authority*, *power*, *decisions*, and *work*. When used as a noun, *delegate* means 'a person sent to represent others, e.g. at a conference, or as a member of a committee'.

Word family *delegation* noun: *the delegation of decision-making.*

deliberate *verb*

to consider carefully and for a long time: *The jury deliberated for five days before finding him guilty.*

Usage As a verb, *deliberate* is mainly used where a group of people, such as a jury in a court, think about and discuss something because they have to make a decision. It is pronounced di-**lib**-uh-rayt. As an adjective, meaning 'done on purpose' or 'careful', it is pronounced di-**lib**-uh-ruht.

Word family *deliberation* noun: *After much deliberation, we have decided to award the title to Springfield College.*

delicate *adjective*

1 very fine or intricate in texture or structure: *a delicate lace shawl.* **2** easily broken or damaged: *The eye is one of the most delicate organs of the body.* **3** (of a colour or flavour) subtle and pleasant: *a delicate shade of blue.*

Usage The word *delicate* also means 'needing skilful, tactful, or sensitive treatment': *the delicate matter of pay* and 'weak': *in delicate health.*

Usage *delicate* or *fragile*? *Delicate*, but not *fragile*, can describe parts of the body: *Babies have very delicate skin.* *Delicate* fabrics, like wool and silk, need special care: *a cool wash for delicate fabrics.* *Fragile* fabrics need even more care, usually because they are very old: *What kind of cleaning method will avoid damaging these fragile old fabrics?*

Word family *delicacy* noun: *miniature pearls of exquisite delicacy.* □ *The crabs are an Australian delicacy* (= a delicious or expensive food).

delight *noun, verb*

noun **1** great pleasure: *The children squealed in delight.* **2** a cause of great pleasure: *The illustrations are a delight.* □ verb **1** to please someone greatly: *This news will delight his fans throughout the world.* **2** (**delight in**) to take great pleasure in: *He was tall, handsome, and amiable and she delighted in his company.*

Word family *delighted* adjective feeling or showing great pleasure: *'Can you stay for dinner?' 'Thank you; I'd be delighted to.'* *delightful* adjective (used to describe times, events, and places) causing delight; very pleasing: *It was a delightful little fishing village.*

deliver *verb*

(especially in journalism or business) to do what you promised to do or what you are expected to do; to produce or provide what people expect you to: *He has promised to finish the job by June and I am sure he will deliver.*

Usage This sense is used in slightly informal contexts. It is usually used to talk about producing what is expected in business or sport: *to deliver a high-quality service/range of benefits/victory.* It derives from the informal phrase *deliver the goods* 'to provide what is promised or expected'.

dependable *adjective*

trustworthy and reliable: *a sturdy, long-lasting dependable watch.*

Usage The word *dependable* is often used to describe products, services, or people: *He's proved himself to be a trusted friend and dependable ally.* □ *The city's ubiquitous trams are frequent and dependable.*

Word family *dependability* noun: *The firm is recognized for the quality and the dependability of its products.* *dependably* adverb: *He is dependably excellent as a performer but his opponent steals the show for being special.*

descriptive *adjective*

saying what someone or something is like; describing: *The text contains some good descriptive passages.* □ *The word I used was meant to be purely descriptive* (= not judging).

Word family *descriptively* adverb: *They rejected the original term in favour of one more descriptively accurate.* *descriptiveness* noun

deserving *adjective*

that deserves help, support, or attention: *Only the more deserving cases ever receive help from the government.*

Usage The opposite of *deserving* is *undeserving*, which is used to describe a person or thing that does not deserve to have or receive something: *The package looked ordinary and unremarkable, undeserving of a second glance.*

design *noun, verb*

noun **1** a plan or drawing produced to show the appearance and workings of something before it is made: *The designs were stolen.* **2** the art or action of producing a design: *the design and development of new products.* **3** a decorative pattern: *abstract designs.* **4** the underlying purpose or planning: *the appearance of design in the universe.* □ *verb* **1** to produce a design for something: *design a new car.* **2** to plan or intend for a purpose: *The reforms were designed to stimulate economic growth.*

Usage The word *designer* 'made by a famous fashion designer' (*designer jeans*) has become a vogue term and it should not be overused.

Word family *designer* noun a person whose job is to decide how things such as clothes, furniture, or tools will look by making drawings, plans, or patterns: *They brought in an interior designer to suggest colour schemes for the house.*

detail *noun, verb*

noun **1** a small individual item or fact: *We shall consider every detail of the bill.* **2** small items or facts as a whole: *Pay close attention to detail.* □ *verb* **1** to give full information about: *The report detailed the environmental and health costs.* **2** to select someone to fulfil a particular task; to assign.

Word family *detailed* adjective giving many details as a lot of information; paying great attention to details: *He gave detailed instructions on what to do in an emergency.*

determined *adjective*

1 having made a firm decision to do or not do something, make something happen, or prevent something from happening, and not being willing to let anyone prevent you: *I'm determined to succeed.* **2** showing that you want very much to do something and trying hard not to let anyone or any difficulties stop you: *The proposal had perished in the face of determined opposition.*

Usage *determination* or *tenacity*? See **tenacity**.

Word family *determination* noun the quality that makes you continue trying to do something even when this is difficult: *The key to his success was courage and determination.*

develop *verb*

1 to gradually become bigger, better, stronger, or more advanced; to start to have a skill or quality that becomes better and stronger: *The village has developed from a small community into a thriving resort.* **2** to think of or produce a new idea or product and make it successful: *The company develops and markets new software.* **3** to start to exist,

experience, or possess: *He developed a passionate interest in fitness.*

Word family *development* noun **1** the process of producing or creating something new or more advanced; a new or advanced product: *the development of vaccines against tropical diseases.* **2** a piece of land with new buildings on it: *a commercial/housing development.* **3** a new event or stage that is likely to affect what happens in a continuing situation: *Are there any further developments in the investigation?* **4** the gradual growth of something so that it becomes more advanced or stronger: *The company offers a number of opportunities for career development.*

devote *verb*

1 to give a lot of your time, effort, attention, or resources to a particular activity or purpose because you think it is important: *Most companies devote resources to quality control and product testing.* **2** (**devote to**) to give an amount of time or attention completely to someone or something: *Many women devote years of their lives to bringing up children.*

Word family *devoted* adjective having great love for someone or something and being loyal to them: *She has left behind a devoted son and many loyal friends.* *devotion* noun great love, care, and support for someone: *His devotion to his wife and family is very touching.*

dialogue *noun*

formal discussion between two groups, especially when they are trying to resolve a problem or end a dispute: *The President told waiting reporters that there had been a constructive dialogue between the two sides.*

Usage In a book, play, or film, the word *dialogue* refers to conversations: *The novel has long descriptions and not much dialogue.* In American English, the word is also spelt *dialog.*

dignity *noun*

the sense you have of your own importance, value, and other people's respect for you: *The prisoners were treated with little regard for human dignity.*

Word family *dignified* adjective calm, serious, and deserving respect: *Throughout his trial, he maintained a dignified silence.* The opposite of *dignified* is *undignified*: *Public outrage at the proposals forced the government to beat an undignified retreat.*

diligent *adjective*
working hard and showing care in your work
or duties: *After a diligent search, police found
the missing child.*
Usage In law, *due diligence* refers to the
investigation process which a buyer (e.g. of
shares in a company) carries out before being
contractually bound so that they are aware of
all relevant issues.
Word family **diligence** noun: *He pursued the
tasks with great diligence.* **diligently** adverb:
*They worked diligently on the task they had
been given.*

dimension *noun*
a feature of something; a way of looking at or
thinking about something: *Her job added a
new dimension to her life.* □ *We should also
consider the social dimension of unemployment.*
Usage The word *dimension* is used especially
to talk about issues in society and history;
common words that combine with it include
*social, economic, political, ideological, cultural,
linguistic, historical, geographical,
environmental, regional, national, international,
human, personal, moral, ethical, religious,* and
spiritual.

diplomatic *adjective*
being skilful in dealing with people in difficult
situations without upsetting or offending
them: *He tried his best to give a diplomatic
answer.*
Usage **diplomatic** or **tactful**? *Tactful* is used to
describe a natural quality that some people
have and that they use in order to avoid
upsetting other people: *She is not exactly
known for being tactful. Diplomatic* is used
to refer more to a skill that can be learnt
through practice and used to get an
advantage for yourself as well as to help
other people.

discern *verb*
to recognize or learn something, especially
something that is not obvious; to manage to
see or hear someone or something that is not
very clear: *It is possible to discern a number of
different techniques in her work.*
Word family **discernible** adjective that can be
noticed, discovered, or understood, especially
when it is not easy to see or understand: *There
is often no discernible difference between the
rival brands.* **discerning** adjective showing
good judgement about the quality of

something: *There is a growing demand for the
product from discerning customers.*
discernment *noun: She saw herself as a woman
of good taste and discernment.*

discover *verb*
1 to find unexpectedly or during a search:
*Police discovered a large stash of drugs while
searching the house.* **2** to become aware of a
fact or situation: *the courage to discover the
truth.* **3** to be the first to find or observe a
place, substance, etc.: *Fleming discovered
penicillin early in the 20th century.* **4** to be the
first to recognize the potential of a performer:
I discovered the band back in the 70s.
Word family **discovery** noun: *a voyage of
discovery.* □ *the discovery of the body.*

discuss *verb*
1 to talk and share ideas on a subject or
problem with other people, especially in order
to decide something: *Have you discussed the
problem with anyone?* **2** to write or talk about
something in detail, showing the different
ideas and opinions about it: *This topic will be
discussed more extensively in the next chapter.*
Word family **discussion** noun: *Discussions are
still taking place between the two leaders.* □ *Her
article is a discussion of the methods used in
research.*

display *verb, noun*
verb **1** to put something in a place where
people can see it easily; to show something to
people: *The exhibition gives local artists an
opportunity to display their work.* **2** to show
signs of something, especially a quality or
feeling: *I have rarely seen her display any sign of
emotion.* □ *These statistics display a definite
trend.* **3** (of a computer etc.) to show
information: *The screen will display the user-
name in the top right-hand corner.* □ *This
column displays the title of the mail message.*
□ *noun* **1** an arrangement of things in a public
place to inform or entertain people or
advertise something for sale: *a beautiful floral
display outside the Town Hall.* □ *a window
display.* **2** an act of performing a skill or of
showing something happening, in order to
entertain: *a firework display.* □ *a breathtaking
display of aerobatics.* **3** an occasion when you
show a particular quality, feeling, or ability by
the way that you behave: *a display of affection/
strength/wealth.* **4** the words, pictures, etc.

shown on a computer screen: *a high-resolution colour display.*
Word family **on display** put in a place where people can look at it: *Designs for the new sports hall are on display in the library.* □ *to put something on temporary/permanent display.*

distinct *adjective*

1 clearly different or of a different kind: *The results of the survey fell into two distinct groups.* □ *We are talking about rural areas, as distinct from major cities.* **2** easy to hear, see, feel, smell, taste, or understand: *His voice was quiet but every word was distinct.*
Word family **distinctly** *adverb*: *The mind is distinctly different from the physical sphere.* □ *I distinctly heard someone calling my name.*

distinctive *adjective*

having a quality or characteristic that makes someone different and easily noticed: *Each subculture developed its own distinctive dress style.*
Usage **distinctive**, **characteristic**, or **typical**? A *distinctive* feature is not necessarily central or typical but serves to distinguish one item or individual from all others: *The system's most distinctive feature is the transferability of votes.* □ *She had a distinctive birthmark on her left knee.* A *characteristic* feature or quality is one that is immediately recognizable as an essential part of the nature of someone or something: *He has behaved with characteristic generosity.* □ *Pinnacles of rock are characteristic of this mountain range.* Something that is a *typical* member of a class of things has all the central defining features of the members of that class: *a typical example of 1930s Art Deco style.* □ *The printing shop is typical of prison industry. Typical* is often used to express annoyance at some regular feature or habit: *He didn't turn up, which was absolutely typical.*
Word family **distinctively** *adverb*: *It's a blue cheese with a distinctively sharp taste.*

distinguish *verb*

1 to recognize or show the difference between people or things: *At what age can children distinguish between right and wrong?* **2** to be a characteristic that makes two people, animals, or things different: *The power of speech distinguishes human beings from animals.*

Usage **distinguished** or **eminent**? See **eminent**.
Word family **distinction** *noun* **1** a clear difference between people or things that are similar or related: *We need to draw a distinction between democratic socialism and social democracy.* **2** the quality of being excellent, important, or special: *She had the distinction of being the first woman to fly the Atlantic.* □ *a writer of great distinction.*
distinguishable *adjective* that can be identified as different: *The male bird is easily distinguishable from the female.* **distinguished** *adjective* successful and respected, especially in a particular profession: *He has had a long and distinguished career in medicine.*

diverse *adjective*

widely varied: *People from diverse backgrounds were invited to the event.* □ *an ethnically diverse part of the city.*
Word family **diversify** *verb* to develop a wider range of products, interests, skills, etc., in order to be more successful or to reduce risks: *Farmers are being encouraged to diversify into new crops.* **diversity** *noun* a group of many people or things that are very different from one another: *There is a need for greater diversity and choice in education.*

document *noun, verb*

noun an official paper or book that gives information about something or that gives evidence or proof of something; a computer file that contains text: *The committee presented a document for discussion.* □ *verb* to record the details of something in writing: *Many aspects of school life have been documented.*
Word family **documentary** *adjective*: *documentary evidence.* **documentation** *noun* **1** documents providing official information or evidence: *You will have to complete the relevant documentation.* **2** written specifications or instructions: *Customers should consult the technical documentation for further help.*

dramatic *adjective*

1 (of events or scenes) exciting and impressive: *The village is set against the dramatic backcloth of Mont Blanc.* **2** (of a change or event) sudden; very great and often surprising: *I need to see a dramatic improvement in your work.*

Word family *dramatically* adverb: *The mountains rose dramatically behind them.* □ *Prices have increased dramatically in recent years.*

drive *noun*
1 the strong desire to do things and to achieve something; great energy: *He'll do very well—he has tremendous drive.* **2** an organized effort by a group of people to achieve something: *She played a crucial role in the drive for greater efficiency.*
Usage As a verb *drive* is used in many senses: *drive a car.* □ *You're driving yourself too hard* (= making yourself work very hard). □ *The urge to survive drove them on* (= forced them to act in a certain, especially extreme, way).

dynamic *adjective, noun*
adjective **1** (of a person) having a positive attitude and a lot of energy and new ideas: *He was a dynamic young advertising executive.* **2** (especially in business) (of a process or situation) always changing and making progress: *The business has managed to change and remain dynamic.* □ *noun* a force that stimulates change or progress: *Evaluation is part of the basic dynamic of the project.*
Word family *dynamically* adverb: *The software allows the user to dynamically recreate any previous point of data.* **dynamism** *noun* (in a person, project, or idea) energy and enthusiasm to make new things happen or to make things succeed: *The fresh dynamism of her approach was welcomed by all her students.*

Ee

economic *adjective*

1 connected with the trade, industry, and development of wealth in a country: *This book deals with the social, economic, and political issues of the period.* **2** (of a process, business, or activity) producing enough profit to continue: *It's simply not economic for these small farmers to start buying large amounts of expensive fertilizer.*

Usage economic or economical? People sometimes describe something as *economic* when they mean *economical*. *Economic* means 'concerning economics': *He's rebuilding a solid economic base for the country's future.* *Economical* means 'thrifty, avoiding waste': *Small cars should be inexpensive to buy and economical to run.*

Word family economically *adverb*: *The factory is no longer economically viable.*

effective *adjective*

successful in producing the result that is wanted or intended: *Aspirin is a simple but highly effective treatment.*

Usage effective or efficient? *Effective* means 'having a definite or desired effect'; *efficient* applies to actions, instruments, etc. and means 'well organized, productive with a minimum waste or effort'; when used to describe a person it means 'capable'. For example, managers need to be not only *efficient*, achieving results with a minimum waste of resources, but also *effective*, achieving the right results.

Word family effectively *adverb*: *The company must reduce costs to compete effectively.*

efficient *adjective*

doing something well and thoroughly with no waste of time, money, or energy: *The more efficient firms have lower costs.* □ *She was helpful, quietly efficient, and tactful.*

Usage efficient or effective? See **effective**.

Word family efficiency *noun*: *The new computer system will cut costs and increase efficiency.* □ *New standards of energy efficiency* (= not wasting energy) *are being introduced.*

efficiently *adverb*: *They began to work harder and more efficiently.*

elegant *adjective*

1 (of people) attractive and showing a good sense of style: *She was tall, slim, and elegant.* **2** (of clothes, places, and things) attractive and designed well: *Guests can dine and relax in comfortable elegant surroundings.*

Word family elegance *noun*: *His writing combines elegance and wit.* **elegantly** *adverb*: *elegantly dressed women.*

eloquent *adjective*

1 (of a person) able to use language and express their opinions well, especially when speaking in public: *She was an eloquent speaker with a beautiful voice.* **2** (of a speech) expressed well: *It was an eloquent and well-informed speech.*

Word family eloquence *noun*: *He was well known for the eloquence of his sermons.* **eloquently** *adverb*: *She spoke eloquently on the subject for about an hour.*

embody *verb*

(especially of a person) to give a visible form to an idea, quality, or feeling: *a politician who embodied the hopes of black youth.* □ *We want to build a national team that embodies competitive spirit and skill.*

Usage embody, represent, or symbolize? Sometimes you can use any of these words, especially when you are talking about a person: *He came to represent/embody/symbolize his country's struggle for independence.* *Embody* is the most physical and visual of these words and is used to talk about real people becoming the basis for other people's hopes: the qualities that someone *embodies* are usually good qualities. *Symbolize* is often more abstract (= existing as an idea rather than as a physical reality), and can be used to talk about objects or things, such as a dove being used to give the idea of peace, but it is a picture or idea of a dove, not a particular dove that really exists. *Represent* is the most general of these words; it can be used to mean *embody* or *symbolize* or it can simply mean 'express': *The comments represent the views of the majority.*

Word family **embodiment** noun a person or thing that represents or is a typical example of an idea or quality: *He is the embodiment of the young successful businessman.*

emerge *verb*
1 to begin to exist; appear or become known: *After the elections, opposition groups began to emerge.* □ *He rapidly emerged as a key figure in the campaign.* □ *The emerging markets of South Asia.* **2** (of facts, ideas, or evidence) to become known: *No new evidence emerged during the investigation.* □ *It emerged that the company was going to be sold.* □ *One thing emerges very clearly from this study.*

Usage The word *emerge* is used especially to talk about changes in politics, economics, technology, and society, with new situations and events, and people and groups playing new roles.

Word family **emergence** noun: *the emergence of new technologies.* **emergent** adjective: *the emergent democracies of eastern Europe.* **emerging** adjective: *a world of emerging economic giants.*

eminent *adjective*
(of a person) famous and respected, especially in a particular profession: *The house was designed by the eminent architect Robert Adam.*

Usage **eminent** or **distinguished**? You can use either word to describe a person in terms of their profession: *a distinguished* or *an eminent scientist/artist/painter/poet/writer/architect/historian/philosopher/scholar/professor. Distinguished* (but not *eminent*) can also describe someone's career, achievement, record, or position, or the record or tradition of an organization or group.

Word family **eminence** noun: *His eminence as a scientist is well known.* **eminently** adverb: *You are eminently well qualified to give talks on this subject.*

emphasis *noun*
special importance that is given to something: *There has been a shift of emphasis from manufacturing to service industries.*

Usage **emphasize** or **stress**? When you are talking about giving particular importance to a fact or issue, you can use either word. *Stress* is slightly more informal and is used more in spoken English and journalism, especially when the subject is human (*I must stress ...*). *Emphasize* is slightly more formal and is used more in written and academic English, especially when the subject is not human (*The report emphasizes ...*). When you are talking about giving extra force to a word, you should use *stress* when you are talking about normal speech patterns, especially syllable stress. You can use *stress* or *emphasize* to talk about giving particular importance to a word.

Word family **emphasize** verb to stress the importance of something: *The report emphasized the need for economic stability.* □ *It should be emphasized that this is only one possible explanation.*

empower *verb*
1 to give someone the authority to do something: *The courts were empowered to impose the death sentence for certain crimes.* **2** to make someone stronger and more confident, especially in controlling their life and claiming their rights: *movements to empower the poor so that they can lead more fulfilled lives.*

Word family **empowerment** noun: *the empowerment of a community to obtain greater self-reliance.*

enchant *verb*
to attract someone strongly and make them feel great pleasure or interest: *The happy family scene had enchanted him.*

Usage The word *enchant* also means 'to put someone under a spell'.

Word family **enchanting** adjective delightfully charming or attractive: *an exhibition that offers an enchanting view of Ireland's heritage and culture.* **enchantment** noun: *To look through one of these shop windows is instant enchantment.*

encourage *verb*
1 to give someone support, courage, or hope: *My parents have always encouraged me in my choice of career.* **2** to persuade someone to do something by making it easier for them and making them believe it is a good thing to do: *Banks actively encourage people to borrow money.* **3** to make something more likely to

happen or develop; make something increase: *The questions are designed to encourage debate.*
Word family **encouragement** noun: *He needs all the support and encouragement he can get.* **encouraging** adjective giving you hope that someone or something will be successful: *The response we received from our readers was extremely encouraging.*

endear verb

to cause to be loved or liked: *Flora's spirit and character endeared her to everyone who met her.*
Word family **endearing** adjective: *I like his honesty—it's one of his most endearing qualities.* **endearingly** adverb: *an endearingly old-fashioned idea.*

endorse verb

1 to declare your approval or support for someone or something: *They fully endorsed a general trade agreement.* **2** to say in an advertisement that you use and like a particular product so that other people will want to buy it: *I wonder how many celebrities actually use the products they endorse.*
Word family **endorsement** noun: *The election victory is a clear endorsement of their policies.* □ *We are happy to give this product our full endorsement.*

energy noun

1 (in a person) the ability to put effort and enthusiasm into something you do: *I admire her boundless energy.* **2** the physical and mental effort that you use to do something: *She concentrated all her energy into her work.*
Word family **energetic** adjective: *He knew I was energetic and would get things done.* **energize** verb: *People are energized by his ideas.*

engage verb

1 to attract or involve someone's attention: *The tasks must engage the children's interest.* **2** (**engage in/with**) to participate or become involved in: *He was engaged in a lively conversation with the barber.*
Word family **engaging** adjective charming and attractive: *She had such an engaging smile.*

enhance verb

to further improve the good quality, status, or value of someone or something: *The images can be enhanced using digital technology.*

Word family **enhancement** noun: *The proposed works contribute to the environmental enhancement of the area.* □ *The aim of the law was to cover future technical enhancements to email.*

enjoy verb

1 to take pleasure in an activity or occasion: *I really enjoyed our evening together.* **2** (**enjoy yourself**) to have a pleasant time: *She travels purely to enjoy herself.* **3** to possess and benefit from: *These professions enjoy a high status.* □ *They enjoyed considerable legal protection.*
Usage **enjoyable** or **pleasurable**? See **pleasurable**.
Word family **enjoyable** adjective that you enjoy: *He always tried to make his lessons enjoyable.* **enjoyment** noun: *I get a lot of enjoyment from gardening.*

enrich verb

to improve the quality of something usually by adding something to it: *Reading good literature can enrich all our lives.* □ *Most breakfast cereals are enriched with vitamins.* □ *The collection was enriched by a bequest of graphic works.*
Word family **enrichment** noun: *personal enrichment.*

enterprise noun

1 a large project, especially one that is difficult: *The music festival is a new enterprise that we hope will become an annual event.* **2** initiative and resourcefulness: *Success came quickly, thanks to a mixture of talent and enterprise.* **3** a business company: *a state-owned enterprise.* **4** the development of business by the people of a country rather than by the government: *They provide grants to encourage enterprise in the region.*
Word family **enterprising** adjective having or showing initiative and resourcefulness: *Some enterprising teachers have started their own recycling programmes.*

enthral verb

to get and keep someone's close attention by being extremely interesting or attractive: *The children watched, enthralled by the bright moving images.*
Usage In American English, the word is spelt *enthrall*.
Usage **enthral**, **captivate**, or **entrance**? See **captivate**.

Word family **enthralling** adjective: *an enthralling best-seller.*

enthusiasm *noun*
1 intense and eager enjoyment, interest, or approval: *her energy and enthusiasm for life.*
2 something that arouses enthusiasm: *They can put their skills and enthusiasms to good use.*
Usage The verb *enthuse* was formed by shortening the noun *enthusiasm*. Like many verbs formed from nouns in this way, especially those from the US, some traditionalists regard it as unacceptable.
Word family **enthusiast** noun: *Railway enthusiasts were given the rare chance to ride on the steam train during the weekend.*
enthusiastic adjective: *They gave her an enthusiastic welcome.* **enthusiastically** adverb: *They responded enthusiastically to the plan.*

entrepreneur *noun*
a person who makes money by starting or running businesses, especially when this involves taking financial risks: *A creative entrepreneur, he was always dreaming up new projects.*
Word family **entrepreneurial** adjective: *As companies have grown larger, the entrepreneurial spirit has been lost.*

envision *verb*
to imagine what a situation will be like in the future, especially a situation that you intend to work towards: *We now have the opportunity to build the world envisioned by the founders of the United Nations.*
Usage The word *envision* is used especially in business and political contexts. In American English, it is also used for 'envisage' ('to imagine what will happen in the future'): *What level of profit do you envisage* (American English, *envision*)?

epitome *noun*
a perfect example of a person or quality: *Her clothes are the epitome of good taste.*
Usage The word *epitome* is almost always used in the phrase *the epitome of someone* or *something.* It is often used to talk about how people look or behave. Although many examples of *epitome* show good qualities, this is not always the case; a common phrase is *the epitome of evil.*
Usage **epitomize** or **typify**? Something can *typify* or *epitomize* a mood, style, or atmosphere, especially of a particular time or

place. *Epitomize* suggests that you cannot imagine a more typical example of something. *Typify* is more neutral, and suggests that the example you are giving has all the usual qualities or features of a particular time, place, or type of person or thing.
Word family **epitomize** verb to be a perfect example of something: *The fighting qualities of the team are epitomized by the captain.* □ *These movies seem to epitomize the 1950s.*

equip *verb*
1 to prepare someone for an activity or task, especially by teaching them what they need to know: *The programme is designed to equip students for a career in nursing.* **2** to provide someone or something with the things that are needed for a particular purpose or activity: *The centre is well equipped for canoeing and mountaineering.*
Usage *Skills*, *professional training*, and *education* are typical things that *equip* people for something or to do something.
Word family **equipment** noun: *supplies of office equipment.*

essential *adjective, noun*
adjective **1** extremely important and completely necessary, because without it something cannot exist, be made, or be successful: *Experience is essential for this job.*
2 connected with the most important aspect or basic nature of someone or something: *The essential character of the town has been destroyed by the new road.* □ noun (**essentials**) **1** things that are absolutely necessary: *The studio had all the essentials like heating and running water.* **2** the most important or basic elements of something: *the essentials of democracy.*
Usage **essential**, **inherent**, **innate**, or **intrinsic**? See **inherent**.
Usage **essential** or **vital**? See **vital**.
Word family **essentially** adverb: *There are three essentially different ways of tackling the problem.*

establish *verb*
1 to find or prove the facts of a situation: *Police are still trying to establish the cause of death.* **2** to start or create an organization or system that is meant to last a long time; start a relationship, especially a formal one: *The*

school has established a successful relationship with the local community.

Usage establish or **ascertain**? See **ascertain**.

Usage You should take care in using the phrase *the Establishment*, because it is usually used with disapproval to refer to the people in a society or profession who have influence and who do not usually support change: *His ideas have not been widely accepted within the academic establishment.*

Word family establishment noun: *His visit facilitated the establishment of diplomatic relations between the two countries.*

ethnic *adjective*

connected with or belonging to a nation, race, or tribe that shares a cultural tradition; happening or existing between people of different groups; typical of a country or culture that is very different from modern western culture and therefore interesting for people in western cultures: *This region of Bulgaria has a large ethnic Turkish population.* □ *The conference strongly condemned the practice of ethnic cleansing* (= mass killing of one ethnic group by another). □ *The country is divided along ethnic lines.* □ *There was a stall selling ethnic jewellery from Afghanistan.*

Usage *Ethnic* has become a more popular word in recent years to describe a person's background or origins, or the group they belong to, in phrases such as *ethnic group/origin/minority*. It is considered more general and less offensive than words such as *race* or *tribe*. It can describe not just the racial background of a group of people but also their religion, customs, and culture. *Ethnic group* is often used as a general term to describe a person's race or nationality. When talking about a group of people living in a place where most people are from a different race and/or nationality, the terms *minority ethnic group* or *ethnic minority* are often used.

Word family ethnically adverb: *an ethnically divided region.*

ethos *noun*

the characteristic spirit of a culture, era, or community as shown in its attitudes and aspirations: *The governing body has responsibility for the ethos of the school.* □ *They tried to develop an ethos of public service.*

evaluate *verb*

to form an opinion of the amount, value, or quality of something after studying it

carefully: *The study will help in evaluating the effects of the recent changes.*

Word family evaluation noun: *Proper evaluation of the results is crucial.*

evoke *verb*

to bring a memory, feeling, or image into your mind: *The music evoked memories of her youth.*

Word family evocation noun a description, film, or work that brings a memory, feeling, or image into your mind: *The film is a brilliant evocation of childhood in the 1940s.* **evocative** adjective: *The song has powerfully evocative lyrics.*

exact *adjective*

1 giving all the details correctly; not vague or inaccurate: *She gave an exact description of her attacker.* □ *Exact details are still being finalized.* 2 (of a person) accurate and careful about minor details: *She was an exact, clever manager.*

Usage exact, **accurate**, or **precise**? See **accurate**.

Word family exactly adverb: *It happened almost exactly a year ago.* **exactness** noun: *In this job, detail and exactness are essential.*

examine *verb*

1 to think about, study, or describe an idea, subject, or piece of work very carefully: *The recession forced us to examine every aspect of our business.* 2 to look at someone or something closely to see if there is anything wrong or to find the cause of a problem: *The goods were examined for damage on arrival.*

Usage The word *examine* also means 'to test someone's knowledge or ability': *Students will be examined in all subjects at the end of term.*

Word family examination noun: *The chapter concludes with a brief examination of what causes family break-up.* □ *Careful examination of the ruins revealed an even earlier temple.* □ *There was an examination at the end of the course.*

excel *verb*

1 to be exceptionally good at an activity or subject: *She excelled at landscape painting.* 2 (**excel yourself**) to perform exceptionally well: *Miss Lodsworth, who organized the flower rota, had excelled herself.*

Usage excel, **outdo**, or **surpass**? *Excel* is most often used without an object, emphasizing someone's outstanding ability: *She excelled at maths and won a scholarship to Cambridge.* *Outdo* indicates that someone is more successful or goes to greater lengths than their competitors. The note of competition with others is strongest in this word: *Not to be outdone, the company also produced its own fully-illustrated catalogue.* Surpass literally means 'go beyond'. It indicates that someone has passed a previous limit, proving themselves greater or better: *He won five races and surpassed all expectations.*

excellent *adjective*

extremely good: *The wine was good and the meal was excellent.*
Usage The word *excellent* is used especially about standards of service or of something that someone has worked to produce. The opposites of *excellent* are *inferior*, *mediocre*, and *poor*.
Word family **excellence** noun: *The college has a reputation for academic excellence.* □ *We want this hospital to be a centre of excellence.* **excellently** adverb: *The couple performed excellently at the Dance Championships.*

exceptional *adjective*

1 unusually good or great: *Exceptional students are given free tuition.* **2** very unusual: *The deadline can be extended only in exceptional circumstances.*
Word family **exceptionally** adverb: *an exceptionally gifted child.* □ *Exceptionally, the director may override the decision of the committee.*

exciting *adjective*

causing great enthusiasm and eagerness: *This is one of the more exciting developments in biology in recent years.*
Usage **exciting**, **thrilling**, or **exhilarating**? *Exhilarating* is the strongest of these words and *exciting* the least strong. *Exciting* is the most general and can be used to talk about any activity, experience, feeling, or event that excites you. *Thrilling* is used particularly to talk about contests and stories where the ending is uncertain. *Exhilarating* is used particularly to talk about physical activities that involve speed and/or danger.
Word family **excitement** noun: *the excitement of seeing a leopard in the wild.*

exclusive *adjective*

1 (of a product or service) of a very high quality and expensive and therefore not often bought or used by most people; (of a group or society) unwilling to allow new people to

become members, especially if they come from a lower social class: *one of Britain's most exclusive clubs.* **2** only to be used by, or given to, one particular person or group: *The hotel has exclusive access to the beach.*
Word family **exclusively** adverb: *paints produced exclusively for independent retailers.*

exemplary *adjective*

providing a very good example of behaviour, which other people should copy: *The medal was awarded for his exemplary conduct and courage.*
Usage An *exemplary punishment* is one that serves as a warning or deterrent to others.

exhaustive *adjective*

including or considering all elements or aspects; fully comprehensive: *The guide outlines every bus route in exhaustive detail.*
Word family **exhaustively** adverb: *his exhaustively researched biography.* **exhaustiveness** noun: *This new exhibition covers the subject with admirable exhaustiveness.*

exhilarating *adjective*

very exciting and enjoyable: *My first parachute jump was an exhilarating experience.*
Usage **exhilarating**, **exciting**, or **thrilling**? See **exciting**.
Word family **exhilaration** noun: *to experience the full exhilaration and despair of the stock market's ups and downs.*

experience *noun, verb*

noun **1** the knowledge, skill, and ability you have gained through doing something for a period of time; the process of gaining this: *I have over ten years' teaching experience.* **2** practical contact with and observation of facts or events: *David gained his first experience of business with his father and brothers.* **3** an event that leaves an impression on you: *an enjoyable experience.* □ verb **1** to encounter or undergo an event or situation: *Police officers can experience harassment and distress.* **2** to feel an emotion.
Word family **experienced** adjective having knowledge, skill, and ability in a particular job or activity through having done it a lot or for a long time: *He's very experienced in looking after animals.* □ *an experienced traveller* (= someone who has travelled a lot).

expert *noun, adjective*

noun a person with special knowledge, skill, or training in something: *She's a leading expert in child psychology.* □ *adjective* done with, having, or involving a lot of knowledge or skill: *It's a good idea to seek expert advice.* □ *She's expert at making cheap but stylish clothes.*

Usage **expert** or **authority**? See **authority**.
Word family **expertise** noun expert knowledge or skill in a particular subject, activity, or job: *They have considerable expertise in dealing with oil spills.* **expertly** adverb: *He tied up the boat and expertly folded down the sails.*

explain *verb*

1 to make something clear to someone by describing it in more detail or in revealing relevant facts: *A technician explained the procedure.* 2 to give a reason for something: *The government now has to explain its decision to the public.*
Word family **explanation** noun: *For a full explanation of how the machine works, turn to page 5.* □ *The most likely explanation for their lateness is that the plane was delayed.* **explanatory** adjective giving the reasons for something; intended to describe how something works or to make something easier to understand: *There are explanatory notes at the back of the book.*

explore *verb*

1 to travel around an area or country in order to learn more about it: *They took advantage of the opportunity to explore the stunning scenery all around them.* 2 to examine or discuss an idea, issue, or possibility completely or carefully in order to find out more about it: *The study explores the differences between the way men and women talk.* □ *They wanted to explore the possibility of achieving a longer-term solution.*
Word family **exploration** noun: *The film is a chronicle of humanity's exploration of space.* **explorer** noun a person who travels to unknown places in order to find out more about them: *Early explorers traded directly with Native Americans for furs.*

exponent *noun*

a person who promotes an idea or theory: *She's well known as an exponent of free-trade policies.* 2 a person who does a particular thing skilfully: *He's the world's leading exponent of country rock guitar.*

Usage You should take care not to overuse the derived form *exponential* meaning (of an increase) 'becoming more and more rapid': *The social security budget was rising at an exponential rate.*

expound *verb*

1 to present and explain a theory or idea in detail: *He was expounding a powerful argument.* 2 to explain the meaning of a literary or doctrinal work: *to expound the scriptures.*
Word family **exposition** noun: *an exposition and defence of Marx's writings.*

expressive *adjective*

1 effectively conveying thought or feeling: *The musical performance was a miracle of expressive freedom and insight.* 2 (**expressive of**) conveying a specified quality or idea: *The spires are expressive of religious aspiration.*
Word family **expressively** adverb: *He gestured expressively with his hands.* **expressiveness** noun: *the emotional expressiveness of the actors' faces.*

exquisite *adjective*

extremely beautiful or carefully made: *Look at the exquisite craftsmanship in this vase.*
Usage The word *exquisite* describes things that are beautiful in a fine, delicate way, rather than in a grand, impressive way.
Word family **exquisitely** adverb: *exquisitely designed jade sculptures.*

extraordinary *adjective*

1 very unusual or remarkable: *the extraordinary plumage of the male.* □ *It is extraordinary that no consultation took place.* 2 unusually great: *Young children need extraordinary amounts of attention.*
Word family **extraordinarily** adverb: *She was an extraordinarily attractive girl.*

exuberant *adjective*

full of energy, excitement, and happiness: *She gave an exuberant performance.*
Word family **exuberance** noun: *Nothing will curb his natural exuberance.* **exuberantly** adverb: *He nodded exuberantly in agreement.*

Ff

facelift *noun*
a procedure carried out to improve the appearance of something: *The railway station has undergone a major multimillion pound facelift.* □ *need/give/receive/have a facelift.*
Usage This use comes from the original meaning of a facelift, a cosmetic surgical operation to remove unwanted wrinkles by tightening the skin of the face.

facilitate *verb*
to make an action or process easy or easier: *The new trade agreement should facilitate faster economic growth.*
Usage *Facilitate* is used with a wide range of nouns that describe a process, such as *passage, flow, transition*, and *transfer*: *Eight residencies are awarded annually to promising young artists to facilitate their transition from formal school training to professional life.*

facility *noun*
1 a piece of equipment, service, or building provided for a particular purpose: *Many shopping centres include car-parking facilities.*
2 a natural ability to do something well and easily: *He had a facility for languages.*
Usage The singular use of sense 1 (*a production facility*) is often jargon and should be used with care.

fact *noun*
1 something that is known to be true, especially something that can be proved: *The most commonly known fact about hedgehogs is that they have fleas.* 2 (**facts**) information used as evidence or as part of a report or news article: *First, let's look at some of the basic facts.*
Usage *In fact* is used to emphasize the truth of a statement, especially one that is opposite to what might be expected or what has been stated before: *You believe you are careful and efficient, but in fact you are not good at organization.*

factor *noun*
a circumstance, fact, or influence that contributes to a result: *Money proved to be the deciding factor.*
Usage It can be preferable to use a more precise word such as *fact* or *influence*: *Ill health was an important factor* (or *influence*) *in his decision to retire early.*

factual *adjective*
based on or containing facts: *The essay contains a number of factual errors.* □ *He fails to distinguish factual information from opinion.*
Word family **factually** adverb: *The comments were factually correct, but I think they were unfair.*

fair *adjective*
1 treating people equally: *Consumers will receive a fair share of the resulting benefits.*
2 just or appropriate in the circumstances: *To be fair, this subject poses special problems.*
3 considerable in size or amount: *I do a fair bit of coaching.* 4 moderately good: *He has a fair chance of success.*
Usage *Fair* is an emotive word, expressing a deep-seated sense of what is basically right and appealing to a general sense of justice: *All we are asking for is a fair wage.*

faithful *adjective*
1 staying with or supporting a particular person, organization, or belief, often in the face of difficulty or some temptation to desert: *He remained faithful to the ideals of the party until his death.* 2 true to the facts or the original: *a faithful copy.*
Usage **faithful** or **loyal**? *Faithful* can be distinguished from *loyal*: a *faithful* friend remains faithful out of affection; a *loyal* friend remains loyal as a matter of principle.
Word family **faithfully** adverb: *She faithfully served the school community as headteacher for years.* □ *She translated the novel as faithfully as*

possibly. **faithfulness** *noun: Here was rock-solid, steadfast faithfulness and integrity.*

famous *adjective*
known by large numbers of people and usually much admired: *The country is famous for its natural beauty.*
Usage **famous**, **celebrated**, **renowned**, or **well-known**? See **celebrate**.
Word family **fame** *noun: She is a designer of international fame.* **famously** *adverb: He held 700 patents, most famously for the electromagnetic motor.*

far-reaching *adjective*
likely to have a lot of influence or many effects: *The decision by the European court will have far-reaching consequences.*

far-sighted *adjective*
showing a prudent awareness of future possibilities: *a far-sighted vision/strategy.*
Usage In American English, *far-sighted* means 'long-sighted'.
Word family **far-sightedness** *noun*

fascinating *adjective*
extremely interesting: *The results of the study make fascinating reading.*
Word family **fascination** *noun: The fascination of the game lies in trying to guess what your opponent is thinking.*

fashion *noun*
1 a popular style of clothes, hair, etc., at a particular time or place: *the new season's fashions.* 2 the production or marketing of new styles of clothing, cosmetics, etc.: *the fashion industry.*
Word family **fashionable** *adjective*
1 following a style that is popular at a particular time: *fashionable clothes/furniture/ideas.* 2 used or visited by people who know what is the current fashion: *It's a very fashionable part of London.*

faultless *adjective*
(of a performance or argument) perfect and without any mistakes: *He gave a faultless performance. □ Her logic was always faultless.*
Word family **faultlessly** *adverb: recite the poem faultlessly word perfect.*

favour *noun, verb*
noun 1 approval or support for someone or something: *The suggestion to close the road has found favour with local people.* 2 an act of

kindness beyond what is due or usual: *I've come to ask you a favour. □ verb* to feel or show approval or support for: *Cutting public spending is a policy that few politicians favour.*
Usage In American English, the word is spelt *favor.*
Usage **favourite** or **preference**? See **preference**.
Word family **favourable** *adjective* 1 making people have a good opinion of someone or something: *He made a favourable impression on her parents.* 2 good for something or making it likely to be successful to have an advantage: *The terms of the agreement are favourable to both sides.* **favourite** *adjective* liked more than others of the same kind: *their favourite Italian restaurant.* **favourite** *noun* a favourite person or thing: *These cakes are great favourites with children.*

feasible *adjective*
possible and practical to be done easily or conveniently: *The Dutch have demonstrated that it is feasible to live below sea level.*
Usage Some people object to the use of *feasible* to mean 'probable or likely' but this sense is long established. However, usage in that sense is best avoided in formal contexts.
Word family **feasibility** *noun: I doubt the feasibility of the plan.* **feasibly** *adverb*

feast *noun*
a plentiful supply of something enjoyable: *The concert season offers a feast of great baroque music.*

feat *noun*
an action or piece of work that needs skill, strength, or courage: *The tunnel is a brilliant feat of engineering.*

feature *noun, verb*
noun 1 something important, interesting, or typical of a place or thing: *The design has many new built-in safety features.* 2 a newspaper or magazine article or broadcast programme devoted to a particular topic: *a special feature on children's books. □ verb* 1 to have as a feature: *The hotel features a swimming pool and spacious gardens.* 2 to have an important or notable part in something: *Floral designs feature prominently in Persian rugs.*

Usage In sense **1** of both the noun and verb, *feature* tends to be used to refer to something noticeable and usually something desirable.

fervent *adjective*

having or showing strong and sincere feelings or beliefs: *a fervent admirer/believer /supporter.* Usage *Fervent* is rather formal and is usually used before a noun: *It is our fervent hope/wish that the new leaders will recognize their responsibilities.*
Word family **fervency** noun: *the fervency of his religious belief.* **fervently** adverb: *He fervently hoped that he wouldn't meet anyone he knew.*

-fest *combining form*

a festival or large meeting involving a particular activity: *a jazzfest.*
Usage The form *-fest* combines with other nouns; it may also be used to express a particular atmosphere: *a love fest.*

festival *noun*

1 an organized series of concerts, films, etc.: *a major international festival of song.* **2** a day or period of celebration, e.g. for religious reasons: *a harvest festival.*
Word family **festive** adjective: *The whole town is in festive mood.* **festivity** noun: *Food plays an important part in the festivities.*

fight *verb, noun*

verb to try very hard to get or achieve something: *Campaigners fought to save the hospital from closure.* □ *We are committed to fighting poverty.* □ *noun* the work of trying to stop or prevent something bad or achieve something good: *Workers won their fight to stop compulsory redundancies.*
Usage **fight** or **campaign**? See **campaign**.

fine *adjective*

1 of a very high quality: *a fine collection of furniture.* **2** satisfactory: *The advertising initiative is fine but it's not enough on its own.* **3** attractive: *a fine figure of a man.* **4** delicate: *fine bone china.* **5** very thin, narrow, or small: *a fine thread.* **6** difficult to see or describe: *The ear makes fine distinctions between different noises.* **7** impressive: *a fine 18th-century house.* **8** used to refer to a person that you have a lot of respect for: *He will be remembered as a fine soldier.*
Word family **finely** adverb: *a finely furnished room.* □ *finely chopped onions.*

finesse *noun*

impressive delicacy and skill: *His acting showed considerable dignity and finesse.*
Usage The verb *finesse* is used especially in American English to mean 'to slyly attempt to avoid blame when dealing with a situation': *Despite the administration's attempts to finesse its mishaps, the public remained wary.*

firm *adjective*

1 with a solid almost unyielding surface: *The mattress should be firm but not too hard.* **2** solidly in place and stable: *We tried to establish the business on a firm financial footing.* **3** having steady power or strength: *a firm grip.* **4** showing determination or strength of character: *He did not like being firm with Lennie but he had to be.* **5** fixed or definite: *She had no firm plans.*
Word family **firm up** verb to make arrangements more final and fixed: *The precise details still have to be firmed up.* **firmly** adverb: *It is now firmly established as one of the leading brands in the country.*

flair *noun*

1 a natural ability or talent: *He has a flair for languages.* **2** stylishness: *She dressed with flair.*
Usage The words *flair* and *flare* should not be confused. The verb *flare* means 'to burn', 'to suddenly become much stronger' (*Tempers flared at the end of the meeting*), or 'to become wider at the bottom' (*flared trousers*). The noun *flare* refers to a bright light: *The flare of the match lit up his face.*

flamboyant *adjective*

1 confident and lively in a way that attracts the attention of other people: *the band's flamboyant lead singer.* **2** brightly coloured or highly decorated: *a flamboyant silk tie.*
Word family **flamboyance** noun: *the flamboyance of the palace.*

flatter *verb*

1 to say nice things about someone, often in a way that is not sincere, because you want them to do something for you or you want to please them: *He was flattered by her attention.* **2** (of a colour or style of clothing) to cause someone to appear to the best advantage: *The fuchsia shade flattered her pale skin.*
Usage When using the verb *flatter*, you should remember that it often refers to insincere praise.

Word family **flattering** adjective full of praise and compliments: *The article began with some flattering words about us.* **flattery** noun excessive or insincere praise: *You're too intelligent to fall for his flattery.*

flavour noun, verb
noun 1 the distinctive taste of a food or drink: *The tomatoes give extra flavour to the sauce.* 2 a particular quality or atmosphere: *The resort has a distinctly Italian flavour.* □ verb to alter or add to the taste of food or drink by adding a particular ingredient: *cottage cheese flavoured with chives.*
Usage In American English, the word is spelt *flavor.*

flawless adjective
(of someone's appearance or action) perfect; without faults or bad features: *The dancer delivered a flawless performance.*
Word family **flawlessly** adverb: *a meticulously planned and flawlessly executed robbery.*

flexible adjective
1 able to change to suit new conditions or situations: *small businesses that are dependent on flexible working hours.* 2 capable of bending easily without breaking: *flexible plastic tubing.*
Usage **flexible** or **adaptable**? See **adaptable**.
Word family **flexibility** noun: *Computers offer greater flexibility in the way work may be organized.*

flourish verb
1 to develop quickly and be successful: *His career flourished under the new manager.* 2 to grow well and be strong: *These plants flourish in a damp climate.*
Usage In sense 1, *flourish* is used to refer to people, their careers and relationships, and also businesses, places, and traditions.
Word family **flourishing** adjective: *a flourishing economy.*

fluctuate verb
to rise and fall irregularly in number or amount: *Her weight fluctuates between eight and eleven stone.*
Word family **fluctuation** noun: *wild fluctuations in interest rates.*

fluent adjective
1 able to speak, read, or write a language, especially a foreign language, easily and well: *He became fluent in German.* 2 (of a language,

especially a foreign language) used easily and well: *She speaks fluent Mandarin.* 3 smoothly graceful and effortless: *His style of play was fast and fluent.*
Word family **fluency** noun: *a job that calls for verbal fluency.* **fluently** adverb: *He is able to speak fluently and without notes.*

focus noun, verb
noun 1 the centre of interest or activity: *This generation has made the environment a focus of attention.* 2 an act of concentrating interest or activity on something: *Our focus is on the needs of customers.* 3 the state or quality of having or producing a clear well-defined image: *The children's faces are out of focus.* □ verb (**focus on**) to concentrate attention on: *The investigation will focus on areas of social need.*
Usage The plural of the noun is either *focuses* or *foci*. In derived forms of the verb, the spelling is *focusing* or *focussing* and *focused* or *focussed*: *many years of hard, focused work.*
Word family **focal point** noun the centre of interest or activity: *A fireplace serves as the focal point of any room.* A focal point is often used to talk about a place in a community which brings people together, for example a school, shop, church, or play area. It can also be used to describe the central point of a discussion, lecture, or someone's political activities; or the main part of a design or arrangement; or the main event in a series of planned events: *The focal point of the policy developed by the government was the construction of a rail network.* **focused** adjective: *It's going to take years of focused effort to deal with these problems.*

foil noun
a person or thing that contrasts with, and so emphasizes or enhances, the qualities of another: *His white cravat was a perfect foil for his bronzed features.*
Usage As a verb, *foil* is often used in journalistic contexts and means 'to prevent something considered wrong or undesirable from happening': *A brave police officer foiled the armed robbery.*

forceful adjective
powerful, assertive, or vigorous: *His mother was a forceful character and had a great influence on him.*
Usage **forceful** or **assertive**? See **assertive**

Word family **forcefully** adverb: *He argued his case forcefully.*

foresee *verb*
to think something is going to happen in the future; to know about something before it happens: *No one could have foreseen that things would turn out this way.* □ *We foresee enormous problems for local authorities.*
Usage The opposite of *foresight* is *hindsight*, the understanding that you have of a situation only after it has happened and that means you would have acted differently: *With hindsight, it is easy to say they should not have released him.*
Word family **foresight** noun the ability to predict and prepare for future events and needs: *She had the foresight to prepare herself financially in case of an accident.*

formative *adjective*
having an important influence on the development of someone or something: *They were a close family during the formative years of his childhood.*

formidable *adjective*
inspiring fear or respect through being impressively large, powerful, or capable: *a formidable opponent.*
Usage There are two acceptable pronunciations of this word. The traditional pronunciation places the stress on the first syllable *for-*; the second puts the stress on the second syllable *-mid-*.
Word family **formidably** adverb: *a formidably talented violinist.*

forum *noun*
a place where people can exchange opinions and ideas on a particular issue: *This Internet forum has been set up to promote political discussion.*
Usage The plural of *forum* in this sense is *forums*; in the original sense of 'a public square in an ancient Roman city', the plural is *fora*.

forward-looking *adjective*
favouring innovation and development; progressive: *a forward-looking company.*
Usage *Forward-thinking* has a similar meaning to *forward-looking*: *an imaginative forward-thinking design.*

foundation *noun*
1 the basis for something; an underlying principle: *The Chinese laid the scientific foundation for many modern discoveries.*
2 justification or reason: *misleading accusations with no foundations.*
Usage **foundation** or **basis**? See **basis**.

fragile *adjective*
easily broken, damaged, or destroyed: *Be careful not to break it—it's very fragile.*
Usage **fragile** or **delicate**? See **delicate**.

fragrance *noun*
1 a pleasant, sweet smell: *The bushes fill the air with fragrance.* 2 a perfume or aftershave: *an exciting new fragrance from Dior.*
Usage **fragrance**, **aroma**, or **scent**?
See **aroma**.
Word family **fragrant** adjective: *She gathered the fragrant blooms.*

framework *noun*
a set of beliefs, ideas, or rules that is used as the basis for making judgements, decisions, etc.: *The report provides a framework for further research.*
Usage The word *framework* is also used to describe the structure of a particular system: *We need to establish a legal framework for the protection of the environment.*

fresh *adjective*
1 made or experienced recently; new or different in a way that adds to or replaces something: *The court has heard fresh evidence.*
2 (especially of food) recently produced or picked; not frozen, dried, or preserved: *fresh bread.* 3 pleasantly clean, pure, or cool: *a toothpaste that leaves a nice fresh taste in your mouth.* 4 looking clear, bright, and attractive: *He looked fresh and neat in a clean white shirt.*
5 full of energy: *feel fresh after a good night's sleep.*
Word family **freshly** adverb: *freshly brewed coffee.* **freshness** noun: *I like the freshness of his approach to the problem.*

fruitful *adjective*
producing good or helpful results: *Memoirs can be a fruitful source of information.*
Usage The opposite of *fruitful* is *fruitless*, a rather formal word meaning 'producing no useful results': *He returned home after weeks of fruitless negotiations.*

Word family **fruitfully** adverb: *The matter of a firm foundation for life could be fruitfully presented in the sermon.* **fruitfulness** noun: *This study demonstrates the fruitfulness of adopting this approach.*

fulfil *verb*

1 to achieve or realize something desired, promised, or predicted: *I fulfilled a childhood dream when I became champion.* **2** to satisfy or meet a requirement or condition: *to fulfil the terms of the agreement.* **3** (**fulfil yourself**) to gain happiness or satisfaction by fully developing your abilities: *His new job enabled him to fulfil himself creatively.*

Usage In American English, the word is spelt *fulfill*.

Usage **fulfilling**, **rewarding**, **or satisfying**? See **rewarding**.

Word family **fulfilled** adjective: *He doesn't feel fulfilled in his present job.* **fulfilling** adjective: *It's been an extremely fulfilling career.* **fulfilment** noun: *the search for personal fulfilment.*

fully-fledged *adjective*

completely developed or established; with all the necessary qualifications for something: *She was now a fully-fledged member of the teaching profession.*

Usage Originally, the word refers to birds with fully developed wing feathers and able to fly.

fulsome *adjective*

1 excessively complimentary: *The press is embarrassingly fulsome in their appreciation.* **2** of large size or quantity; generous or plentiful: *the fulsome details of the legend.*

Usage The modern, generally accepted meaning of *fulsome* is 'excessively complimentary or flattering', but it is also often used to mean simply 'abundant': *Critics have been fulsome in their praise.* Although this is in line with its earliest use, some people consider it to be incorrect.

functional *adjective*

1 practical and useful; with little or no decoration; utilitarian: *Bathrooms don't have to be purely functional.* **2** having a special purpose: *These units played a key functional role in the military operation.* **3** working or operating: *The hospital will soon be fully functional.*

Word family **functionality** noun: *Manufacturing processes might be affected by the functionality of the product.*

fundamental *adjective, noun*

adjective of central importance: *a fundamental difference of opinion.* □ *noun* a central or basic rule or principle: *the fundamentals of modern physics.*

Usage **fundamental** or **basic**? See **basic**.

Word family **fundamentally** adverb **1** in central or underlying respects: *two fundamentally different concepts of democracy.* **2** used to make an emphatic statement about the basic truth of something: *Fundamentally, this is a medical matter.*

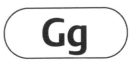

galvanize *verb*
(of a person or event) to encourage someone to do something or to try harder to achieve something: *The urgency of the task galvanized them into action.*
Word family **galvanization** noun: *The energy crisis needs a grass-roots galvanization of citizens throughout the world.*

generic *adjective*
characteristic of or relating to a class or group of things; not specific: *'Vine fruit' is the generic term for currants and raisins.*
Usage The word *generic* is also used to refer to goods, especially medicinal drugs, having no brand name, i.e. they are not protected by a registered trademark: *Generic drugs are generally cheaper than branded drugs.*
Word family **generically** adverb: *The term 'assessment' applies generically to a wide range of approaches that measure educational effectiveness.*

generous *adjective*
1 (of a person) giving or willing to give freely: *He's a kind and generous man.* □ *They were very generous with their time.* **2** (of a gift) given freely or in large amounts: *That's a very generous offer.* **3** (of an amount) large: *He took a very generous helping of pasta.* **4** kind in the way you treat people; willing to see what is good about someone or something: *Her generous spirit shone through in everything she did.* □ *He wrote a very generous assessment of my work.*
Word family **generosity** noun: *He treated them with great generosity.* **generously** adverb: *Please give generously.*

genre *noun*
a particular style or type of literature, art, music, or film that can be recognized because of its special features: *Crime fiction is a genre that seems likely to stay with us for many years.*
Usage The initial consonant of this word is pronounced *zh-*, as in *vision.*

genuine *adjective*
1 exactly as it appears to be; that really belongs to a group of people or things of the same kind; not artificial: *Is the painting a genuine Picasso?* □ *Only genuine refugees can apply for asylum.* **2** (of people, their feelings, or intentions) sincere and honest: *He came across as a very genuine person.*
Usage **genuine** or **sincere**? In many cases you can use either word. However, *sincere* is more likely to be used by someone about their own feelings and intentions; *genuine* is more likely to be used to express a judgement on someone else's feelings and intentions: *She insisted that they were making a sincere attempt to resolve the problem.* □ *He made a genuine attempt to improve conditions.*
Word family **genuinely** adverb: *He is genuinely interested in what you say to others.* □ *They seemed genuinely sorry for what had happened.*

germane *adjective*
(*formal*) relevant to a subject under consideration: *This is not germane to our theme.*
Word family **germanely** adverb **germaneness** noun: *The topic is of great germaneness to world politics.*

glamour *noun*
1 the attractive and exciting quality that makes a person, job, or place seem special, often because of wealth or status: *Hopeful young actors are drawn by the glamour of Hollywood.* **2** physical beauty that also suggests wealth or success: *Add a cashmere scarf under your jacket for a touch of glamour.*
Usage In American English, the word is spelt *glamor.*
Usage The word *glamour* is often used when people are talking about the fashion and elegance associated with famous people.
Word family **glamorous** adjective especially attractive and exciting, and different from ordinary things or people: *glamorous movie*

stars. **glamorously** *adverb*: *glamorously dressed.*

glory *noun, verb*

noun **1** great beauty; special cause for pride, respect, or pleasure: *The temple is one of the glories of ancient Greece.* □ *The railway engine had been restored to all its former glory.* **2** fame, praise, respect, or admiration that is given to someone because they have achieved something important: *He began his pursuit of Olympic glory with the 100 metres.* □ *verb* (**glory in**) to take great pride or pleasure in: *They gloried in their independence.*

Usage The word *glorious* is used especially to describe things that are bright and connected with summer or the colours of the sun (yellow, orange, and red).

Word family **glorious** *adjective* **1** extremely beautiful and impressive: *We sat on the beach and gazed at the glorious sunset.* **2** hot, with the sun shining: *They had three weeks of glorious sunshine.* **3** having or bringing fame or admiration: *His glorious career with Chelsea is coming to an end.* **4** (*informal*) very enjoyable: *glorious platters of succulent crabs.* **gloriously** *adverb*: *The game that began so gloriously for United ended in disappointment.*

go-ahead *adjective*

willing to consider new ideas; enterprising and ambitious: *a young and go-ahead managing director.*

Usage The noun *go-ahead* means 'permission to proceed': *The government gave the go-ahead to build the new power station.*

goal *noun*

something that you hope to achieve: *He continued to pursue his goal of becoming a photographer.* □ *Their goal was to eradicate malaria.*

Usage **goal**, **objective**, or **target**? See **target**.

Usage In football, rugby, hockey, and some other games, a *goal* is a pair of posts linked by a crossbar and typically with a net between, forming a space into or over which the ball has to be sent in order to score.

grace *noun*

1 an attractive quality of movement that is smooth, elegant, and controlled: *She moves with the natural grace of a ballerina.* **2** a quality of behaviour that is polite and pleasant and deserves respect: *He conducted himself with grace and dignity throughout the trial.* □ *We will*

simply have to accept the situation with good grace.

Word family **graceful** *adjective* moving in a smooth, elegant, and controlled way: *He gave a graceful bow to the audience.* **gracefully** *adverb* **gracious** *adjective* kind, polite, and generous: *He has not yet learnt how to be gracious in defeat.* **graciously** *adverb*

grand *adjective*

1 impressive and large or important: *The wedding was a very grand occasion.* **2** large or ambitious in scope or scale: *a grand plan to bring Las Vegas to Blackpool.*

Usage When *grand* is used to describe a thing, it is usually something relating to a building or part of a building such as a *house*, *villa*, *hotel*, *castle*, *palace*, *staircase*, or *entrance*. When *grand* is used to describe an occasion, it is usually one that involves rich people or the spending of a large amount of money. *Grandeur* is used especially to talk about old buildings and wild, impressive landscapes. It is used more to talk about how impressive something is, rather than its beauty. Typical adjectives that combine with *grandeur* are *classical*, *faded*, *former*, *imperial*, *scenic*, *rugged*, and *natural*.

Word family **grandeur** *noun* the quality of being great and impressive in appearance: *The hotel had an air of faded grandeur.* □ *We admired the rugged grandeur of the mountain scenery.*

gratify *verb*

to please someone by making them feel that they are good at something, liked, or valued: *I was gratified to receive their invitation.*

Word family **gratifying** *adjective* that gives you pleasure, especially because it makes you feel that you have done well: *It is gratifying to see such good results.*

gravitas *noun*

dignity, seriousness, or solemnity of manner: *a post for which he has the expertise and the gravitas.* □ *Its height and remoteness give the mountain a distinct air of gravitas.*

Usage You should take care in using this expression as some people consider it a vogue word.

guarantee *noun, verb*

noun **1** a formal assurance (typically in writing) that certain conditions will be fulfilled, especially that a product will be repaired or replaced if not of a specified quality: *We offer a ten-year guarantee against rusting.* **2** a firm promise, especially in business contexts, that you will do something or that something will happen: *The union wants cast-iron guarantees that there will be no job losses.* See also **warranty**. □ *verb* **1** to provide a formal assurance (typically in writing) that certain conditions will be fulfilled, especially that a product will be repaired or replaced if not of a specified quality: *The cooker is guaranteed for five years.* **2** to tell someone that something definitely will or will not happen or that you definitely will or will not do something: *Basic human rights, including freedom of speech, are now guaranteed.* **3** to make something certain to happen: *Getting a degree doesn't guarantee you a job.* **4** (**be guaranteed**) to be certain to happen: *The film is virtually guaranteed to do well at the box office.* **5** (*finance*) to agree to be legally responsible for repaying an amount of money if the person who owes it fails to repay it: *His father agreed to guarantee the loan.*

Usage **guarantee** or **promise**? When you *promise* something, you make a personal commitment to the person you are talking to, usually to do something: *I promise to pay you back at the end of the week.* □ *He promised the money to his grandchildren.* Guarantee is less personal: when you *guarantee* something, you mean that you will make sure that it happens; it is a stronger form of promise: *We guarantee to deliver your goods within a week.*

guide *noun, verb*

noun **1** a person who advises or shows the way to other people: *His sister has been his guide, counsellor, and friend.* **2** something that helps a person make a decision or form an opinion: *Your resting pulse is a rough guide to your physical condition.* **3** a book providing information on a subject: *a comprehensive guide to British hotels and restaurants.* □ *verb* **1** to show someone the way, e.g. to a place you know well, by going with them: *She guided us through the busy streets.* □ *Information is available to guide you through the planning and development process.* **2** to direct the positioning or movement of something: *The groove in the needle guides the thread.* **3** to direct or influence the behaviour or development of: *His entire life was guided by his religious beliefs.*

Usage **guide** or **guideline**? There is very little difference in meaning between these two words. *Guide* is often used in situations where being exact is less important: *As a general guide, large dogs need more exercise than small ones.* □ *These figures should be taken as a rough guide.* Guideline is often used in business situations, where it is impossible to be exact, but still important to be as nearly right as possible: *These prices are a guideline only.* Guide is not usually used in the plural.

Word family **guideline** *noun* something that helps a person make a decision or form an opinion: *It might help to have a few guidelines to follow.*

g

Hh

halcyon *adjective*
referring to a period of time in the past that was idyllically happy and peaceful: *the halcyon days when profits were soaring.*
Usage The adjective derives from the noun sense referring to a mythical bird said by ancient writers to breed in a nest floating at sea at the winter solstice, charming the wind and waves into calm, by association with Greek *hals* 'sea' and *kuōn* 'conceiving'.

hallmark *noun*
(*journalism*) a feature or quality that is typical of someone or something: *The tiny bubbles are the hallmark of fine champagne.* □ *Police said the explosion bore all the hallmarks of a terrorist attack.*
Usage A *hallmark* is a mark stamped on articles of gold, silver, or platinum by the British assay offices, certifying their standard of purity.

harmony *noun*
1 a state of peaceful existence and agreement: *The measures are designed to promote racial harmony.* 2 a pleasing quality when things are arranged together well to form a consistent whole: *delightful cities where old and new blend in harmony.*
Word family *harmonious adjective*: *harmonious relationships.* □ *The décor is a harmonious blend of traditional and modern.* *harmoniously adverb*: *human beings and machines working harmoniously together.*

harvest *noun, verb*
noun the product or result of an action; return or output: *The successful expedition brought the company a rich harvest of favourable publicity.* □ *verb* to obtain as a result: *He harvested a hat trick of honours.*
Usage These figurative senses derive from the literal sense of gathering in a harvest of crops.

health *noun*
someone's good or bad physical or mental state; the state of being physically and mentally healthy: *Smoking can seriously damage your health.*
Word family *healthily adverb*: *Try to eat healthily.* *healthy adjective* 1 good for your health: *More public awareness of healthy eating has made us think more about our diet.* 2 in good health and not likely to become ill: *Here are ten tips for a healthy heart.*

heart *noun*
1 the central or innermost part of a place: *'Hillsdown' is a quiet hotel in the heart of the city.* 2 the most important part of a problem: *Cost is at the heart of the matter.* □ *The committee's report went to the heart of the government's dilemma.*
Usage In sense 1, the word *heart* is often used in advertising to try to attract people to the central part of a city, country, or region.
Usage *heart* or *core*? See **core**.
Usage *heart* or *hub*? See **hub**.

heighten *verb*
to increase an effect or feeling or make it stronger; (of an effect or feeling) to increase or become stronger: *Fears of further racial conflict were heightened by news of the riots.*
Usage *heighten* or *intensify*? Although both verbs can be used with or without an object, *heighten* is more often used with an object. *Heighten* is used especially to talk about feelings and attitudes; *intensify* can apply to actions too: *a heightened sense of loneliness/well-being.* □ *to intensify the campaign/battle.*
Word family *heightened adjective*: *heightened awareness/interest/security measures.*

herald *verb, noun*
verb to be a sign that something is going to happen, especially something new and positive: *These talks could herald a new era of peace.* □ *noun*: *The government claims that the*

fall in unemployment is the herald of economic recovery.

heritage *noun*
the history, traditions, and qualities that a country or society has had for many years and that are considered an important part of its character: *Spain's rich cultural heritage.* □ *The building is part of our national heritage.*
Usage When used in front of a noun, the word *heritage* means 'relating to the things of special architectural, historical, or natural value that are preserved for the nation': *a heritage centre.* Typical verbs that are used with *heritage* include: *appreciate, celebrate, preserve, protect,* and *reflect.*

highlight *noun, verb*
noun the best, most interesting, or most exciting part of something: *The highlight of the trip was seeing the Taj Mahal.* □ *Highlights of the game will be shown later this evening.*
□ *verb* 1 to mark part of a text, especially to emphasize it: *I've highlighted the important passage in yellow.* 2 to emphasize something, especially a problem, so that people give it more attention: *The report highlights the major problems facing society today.*
Usage Reports, studies, surveys, and figures most often *highlight* a *problem, need, issue, danger,* or *difficulty.* People might deliberately *highlight* a problem because they want more people to notice it; or an event might have the effect of *highlighting* a problem by making people notice it.

high-profile *adjective*
attracting much attention or publicity: *a high-profile military presence.* □ *a fiercely contested high-profile legal battle.*
Usage As a noun, *high profile* (without a hyphen) means 'a position attracting much attention or publicity': *people who have a high profile in the community.* □ *This issue has had a high profile in recent months.*

historic *adjective*
important in history; likely to be thought of as important at some time in the future: *a historic building/monument.* □ *The party has won a historic victory at the polls.*
Usage *Historic* and *historical* are used in slightly different ways. *Historic* means 'famous or important in history': *a historic occasion,* whereas *historical* means 'concerning history or historical events': *historical evidence.* Thus a

historic event is one that was very important, whereas a *historical event* is something that happened in the past.

holistic *adjective*
(*medical*) treating the whole person, considering mental and social factors, rather than just the symptoms of a disease: *Research shows that the consultation process and holistic approach adopted by practitioners of complementary medicine make patients feel in more control of their illness.*
Usage In informal English, the word *holistic* is used when you are considering a whole thing or being as more than simply a collection of parts: *a holistic approach to life.* This adjective derives from *holism,* the theory that parts of a whole are in intimate interconnection, such that they cannot exist independently of the whole, or cannot be understood without reference to the whole, which is thus regarded as greater than the sum of its parts. *Holism* is often applied to mental states, language, and ecology.
Word family *holistically* adverb: *I have learned to approach patients holistically, and to appreciate the power of communication in healing.* □ *What's needed is properly trained admissions people who can evaluate applicants more holistically and take into consideration their background.*

honest *adjective*
1 not hiding the truth about something; truthful and sincere: *I've not been totally honest with you.* 2 morally correct or virtuous: *He did the only right and honest thing and offered his resignation.* 3 fairly earned, especially through hard work: *struggling to make an honest living.* 4 (of an action) done with good intentions even if unsuccessful or misguided: *He made an honest mistake.* 5 simple, unsophisticated, and unpretentious: *good honest food with no gimmicks.*
Word family *honestly* adverb: *She honestly believed she was making life easier.* □ *Honestly, I'm not upset.* **honesty** noun: *I always expect total honesty from my staff.*

honour *noun, verb*
noun 1 great respect: *His portrait hangs in the place of honour.* 2 a clear sense of what is morally right: *As a matter of honour, I must avoid any taint of dishonesty.* 3 something that is a privilege and a pleasure: *She had the*

honour of being received by the Queen.
4 a person or thing that brings credit to
something: *You are an honour to our
profession.* **5** an award or title given as a
reward for achievement: *gain the highest
military honour.* □ *verb* **1** to regard with great
respect: *She has now learnt to honour her
father's memory.* **2** to pay public respect to:
*Talented writers were honoured at a special
ceremony.* **3** to fulfil a duty; to keep an
agreement: *honour the terms of the contract.*
Usage **honour** or **integrity**? See **integrity**.
Usage In American English, *honour* is spelt
without the *u*: *honor.*
Word family **honourable** *adjective* **1** showing
high moral standards; behaving in a way that
means you keep the respect of other people:
The only honourable thing is to resign.
2 deserving respect; not bringing shame: *The
team managed an honourable 2–2 draw.*
honourably *adverb*: *He served honourably
during his 44 years in office.*

hope *noun, verb*

noun **1** a feeling of expectation and desire for
something to happen: *He looked through her
belongings in the hope of coming across some
information.* **2** a cause or source of hope: *Her
only hope is surgery.* **3** a reason for believing
that something good may happen: *He does
see some hope for the future.* □ *verb* **1** to expect
and want something to happen: *He's hoping
for an offer of compensation.* **2** to intend if
possible to do something: *We're hoping to
address all these issues.*
Usage The traditional sense of *hopefully*, 'in a
hopeful manner', has been used since the
17th century. In the second half of the 20th
century a new use, commenting on the whole
sentence, arose, meaning 'it is to be hoped
that', as in *Hopefully, we'll see you tomorrow.*
This second use is now very much commoner
than the first use, but it is still widely believed
to be incorrect, and it may be wise to avoid its
use in formal or written contexts.
Word family **hopeful** *adjective* feeling or
inspiring hope: *They remained hopeful that*

something could be worked out. □ *This is the
first hopeful sign that the hostages might be
released soon.* **hopefully** *adverb*

horizon *noun*

(often **horizons**) the limit of a person's
mental perception, experience, or interest:
*She wanted to leave home and broaden her
horizons.* □ *expand/widen your horizons.*
Usage You should not overuse the phrase
widen your horizons, as some people consider
it a cliché.

hub *noun*

the central and most important part of a
particular place or activity: *The bank is situated
in the commercial hub of the city.* □ *a hub
airport* (= a large important one where people
often change from one plane to another).
Usage **hub** or **heart**? In some cases you can
use either word: *the commercial heart/hub of
the city.* However, *the heart of the village/the
town/the city/England* usually suggests an
attractive, historic place; *the hub of the city/
operations/business activity* suggests a busy
place where a lot of business is undertaken.

humane *adjective*

showing kindness towards people or animals
by making sure that they do not suffer more
than is necessary: *The animals must be reared
in human conditions.* □ *campaigns for a more
humane penal system.*
Word family **humanely** *adverb*: *to ensure that
the whales were killed as humanely as possible.*
humaneness *noun*

hygiene *noun*

the conditions or practices that help to
maintain health and prevent illness or
disease, especially the keeping of yourself and
your surroundings clean: *poor standards of
food hygiene.* □ *personal hygiene.*
Word family **hygienic** *adjective*: *Food must be
prepared in hygienic conditions.* **hygienically**
adverb: *Medical supplies are disposed of
hygienically.*

icon *noun*

a famous person or thing that people admire and see as a symbol of a particular idea or way of life: *Madonna and other pop icons of the 1980s.* □ *The Routemaster bus has become a global transport icon.*

Usage In religion, an *icon* is a painting of Christ or another holy figure, typically in a traditional style on wood, venerated and used as an aid to devotion in the Byzantine and other Eastern churches. In computing, an *icon* is a symbol or graphic representation on a VDU screen of a program, option, or window, especially one of several for selection.

Word family *iconic* adjective: *attain iconic status.* □ *He became an iconic figure for film directors around the world.*

ideal *adjective, noun*

adjective 1 exactly right for someone or something; most suitable or perfect: *This beach is ideal for the children.* 2 desirable or perfect, but existing only in the imagination: *In an ideal world, we might have made a different decision.* □ *noun* 1 a person or thing that you think is perfect: *It's my ideal of what a family home should be.* 2 an idea or standard that seems perfect and worth trying to achieve or obtain: *His followers sometimes found it hard to live up to his high ideals.* □ *the liberal ideals of tolerance and freedom.*

Word family *ideally* adverb: *Ideally, I'd like to live abroad, but that's not possible at the moment.*

identify *verb*

1 to be able to say who or what someone or something is: *The judge ordered that the girl should not be identified.* 2 to find a connection, cause, or solution to a problem by studying the matter carefully; to recognize or distinguish: *They are trying to identify what is wrong with the present system.* 3 (**identify with**) to feel that you can understand and share the feelings of someone else, especially because you feel that you are similar to them or in a similar situation: *Children normally identify with the hero.* 4 (**identify with**) to associate someone or something closely with: *He was equivocal about being identified too closely with the peace movement.*

Word family *identifiable* adjective (especially of a place or thing) that you know and can find and/or name because you know its features: *There are several clearly identifiable ethnic groups in the community.* *identification* noun: *Each product has a number for easy identification.* □ *His identification with the music is evident from the opening moments.*

identity *noun*

1 the fact of being who or what a person or thing is: *He knows the identity of the bombers.* □ *She believes she is the victim of mistaken identity.* 2 the characteristics, feelings, and beliefs that make a person or group of people seem or feel different from others: *a sense of national identity.* 3 the state of feeling or being very similar to and able to understand someone or something: *The close identity between the fans and the team has been eroded.*

idyllic *adjective*

extremely happy, peaceful, or picturesque: *an attractive hotel is an idyllic setting.*

Usage The word *idyllic* derives from *idyll* 'a short description in verse or poem of a picturesque scene or incident, especially in rustic life' and 'an extremely happy, peaceful, or picturesque episode or scene, typically an idealized or unsustainable one': *The rural idyll remains strongly evocative in most industrialized societies.*

Word family *idyllically* adverb: *an idyllically located cottage on the riverbank.*

illuminate *verb*

to help to clarify or explain something: *Documents often illuminate people's thought processes.*

Word family **illuminating** adjective: *a most illuminating discussion.*

illustrate *verb*

1 to make the meaning of something clearer by using examples, pictures, diagrams, etc.: *Last year's sales figures are illustrated in figure 2.* □ *To illustrate my point, let me tell you a story.* **2** to show that something is true or exists: *This incident illustrates the need for better security.*

Word family **illustration** noun a story, event, or example that clearly shows the truth about something: *The statistics are a clear illustration of the point I am trying to make.* **illustrative** adjective helping to explain something or show it more clearly: *The history text book provides plenty of illustrative details and examples.*

image *noun*

1 an idea of what someone or something is like that appears as a picture in your mind: *Do people think in words or images?* **2** a picture in the mind that is produced when you read something: *Her writings are full of poetic images of the countryside.* **3** the impression that a person, organization, or product presents to the public; reputation: *The advertisements are intended to improve the company's image.*

imagine *verb*

to form an idea in your mind of what someone or something might be like: *I can't imagine life without the children now.*

Usage **imagine** or **visualize**? *Imagine* is the more general of these words and is used for any idea that you form of how a person, place, thing, or experience might look or feel. *Visualize* is used particularly for imagining something in a picture or series of pictures. *Visualize* is slightly more formal and is often used to talk about a deliberate attempt to imagine something for a particular purpose: *Try to visualize yourself walking into the interview room calmly and confidently.*

Usage **imaginative**, **ingenious**, **innovative**, **inventive**, or **original**? See **inventive**.

Word family **imagination** noun: *His writing lacks imagination.* □ *She has a vivid imagination.* **imaginative** adjective having or sharing new, different, and interesting ideas; creative: *recipes that make imaginative use of seasonal vegetables.* **imaginatively** adverb: *The*

stables have been imaginatively converted into offices.

immaculate *adjective*

1 (of the appearance or condition of someone or something) so clean and neat that it is perfect: *She always looks so immaculate.* **2** (of someone's record or achievement) containing no mistakes: *The incident ruined an otherwise immaculate safety record.*

Usage In the Roman Catholic Church, the *Immaculate Conception* is the belief that Mary (the mother of Jesus Christ) was free from all sin when she was conceived.

Word family **immaculately** adverb: *He was immaculately dressed in a white dinner jacket.*

impact *noun, verb*

noun the powerful effect that something has on someone or something: *Her speech made a profound impact on everyone.* □ *We are trying to minimize the impact of price rises on customers.* □ *verb* to have an effect on, especially a bad one: *The company's performance was impacted by the high value of the pound.*

Usage The verb *impact on*, as in *When produce is lost, it always impacts on the bottom line*, has been in the language since the 1960s. Many people disapprove of it, despite its relative frequency, saying that *make an impact on* or other equivalent wordings should be used instead. This may be partly because, in general, new formations of verbs from nouns (as in the case of *impact*) are regarded as somehow inferior. In addition, since the use of *impact* is associated with business and commercial writing, it has the unenviable status of jargon, which makes it doubly disliked.

impartial *adjective*

not supporting one person, group, or idea more than another: *Teenagers need access to confidential and impartial advice.*

Word family **impartiality** noun: *The BBC is supposed to maintain strict impartiality in its broadcasts.* **impartially** adverb: *There are fears that the matter will not be investigated impartially.*

impeccable *adjective*

without any faults or mistakes: *impeccable manners/taste.* □ *She came to the company with impeccable credentials.*

Word family *impeccably* adverb: *a richly
detailed and impeccably researched account.*

impetus *noun*

something that encourages a process or
activity to develop more quickly: *The debate
seems to have lost much of its initial impetus.*
□ *Each new rumour added a fresh impetus to
the smear campaign.*
Usage *impetus* or *stimulus*? The word
stimulus is often used to talk about starting
things off; *impetus* is used to talk about how
things develop: processes or activities can
gain/maintain/lose impetus, or they can *gain
added/new/further/fresh impetus. Stimulus* is a
more formal word, often used in academic or
business contexts; *impetus* is often used in
journalism or broadcasting when discussing
trends and developments.

implement *verb*

to make something that has been officially
decided start to happen or be used: *We are
implementing a new system of stock control.*
Word family *implementation* noun: *As
manager, he was responsible for the
implementation of the proposals.*

imply *verb*

1 to suggest that something is true or that
you feel or think something, without saying
so directly: *His silence seemed to imply
agreement.* 2 to make it seem likely that
something is true or exists: *The survey implies
that more people are moving house than was
thought.* 3 (of an idea or action) to make
something necessary in order to be
successful: *The project implies an enormous
investment in training.* □ *Sustainable
development implies a long-term perspective.*
Usage *imply* or *suggest*? Often you can use
either word. However, *suggest* is often used to
talk about how a piece of research, a report,
or evidence shows a link, relationship, or
similarity between things: *Research suggests a
link between a person's outlook and the immune
system. Imply* is more usually used to talk
about how data or facts show things such as
the need for something or the existence or
possibility of something: *Campaigners said the
data implies the existence of 'a pressing
social need'.*
Word family *implication* noun: *They failed to
consider the wider implications of their actions.*

important *adjective*

1 having a great effect on people or things; of
great value: *Listening is an important part of
the job.* 2 (of people or groups) having a lot of
power or influence: *Some disabled people hold
important jobs in industry.*
Usage *important* or *significant*? *Important* is
the more general of these words. Things that
are *significant* are important within a
particular context or from a particular point
of view. *Significant* is often used when
someone wants to suggest that the level of
importance of something has been measured
in some way. Figures can be *statistically
significant* but not *statistically important.
Significant* but not *important* can mean 'great
in degree': *a significant* (not: *important*)
proportion of the population.
Word family *importance* noun: *The signing of
the trade agreement was an event of immense
importance.* **importantly** adverb: *More
importantly, how much will it cost?*

imposing *adjective*

impressive to look at; making a strong
impression: *an imposing 17th-century
manor house.*
Usage If you describe a person or thing as
imposing, you are likely to feel respect for
them, but you are also likely to feel rather
small or unimportant.
Word family *imposingly* adverb: *Imposingly
tall and handsome, he is the archetypal prince.*

impressive *adjective*

1 (especially of an achievement) making you
feel admiration because it is extremely good
or skilful: *The team are 12 points ahead after an
impressive victory last night.* □ *She was very
impressive in the interview.* 2 making you feel
admiration, because it is very large,
attractive, or well or expressively made or
built: *A large portico provides a suitably
impressive entrance to the chapel.*
Usage The word *impressive* is often used
when you feel great admiration for a place or
thing but do not necessarily find it beautiful.
Word family *impressively* adverb: *Although
very old, the maps are impressively accurate.*

improve *verb*

1 to make someone or something better than
before: *You can significantly improve your
chances of getting a job by compiling a good CV.*

2 to become better: *His quality of life has improved dramatically since the operation.* Word family **improved** adjective: *We now offer a much improved service to our customers.* **improvement** noun: *Sales figures continue to show significant improvement.* □ *improvements to the bus service.*

incentive *noun*
something that encourages you to do something, especially because you will get something in return: *There are no incentives for people to save fuel.* □ *The government has created tax incentives to encourage investment.* □ *There is little incentive for firms to increase the skills of their workers.* Usage The opposite of *incentive* is *disincentive,* something that makes you less willing to do something, especially because you will not gain much if you do: *A sudden fall in profits provided a further disincentive to investors.*

incisive *adjective*
showing clear thought, a good understanding of what is important, and the ability to express this: *He had a clear incisive mind.* □ *She is an incisive critic of the current education system.* Word family **incisively** adverb: *to comment incisively on the subject.* **incisiveness** noun: *The film lacks incisiveness.*

inclusive *adjective*
1 having the total cost, or the cost of something that is mentioned, contained in the price: *The fully inclusive fare for the trip is £320.* □ *These services offer inclusive insurance cover of up to $5,000.* □ *The rent is inclusive of* (= includes the cost of) *water and heating.* **2** not excluding any section of society or any party involved in something: *Only an inclusive peace process will end the conflict.* Usage *Inclusive language* is the deliberate use of non-sexist terms, especially avoiding the use of masculine pronouns to refer to both men and women: *a gender-inclusive version of the Bible.*

incomparable *adjective*
1 without an equal in quality or extent; matchless: *the incomparable beauty of Venice.* **2** unable to be compared; totally different in nature or extent: *Censorship still exists, but now it's absolutely incomparable with what it was.*

Word family **incomparably** adverb: *Gutenberg's invention was incomparably the greatest event in the history of the world.*

incontrovertible *adjective*
not able to be denied or disputed: *Their judgement is based on the evidence of incontrovertible facts.* □ *incontrovertible evidence/proof.*
Word family **incontrovertibly** adverb: *The documents incontrovertibly establish that they were responsible for the terrorist attack.*

independent *adjective*
1 (especially of groups and organizations) not connected with or influenced by something; not connected with each other: *The police force should be independent of direct government control.* □ *Two independent research bodies reached the same conclusions.* **2** confident and free to do things without needing help from other people: *Going away to college has made me much more independent.*
Word family **independence** noun **1** a country's freedom from political control by other countries: *Cuba gained independence from Spain in 1898.* **2** freedom to make decisions, organize your life, do your job, etc., without needing help from other people or being controlled by others: *Some people have questioned the independence of the inspectors.* □ *Her work gave her some financial independence.* **independently** adverb: *the ability to work independently.*

in-depth *adjective*
knowing or considering a subject in a lot of detail: *We will be providing in-depth coverage of the election as results come in.* □ *Tonight's programme is an in-depth look at the long-term effects of unemployment.*

indigenous *adjective*
(of people or their culture, animals, or plants) belonging to a particular place rather than coming to it from somewhere else: *Antarctica has no indigenous population.*
Usage The word *indigenous* is preferred to *native* in the sense: *The indigenous* (rather than: *native*) *peoples depend on the forest for their livelihoods.* Note also that *Native American* is still the preferred term for members of the races of people who were the original people living in America.

indispensable *adjective*

essential; too important to be without: *Cars have become an indispensable part of our lives.*
Usage The opposite of *indispensable* is *dispensable*: *dispensable* things are not necessary and can be got rid of: *They looked on music and art lessons as dispensable.*
Word family **indispensability** noun: *the indispensability of tackling global threats.* **indispensably** adverb: *indispensably necessary to support life.*

indisputable *adjective*

that is definitely true: *It is indisputable that the crime rate has been rising.* □ *The report should distinguish clearly between indisputable facts and mere speculation.*
Word family **indisputably** adverb: *The painting is indisputably one of his finest works.*

individual *adjective*

adjective 1 connected with one person; designed for one person: *Respect for individual freedom is a cornerstone of our culture.*
2 considered separately rather than as part of a group: *The minister refused to comment on individual cases.* 3 typical of one particular person or thing in a way that is interesting and different from others; unique: *She creates her own, highly individual, landscapes.*
Word family **individuality** noun the qualities in a person or thing that make them clearly different from others; uniqueness: *She expresses her individuality through her clothes.* **individually** adverb: *The manager spoke to them all individually.* □ *individually wrapped chocolates.*

induce *verb*

to persuade or influence someone to do something: *Nothing would induce me to accept that job.*
Usage **induce**, **convince**, or **persuade**? See **convince**.
Word family **inducement** noun something, especially money, given to someone to persuade them to do something, especially something they would not normally do: *The higher payments were offered as an inducement.*

industrious *adjective*

diligent and hard-working: *she was surrounded by energetic, industrious people.*
Word family **industriously** adverb: *The three of them worked industriously, cutting, stitching,*

and shaping the leather. **industriousness** noun: *That country is known for the industriousness of its workers.*

inescapable *adjective*

(of a fact or situation) that you cannot avoid or ignore: *It is an inescapable fact that how we eat affects how we feel.*
Word family **inescapably** adverb: *Despite its remodelling, the building remains inescapably linked to the past.*

inevitable *adjective, noun*

adjective (especially of something unpleasant) that you cannot avoid or prevent: *It was an inevitable consequence of the decision.* □ *It was inevitable that there would be job losses.*
□ *Change is inevitable.* □ noun (**the inevitable**) an unavoidable situation: *You have to accept the inevitable.*
Usage **inevitable** or **unavoidable**? *Inevitable* is much more frequently used than *unavoidable* and combines with a much wider range of other words. *Unavoidable* always describes something unpleasant, especially *delays* and *consequences*. Things that are *inevitable* are often unpleasant, but do not have to be; words that combine with *inevitable* include *change, comparison, conclusion, development, effect, outcome, part, product, question, response, result, tendency, conflict, tension*, and *disappointment*.
Word family **inevitability** noun something that will definitely happen and cannot be avoided: *We must all, sooner or later, confront the inevitability of death.* **inevitably** adverb: *Inevitably, the press exaggerated the story.*

inexorable *adjective*

(of a process) that cannot be stopped or changed; (of logic) that cannot be argued against: *What is the reason for the inexorable rise in crime?* □ *This is where the inexorable logic of the theory breaks down.*
Word family **inexorably** adverb: *Pressure of population is leading inexorably towards a crisis.*

influence *noun, verb*

noun 1 a person or thing that affects the way someone behaves or thinks: *She was by far the biggest influence on my writing.* 2 the effect that someone or something has on the way a person thinks or behaves, or on the way something works or develops: *The artist exerted a strong influence on the younger*

generation. □ *verb* **1** to have an effect on the way that someone thinks or behaves, especially by giving them an example to follow: *His writings have influenced the lives of millions.* **2** to have an effect on a particular situation and the way it develops: *A number of social factors influence life expectancy.*
Word family **influential** *adjective* (of people, groups, and ideas) having a lot of influence on someone or something, especially within a particular area of interest: *The committee was influential in formulating government policy on employment.* **influentially** *adverb*: *Such ideas were to be revived perhaps most influentially in Renaissance Italy.*

inform *verb*

to tell someone about something, often in a formal or official way: *The leaflet informs customers about healthy eating.*
Usage **informative** or **instructive**? See **instructive**.
Word family **information** *noun* things you know, are told, or can find out about someone or something: *For further information, contact us at the above address.* **informational** *adjective* providing or containing information about something: *set up a simple informational website.* **informative** *adjective* (of a written or spoken source of information) giving useful information: *The talk was both entertaining and informative.* **informed** *adjective* knowing a lot about something; based on a lot of knowledge about a particular subject or situation: *The newspaper's readership is generally well informed and intelligent.*

ingenious *adjective*

having or showing clever new ideas; good at inventing things: *an ingenious device /invention.*
Usage Do not confuse *ingenious*, meaning 'clever; creative' and *ingenuous*, which means 'innocent, unsuspecting, and straightforward': *His love for her was plain on his ingenuous face.*
Usage **ingenious**, **imaginative**, **innovative**, **inventive**, or **original**? See **inventive**.
Word family **ingeniously** *adverb*: *an ingeniously designed gadget.* **ingenuity** *noun* the ability to invent things or solve problems in clever new ways: *Considerable ingenuity must be employed in writing software.*

inherent *adjective*

existing in something or a permanent, essential, or characteristic quality: *Any form of mountaineering has its inherent dangers.*
Usage **inherent**, **essential**, **innate**, or **intrinsic**? These words are all applied to qualities or features that are a central element in the nature of something or someone. *Inherent* is typically used to qualify words having negative connotations: *Violence is inherent in our society.* It tends to be used as a warning, indicating the undesirable features or consequences of something. An *essential* feature of someone or something is one that is so important to their nature that without it they would not be the same person or thing: *Ensuring that others have their turn is an essential feature of citizenship.* □ *Human expertise is essential to any organization.* Something may therefore be defined or summarized by reference to an essential element: *The essential point is those who hold information hold power.* Essential may be used to suggest that a characteristic is in fact fundamental to someone, even if more superficial characteristics conceal or contradict it: *a belief in the essential goodness of human nature.* An *innate* characteristic is literally one with which someone is born, contrasted with one that is acquired at some later stage in life: *students with innate ability.* Innate is also used in a weakened sense of 'great' or 'deep-seated': *He had an innate respect for a fellow professional sportsman.* Intrinsic is a more general term for an element regarded as central to something's nature. A feature or quality described as *intrinsic* is typically either neutral or good: *Access to the arts is intrinsic to a high quality of life.* Intrinsic is often used to emphasize that something possesses a quality in its own right, not through external or incidental factors: *The analysis is worthwhile because of its intrinsic interest.*
Word family **inherently** *adjective*: *nothing inherently improper about the system.*

inimitable *adjective*

so good or unusual as to be impossible to copy; unique: *The band took the chart by storm in their own inimitable style.*
Word family **inimitably** *adverb*: *in his usual inimitably, inspiringly different way.*

initiative *noun*

1 the ability to assess and initiate things independently: *Use your initiative, imagination,* *and common sense.* **2** the power or opportunity to act or take charge before others do: *Anti-hunting groups have seized the initiative in the dispute.* **3** an act or strategy intended to resolve a difficulty or improve a situation; a fresh approach to something: *a new initiative against car crime.* **4** a proposal made by one nation to another in an attempt to improve relations: *a Middle East peace initiative.*

innate *adjective*
(of behaviour, qualities, or feelings) part of the character that a person or animal was born with: *Many children seem to have an innate sense of justice.*
Usage **innate** or **natural**? There is little difference in meaning or use between these words. *Natural* is more frequent and less formal. You might use *innate* in cases where there might be confusion with a different meaning of *natural*: for example, *an innate response* is a response that someone or something makes because it is in their character; *a natural response* is more likely to be a response that someone else expects or understands: *Anxiety at a perceived threat is an innate response in any animal.* □ *It's a natural response to keep your troubles quiet.*
Usage **innate**, **inherent**, **essential**, or **intrinsic**? See **inherent**.
Word family **innately** adverb: *Some philosophers view human nature as innately good.*

innovation *noun*
the introduction of new things, ideas, or ways of doing something; a new idea or way of doing something: *recent innovations in steel-making technology.*
Usage The verb *innovate* 'to introduce new methods, ideas, or products' is used, but it is less common than the noun *innovation*: *We must constantly adapt and innovate to ensure success in a changing market.*
Usage **innovative**, **imaginative**, **ingenious**, **inventive**, or **original**? See **inventive**.
Word family **innovative** adjective introducing or using new ideas or ways of doing something: *their innovative use of existing technology.* **innovator** noun a person or organization that introduces new things, ideas, or ways of doing things: *The company is a global innovator in science and technology.*

insight *noun*
the ability to understand the truth about people or situations; the understanding of what something is like: *I hope you've gained some insight into the difficulties we face.*
Word family **insightful** adjective having a clear understanding of a person or situation; perceptive: *an insightful analysis.* **insightfully** adverb: *As he has insightfully observed . . .*

inspect *verb*
to look at someone or something closely to make sure that everything is satisfactory; to officially visit a school, factory, etc. in order to check that rules are being kept and that standards are acceptable: *The Tourist Board inspects all recommended hotels at least once a year.*
Word family **inspection** noun: *The documents are available for public inspection.* **inspector** noun: *US weapons inspectors have been called in to verify the claims.*

inspire *verb*
1 to make someone want to do something well or do something new by giving them the necessary desire, confidence, or enthusiasm: *The actors visit schools and hope to inspire the children to put on their own productions.* **2** (especially of a person's actions or the way they behave) to make someone have a particular feeling: *As a general, he inspired great loyalty in his troops.*
Word family **inspiration** noun **1** the process that takes place when someone sees or hears something that causes them to have exciting new ideas or that makes them want to create something new, especially in art, music, or literature: *If you're looking for inspiration for a new dessert, then try this recipe.* **2** a person or thing that is the reason why someone creates or does something: *Clark was the inspiration behind Saturday's victory.* **3** a person or thing that makes you want to be better or more successful: *Her charity work was an inspiration to us all.* **inspirational** adjective: *the team's inspirational captain.* **inspired** adjective displaying creativity or excellence: *give an inspired performance.* **inspiring** adjective: *an inspiring evening of wine and music.*

instructive *adjective*
(of an experience or activity) giving useful information: *It was a most instructive*

experience. □ *He said he had found the meeting extremely instructive.*

Usage *instructive* or *informative*? Things that you do or experience may be *instructive*: *It is instructive to compare the two projects.* Things that you read or hear may be *informative*: *The book is not very informative about local customs.*

Word family *instructively* adverb: *instructively annotated texts.*

integral *adjective*

1 necessary to make a whole complete; essential or fundamental: *Games are an integral part of the school's curriculum.* □ *Systematic training should be integral to library management.* **2** included as part of a whole rather than supplied separately: *The unit comes complete with integral pump and heater.*

integrate *verb*

to combine two or more things so that they work together; to combine with something else in this way: *The department has successfully integrated new ideas into the traditional course structure.*

Word family *integrated* adjective with various parts or aspects linked or coordinated: *an integrated public transport system.* *integration* noun: *The aim is to promote closer economic integration.*

integrity *noun*

the quality of knowing and doing what is morally right: *As a leader he was a man of great integrity.*

Usage Other senses of *integrity* include reference to something whole, undivided, or unbroken: *the structural integrity of the novel.*

Usage *integrity* or *honour*? With *integrity* the emphasis is mainly on how you see yourself: being good and honest so that you can approve of your own character and actions. With *honour* the emphasis is more on how others see you: being good and honest in order to keep your reputation in a community. *Integrity* is mostly individual, although you can talk about the *integrity* of the company or profession: *preserve your professional integrity.* *Honour* can be individual or collective: *to defend the family honour.*

intelligent *adjective*

good at learning, understanding, and thinking in a logical way about things; showing this

ability: *He's a highly intelligent man.* □ *She asked a lot of intelligent questions.*

Word family *intelligence* noun: *Most people of average intelligence would find this task quite difficult.* *intelligently* adverb: *to invest your money more intelligently.*

intensify *verb*

to increase an activity or feeling in degree or strength; (of an activity or feeling) to increase in degree or strength: *Pressure to stop the process had intensified efforts to form a constitutional commission.*

Usage *intensify* or *heighten*? See **heighten**.

Word family *intensification* noun: *He warned of the intensification of terrorist activity.*

intention *noun*

what you plan or have decided to do: *It is his intention to be leader.* □ *I have every intention of paying her back what I owe her.*

Word family *intentional* adjective deliberate: *There must be no intentional contact between teams.* *intentionally* adverb: *Intentionally or not, police procedures may be biased.*

interactive *adjective*

(of two or more people or things) influencing each other: *fully-sighted children in interactive play with others with defective vision.*

Word family *interactively* adverb: *You can use your computer to learn interactively.*

interest *noun, verb*

noun the quality something has when it attracts someone's attention or makes them want to know more about it: *There are many places of interest around Oxford.* □ *verb* to catch and keep your attention: *The museum has something to interest everyone.*

Usage You may find you overuse the words *interested* and *interesting*. Synonyms for *interested* are: *absorbed, engrossed, fascinated, gripped, intrigued*; and for *interesting*: *absorbing, fascinating, intriguing, stimulating, thought-provoking.*

Word family *interested* adjective giving your attention to something because you enjoy finding out about it or doing it; showing interest in something and finding it exciting: *I'm very interested in history.* *interesting* adjective attracting your attention because it is exciting, unusual, or full of good ideas: *Our survey produced some interesting results.* *interestingly* adverb: *Interestingly, there are very few recorded cases of such attacks.*

interface *noun, verb*

noun the point when two systems, subjects, organizations, etc. meet or interact: *the interface between accountancy and the law.* □ *verb* to interact with another person, system, etc.: *You will interface with counterparts from other companies in the same group.*

Usage The word *interface* is a relatively new word, having been in the language (as a noun) since the 1880s. However, in the 1960s it became widespread in computer use and, by analogy, began to enjoy a vogue as both a noun and a verb in all sorts of other spheres. Some people object to it on the grounds that there are plenty of other words that could be used instead. Although it is now well established in standard English, if you wish to avoid it in certain contexts you could use such words as *interaction*, *dialogue*, and *contact* and their related verbs.

interlude *noun*

a period of time between two events during which something different happens: *Apart from a brief interlude of peace, the war lasted nine years.*

Usage The word *interlude* is often used to talk about a calm or more peaceful time between two periods of war, or between two busier periods. Typical adjectives that are combined with *interlude* are *brief*, *little*, *musical*, *peaceful*, and *romantic*.

interpersonal *adjective*

relating to relationships or communication between people: *The successful candidate will have energy, enthusiasm, and excellent interpersonal skills.*

Word family **interpersonally** adverb: *interpersonally sensitive.*

interpret *verb*

1 to explain the meaning of something such as a text or work of art, especially when it is possible to understand or explain it in several different ways: *The students were asked to interpret the poem.* 2 to understand as having a particular meaning: *He interpreted her silence as indifference.*

Word family **interpretation** noun the particular way in which someone understands or explains something: *The evidence may suggest a different interpretation.* □ *Dreams are open to interpretation* (= can be explained in different ways). **interpretative** adjective (*formal*) connected with the particular way in which something is understood, explained, or performed: *activities designed to increase students' interpretative skills.*

intimate *adjective*

1 close and friendly: *They are intimate friends.* 2 (of a place or setting) having a cosy and private or relaxed atmosphere: *an intimate little Italian restaurant.* 3 involving very close connection: *their intimate involvement with the community.* 4 (of knowledge) detailed or thorough: *an intimate knowledge of the software.*

Usage You should take care using the word *intimate* because it can also mean 'private and personal' (*intimate details*) and euphemistically to refer to a sexual relationship.

Word family **intimately** adverb: *intimately familiar with his writings.*

intrepid *adjective*

very brave and not afraid of danger; adventurous: *an intrepid explorer/traveller.*

Usage You should take care when using this word because it is often used for humorous or rhetorical effect.

Word family **intrepidly** adverb: *set off intrepidly into the unknown.* **intrepidity** noun: *the intrepidity of their odyssey across the ocean.*

intricate *adjective*

having a lot of different parts and small details that fit together: *The building has intricate geometric designs on several of the walls.* □ *It is difficult to describe the intricate network of loyalties and relationships.*

Word family **intricacy** noun: *the intricacy of the craftsmanship.* **intricately** adverb: *intricately carved/decorated/patterned.*

intrigue *verb*

to make someone very interested and want to know more about something, usually because it seems unusual or mysterious: *There was something about him that intrigued her.*

Usage As a noun, *intrigue* refers to 'the plotting of something illegal or harmful' or 'a secret love affair'.

Word family **intrigued** adjective: *I am intrigued by her story.* **intriguing** adjective: *an intriguing possibility/question/idea/story.*

intrinsic *adjective*
belonging naturally; essential: *Pride was an intrinsic component of his personality.*
Usage **intrinsic**, **essential**, **inherent**, or **innate**? See **inherent**.
Word family **intrinsically** adverb: *There is nothing intrinsically wrong with such an approach.*

intuition *noun*
1 the ability to know something by using your feelings rather than by considering the facts: *Intuition told her that he was telling the truth.*
2 an idea or strong feeling that something is true even though you cannot explain why: *I had an intuition that something terrible was going to happen.*
Word family **intuitive** adjective (of ideas) obtained by using your feelings rather than by considering the facts; (of people) able to understand something by using feelings rather than by considering the facts: *Our approach to the subject can be strictly rational or wholly intuitive.*

inventive *adjective*
having or showing new, different, and interesting ideas; good at inventing things: *she is one of the most inventive of modern writers.* □ *This is a courageous and inventive piece of film-making.*
Usage **inventive**, **innovative**, **original**, **imaginative**, or **ingenious**? *Innovative* is often used in practical and business contexts and is as much about using new ideas as having them; *original*, *imaginative*, and *inventive* are often used in more artistic contexts. *Original* or *imaginative* ideas are interesting whether they work in practice or not; things that are *ingenious* are clever and must work, or they are not *ingenious*; however, they may not be as big or important as things that are *innovative* or *original*.
Word family **inventiveness** noun: *the inventiveness of modern advertising.*

irreplaceable *adjective*
too valuable or special to be replaced: *These paintings are irreplaceable.*
Word family **irreplaceably** adverb: *irreplaceably precious/unique.*

irresistible *adjective*
(of a feeling, event, or argument) so powerful that it cannot be stopped or resisted: *He found the delicious-looking cakes irresistible.* □ *Her arguments were irresistible.*
Word family **irresistibly** adverb: *irresistibly drawn to her vitality.*

key *adjective*
most important; essential: *Caution is the key word in this situation.* □ *The key issue here is taxation.* □ *Attitude is a key concept in social psychology.*
Usage **key**, **central**, **major**, or **principal**? See **central**.

keynote *noun*
the central idea of a book, speech, etc.: *Individuality was the keynote of the nineties.* □ *Choice is the keynote of the new education policy.*
Usage The word *keynote* is often used in front of a noun: a *keynote speech* sets out the central theme of a conference.

LI

landmark *noun*
an event, discovery, or invention that is an important stage in a process of the development of something: *The ceasefire was seen as a major landmark in the fight against terrorism.*
Usage The word *landmark* is sometimes used before a noun such as *case*, *decision*, *ruling*, *study*, *victory*, or *judgment* to refer to an important stage or turning point.

lavish *adjective, verb*
adjective large in amount, or impressive, and usually costing a lot of money: *He willingly accepted their lavish hospitality.* □ *a lavish dining room.* □ *verb* (**lavish on**) to give a lot of something, sometimes too much, to someone or something: *She lavishes most of her attention on her youngest son.*
Usage Typical things that are *lavished* on someone are *gifts*, *praise*, and *attention*.
Word family **lavishly** adverb: *a lavishly decorated banqueting hall.* □ *a lavishly illustrated book.*

leader *noun*
1 a person who leads a group of people, especially a country or organization: *He resigned as leader of the Democratic Party.* □ *Discuss any problems with your team leader.* □ *A strong leader is one who is not afraid of listening to people.* □ *She's a born leader* (= she has the skills needed to be a good leader). **2** a person or thing that is the best or in first place in a race, competition, or area of business: *The company is a world leader in electrical goods.* □ *They are the brand leader* (= most successful brand) *for herbs and spices in the UK.*

leadership *noun*
1 the activity or position of being a leader; abilities or qualities needed to be a leader: *The party thrived under her leadership.* □ *In the crisis he showed real leadership.* **2** the people who control or run an organization, political party, or country: *The party leadership is divided.* □ *There have been disagreements within the leadership of the union.*
Usage In sense **2** of *leadership*, when used to talk about the people who run a country, the word usually refers to governments that are not elected or are not considered to be democratic: *the Communist/military leadership.*

leading *adjective*
most important or most successful: *She was offered the leading role in the new TV series.* □ *He's a leading business analyst.*
Usage The word *leading* is often used in publicity for companies that produce products or provide services: *a leading brand/manufacturer/supplier.* The *leading edge* of something is the forefront or vanguard, especially of technological development: *The research company is at the leading edge of scientific innovation.*

learning curve *noun*
the rate of a person's progress in gaining experience or new skills: *We are on a steep learning curve with the latest software packages.* □ *The control system has a steep learning curve to it, but with enough practice, it becomes amazingly intuitive.*
Usage You should take care in using this expression because some people consider it to be jargon.

legend *noun*
a very famous person, especially in sport, music, or acting, who is admired by other people: *She was a legend in her own lifetime.* □ *Many of golf's living legends were playing.*
Usage A *legend* has a higher level of fame and a higher status than other types of famous people. The word suggests that someone has shown real talent over a long career, and that

they are famous because of this rather than because of their appearance or personality. Usage The word *legendary* is often used to talk about people who are dead or old, but who are still talked about and admired: *We once received a visit from the legendary Orson Welles.*
Word family **legendary** adjective very famous and talked about a lot by people, especially in a way that shows admiration: *Her patience and tact are legendary.*

legitimate *adjective*

1 based on a fair and acceptable reason; able to be defended with logic or justification; valid: *All legitimate grievances should be raised with your line manager.* □ *The court ruled that celebrities' children were not a legitimate target for press intrusion.* 2 allowed and acceptable according to the law: *The legitimate government was reinstated after the uprising.* □ *Is his business strictly legitimate?*
Word family **legitimately** adverb: *Given the deadly consequences of their deployment, use of the cluster bombs can legitimately be considered to constitute murderous intent.*

leverage *noun*

(*formal*) the ability of someone to influence someone or something, especially because of their position: *Retailers can exert leverage over producers by threatening to take their business elsewhere.* □ *The right wing had lost much of its political leverage in the assembly.*
Usage In finance, *leverage* is a term used especially in North America for the British term *gearing*, referring to the ratio of a company's loan capital (debt) to the value of its ordinary shares (equity).

logical *adjective*

1 based on the rules of logic; showing clear thinking based on facts and reason: *The problem can be solved using a process of logical reasoning.* □ *A contradiction is a logical impossibility.* 2 (of a course of action or line of reasoning) seeming natural, reasonable, or

sensible: *It was a logical thing to do in the circumstances.* □ *It seemed logical to try and contact the child's mother.*
Word family **logically** adverb: *If you look at it logically his argument makes no sense.* □ *The problem is that you can never trust them to act logically.*

loyal *adjective*

(of a person) staying with or supporting a particular person, organization, or belief, especially as a matter of principle: *She has always remained loyal to her political principles.* □ *He is one of the president's most loyal supporters.*
Usage **loyal** or **faithful**? See **faithful**.
Word family **loyally** adverb: *He loyally supported the government through the crisis.* **loyalty** noun: *They swore their loyalty to the king.* □ *a case of divided loyalties* (= with strong feelings of support for two different people or causes).

lucrative *adjective*

(of business or work) producing or paying a large amount of money; making a large profit: *The firm has a lucrative business contract with the Scottish Executive.* □ *Many of the engineers left the service for more lucrative jobs abroad.*
Word family **lucratively** adverb: *lucratively paid specialists.*

luxury *noun*

1 a situation in which you are very comfortable because you have special and expensive things to enjoy, especially food and drink, clothes, and surroundings: *He was used to living a life of luxury.* □ *You've just won three weeks in a luxury hotel.* □ *They stock a wide range of luxury goods.* 2 an inessential, desirable item which is expensive or difficult to obtain: *Luxuries like chocolate, scent, and fizzy wine.* 3 a pleasure obtained only rarely: *They had the luxury of a whole day together.*
Word family **luxurious** adjective: *a luxurious hotel.* □ *luxurious surroundings.*

magnanimous *adjective*
generous or forgiving, especially towards a rival or less powerful person: *She was magnanimous in victory.*
Word family **magnanimity** *noun*: *He has the magnanimity to listen to divergent opinions.* **magnanimously** *adverb*: *magnanimously agree to forgo the additional income.*

magnificent *adjective*
extremely good or beautiful in a way that makes you feel wonder and admiration: *The Taj Mahal is a magnificent building.* □ *a magnificent act of heroism.* □ *It was a magnificent performance.*
Word family **magnificence** *noun*: *the magnificence of the scenery.* **magnificently** *adverb*: *The city boasts a wealth of magnificently preserved temples and palaces.*

majestic *adjective*
very impressive because of its size or beauty: *The college is close to Edinburgh's majestic castle.* □ *The Rockies are majestic in size.*
Usage The word *majestic* is usually used to describe large and impressive buildings such as castles, mansions, or hotels, or high natural features such as mountains or cliffs.
Word family **majestically** *adverb*: *The cliffs rise majestically from the ocean.*

major *adjective*
important, serious, or significant: *A major road runs right through the centre of the town.* □ *He played a major role in setting up the system.* □ *We have encountered major problems.*
Usage **major**, **central**, **key**, or **principal**? See **central**.

manage *verb*
1 to be in charge of people or an organization: *Organizers are looking for someone to manage the project.* **2** to control the use of money, time, or other resources: *This computer program helps you manage data efficiently.* **3** to succeed in doing or dealing with something: *She eventually managed to buy a horse.* **4** to succeed or cope despite difficulties: *Many people find it difficult to manage on their weekly income.*
Usage **manage** or **run**? These two verbs can often be used in the same way: *The hotel is run/ managed by two brothers.* *Run* emphasizes the tasks involved in the operation of a business—planning, ordering stock, organizing transport of goods, etc. Someone can *run* a small business (without any employees), part of a business, a department, or a larger organization. *Manage* often refers to organizing other workers. A *manager* makes decisions about how a business, department, etc. is *run*, but they usually tell other people what to do rather than doing it themselves.
Word family **management** *noun* **1** the people who run a business or other organization: *Union leaders are seeking talks with management over the proposed layoffs.* □ *It is a one-day workshop for senior and middle management.* □ *The store is now under new management.* **2** the activity of running and controlling a business or other organization; the way in which it is run: *She studied hotel management in Munich.* □ *The report blames bad management.* □ *The company's top-down management style made decision-making slow.*
manager *noun* a person who is in charge of running a business, store, or similar organization; a person who is in charge of a particular activity or department in a company: *Sales manager Chris Jones says, 'We're thrilled with the results.'* □ *There's a meeting of area managers next Tuesday.*
managerial *adjective* relating to management or managers: *the division of managerial responsibilities.*

mandatory *adjective*
(*formal*) that must be done because of a law: *It is mandatory for blood banks to test all*

donated blood for the virus. □ *The offence carries a mandatory life sentence.*

marginal *adjective*

minor or not important; not central: *The story will be of only marginal interest to our readers.* □ *It seems likely to make only a marginal difference.* □ *The difference between the two estimates is marginal.*
Usage In politics, the word *marginal* means won or lost by a very small number of votes in the last election and therefore significant politically: *Their campaign targeted marginal constituencies.* □ *They risk losing key marginal seats at the next election.*
Word family *marginally* adverb: *He's in a new job but he's only marginally better off.*

masterly *adjective*

showing great skill or understanding: *Her handling of the situation was masterly.* □ *As a performer he shows a masterly sense of timing.*

mastermind *noun, verb*

noun 1 a person with an outstanding intellect: *an eminent musical mastermind.* 2 a person who plans and directs a complicated project or activity, often a criminal one: *There's a criminal mastermind behind all this.* □ *verb* to plan and direct a complicated project or activity: *He masterminded the whole campaign.*

masterpiece *noun*

a work of art, literature, film, etc. that is an excellent, or the best, example of the artist's work: *the work has been described as a literary masterpiece.* □ *This is an excellent production of Verdi's masterpiece.* □ *Her work is a masterpiece of simplicity* (= an excellent example of something simple).

mature *adjective, verb*

adjective 1 (of a child or young person) behaving in a sensible way, like an adult: *Jane is very mature for her age.* □ *He shows a mature and sensible attitude.* 2 (of a person, tree, bird, or animal) fully grown and developed: *a mature oak/eagle/elephant.* 3 (of thought or planning) careful and thorough: *On mature reflection he decided they should not go.* 4 having reached the most advanced stage in a process: *Van Gogh's mature work.* 5 denoting an economy, industry, or market that has developed to a point where substantial expansion and investment no longer takes place. 6 (of certain foodstuffs or

drinks) ready for consumption: *mature cheese/ wine.* □ *verb* 1 (of a person or animal) to become physically mature: *Children mature at different ages.* □ *She matured into a woman.* 2 to develop fully: *The trees take at least thirty years to mature.* 3 (of a person) to reach an advanced stage of mental or emotional development: *Men mature as they grow older.* 4 (with reference to certain foodstuffs or drinks) to become or cause to become ready for consumption: *Leave the cheese to mature.* 5 (of an insurance policy, security, etc.) to reach the end of its term and hence become payable.
Usage You should take care when using the word *mature* because it is also used as a polite or humorous way of saying that someone is no longer young: *The shop specializes in clothes for the mature woman.* □ *He's a man of mature years.*
Word family *maturely* adverb: *She talked very maturely for a girl of her age.* *maturity* noun: *He has maturity beyond his years.*

meaningful *adjective*

1 having meaning: *meaningful elements in a language.* □ *words likely to be meaningful to pupils.* 2 having a serious, important, or useful quality or purpose: *The new structure would bring meaningful savings.* 3 communicating something that is not directly expressed: *meaningful glances and repressed passion.*
Word family *meaningfully* adverb: *She glanced meaningfully at him.* *meaningfulness* noun: *The research questions the meaningfulness of studying racial comparisons.*

measure *noun*

1 a way of judging or measuring something; a sign of the size or strength of something: *Exam results are only one measure of a school's success.* □ *Is this test a good measure of reading comprehension?* 2 an official action that is done in order to achieve a particular aim: *Special measures are being taken to protect the local water supplies.* □ *Tougher measures against racism are needed.* □ *This is just a temporary measure, while the emergency exists.* □ *The government introduced emergency measures to stave off an economic crisis.*
Word family *measured* adjective (usually of the way someone talks or walks) slow and controlled: *She replied in a measured tone to his threat.* □ *He walked down the corridor with measured steps.*

mediate *verb*

to try to end a disagreement between two or more people or groups by talking to them and trying to find things that everyone can agree on: *An independent body was brought in to mediate between workers and management.* □ *The UN attempted to mediate a solution to the conflict.*

Usage **mediator** or **intermediary**? A *mediator* or *intermediary* can play a similar role. Usually a *mediator* is involved in a discussion where the opposing people or groups meet to try to settle their dispute. The role of the *mediator* is to try to help the discussions. An *intermediary* is often involved in a situation where the two people or groups do not want to meet and the role of the *intermediary* is to act as a neutral person who can pass messages between them.

Word family **mediator** *noun* a person or organization that helps to get an agreement between people or groups who disagree with each other: *A Swedish diplomat acted as mediator between the government and the rebels.*

medley *noun*

1 a varied mixture of people or things; a miscellany: *an interesting medley of flavours.*
2 a collection of songs or other musical items performed as a continuous piece: *a medley of Beatles songs.*

Usage In swimming, a *medley* is a race in which contestants swim sections in different strokes, either individually or in relay teams.

mellow *adjective, verb*

adjective 1 (especially of a sound, taste, or colour) pleasantly smooth or soft; free from harshness: *She was hypnotized by the mellow tone of his voice.* □ *Slow cooking gives the dish a sweet, mellow flavour.* 2 (of a person's character) softened or matured by age or experience: *a more mellow personality.*
3 relaxed and good-humoured: *Jean-Claude was feeling mellow.* 4 (of wine) well-matured and smooth: *delicious, mellow, ripe, fruity wines.* □ *verb* to make or become mellow: *Eight years had done nothing to mellow him.*

Usage You should take care in using the word *mellow,* as in informal contexts it can mean 'relaxed and cheerful through being slightly drunk': *Everybody got very mellow and slept well.*

memorable *adjective*

worth remembering or easily remembered, especially because of being special or unusual: *This victory was one of the most memorable of his career.*

Word family **memorably** *adverb*: *Gothic has been memorably described as the epitome of the 'church triumphant' rather than the earlier 'church militant'.*

merge *verb*

(of two or more groups) to combine to form a single larger group; (of qualities) to combine in a way that makes them hard to separate; to combine groups or qualities in these ways: *His department will merge with mine.* □ *Fact and fiction merge together in his latest thriller.* □ *The company was formed by merging three smaller firms.*

Usage The word *merge* is used especially in business and political contexts to talk about groups or organizations that join together.

Word family **merger** *noun*: *a merger between the two banks.*

methodical *adjective*

doing things or done in a careful and logical way: *He was slow, methodical, and reliable.* □ *Police carried out a methodical search of the premises.*

Word family **methodically** *adverb*: *The investigation was proceeding slowly but methodically.*

meticulous *adjective*

paying careful attention to every detail: *He's always meticulous about keeping the records up to date.* □ *The room had been prepared with meticulous care.*

Word family **meticulously** *adverb*: *a meticulously planned schedule.* **meticulousness** *noun*: *She sets a high standard with the meticulousness of her research.*

milieu *noun*

the social environment that you live or work in: *The findings of the report refer to a particular social and cultural milieu.*

Usage The word *milieu,* which comes from French, has two plural forms: *milieux* or *milieus.* Each is pronounced either as the singular form (**mee**-lyer) or **mee**-lyers.

minded *adjective*

inclined to do something; wishing or intending: *The committee declared that they*

were minded to grant planning permission. □ *He was minded to reject the application.*
Usage This usage is found in formal contexts, for example reports. The word *minded* is also used in combination with another word to mean inclined to think in a particular way or interested in or enthusiastic about the thing specified: *I'm not scientifically minded.* □ *conservation-minded citizens.*

mindful *adjective*
aware of someone or something and considering them when you do something: *mindful of his advice, I decided to return to my hotel.* □ *The judge said that he was not mindful to postpone the eviction again.*
Word family **mindfully** *adverb*
mindfulness *noun*

mission *noun*
1 an important official job that a person or group of people is given to do, especially when they are sent to another country: *a trade mission to China.* □ *They undertook a fact-finding mission in the region.* **2** particular work that you feel it is your duty to do: *Her mission in life was to work with the homeless.* □ *We will continue our mission to close the gap between customers' expectations and the reality.*
Word family **mission statement** *noun* a formal summary of the aims and values of an organization.

mobilize *verb*
1 to organize and encourage people to act in a concerted way in order to bring about a particular, especially political, objective: *He used the press to mobilize support for his party.* **2** to bring resources into use in order to achieve a particular goal: *At sea we will mobilize any amount of resources to undertake a rescue.*
Word family **mobilization** *noun*: *the mobilization of the working class.*

model *noun*, *verb*
noun **1** an excellent example of a quality: *She was a model of self-control.* □ *Her essay was a model of clarity.* **2** an example of something such as a system that can be copied by other people: *The nation's constitution provided a model that other countries followed.* □ *a mathematical model for determining the safe level of pesticides in food.* **3** a particular design or type of product, especially a vehicle or machine, that is made by a particular

company: *The latest models will be on display at the motor show.* **4** a copy of something, usually smaller than the original object: *They have a working model* (= one in which the parts move) *of a water mill.* □ *The architect had produced a scale model of the proposed shopping complex* (= in which all the parts are the correct size in relation to each other).
□ *verb* **1** to use a system, procedure, etc. as an example to follow or imitate: *The research method will be modelled on previous work.*
□ *The program can model a typical home page for you.* **2** (**model yourself on**) to copy the behaviour or style of someone you like and respect in order to be like them: *As a politician, he modelled himself on Churchill.*
Usage **model** or **pattern**? A system or organization *is/provides a model* but *sets a pattern* for people to follow. A *pattern* is always an excellent example and one that people should follow; a *model* is an example that people do follow, although this is usually because it works well.

moderate *adjective*, *verb*
adjective **1** average in amount, intensity, or degree: *We walked at a moderate pace.* **2** (of a political position) not radical or extreme. **3** staying within limits that are considered reasonable by most people: *I class myself as a moderate drinker.* □ *verb* to become or make something become less extreme, severe, or strong: *She apologized immediately and moderated her voice.* □ *By evening the wind had moderated slightly.*
Usage The verb *moderate* is often used to talk about things that are done by people, for example *behaviour*, *criticism*, or *language*, and usually has a person as the subject of the verb: *We agreed to moderate our original demands.*
Word family **moderately** *adverb*: *He only drinks moderately.* □ *The plan was only moderately successful.* **moderation** *noun*: *to drink in moderation.* □ *He urged the police to show moderation.* □ *the moderation of the union's demands.*

modern *adjective*
1 of the present time or recent times: *modern European history.* □ *Stress is a major problem of modern life.* **2** using the most recent technology, methods, designs, or materials: *The company needs to invest in a modern computer system.* □ *It is the most modern, well-*

m

equipped hospital in the country. **3** (of ways of behaving or thinking) new and intended to be different from traditional ways, and therefore not always accepted by most members of society: *She has very modern ideas about educating her children.* **4** (of styles in art, music, fashion, etc.) new and intended to be different from traditional styles: *The gallery has regular exhibitions of modern art.*
Usage **modern** or **contemporary**? See **contemporary**.
Word family **modernize** verb to make a system, methods, etc. more modern and more suitable for use at the present time; to start using modern equipment, ideas, etc.: *The company is investing millions of pounds to modernize its factories.*

modest *adjective*
1 not talking much about your own abilities or status: *She's very modest about her success.* □ *Don't be so modest! You're a very talented player.* **2** not very large, expensive, or grand: *There has been a modest improvement in the situation.* □ *He charged a relatively modest fee.* □ *She grew up in a modest little house in the suburbs.* □ *The research was carried out on a modest scale.*
Usage The word *modest* is used especially to talk about aims and achievements: *a modest aim/achievement/ambition/goal/success*; amounts of money that people spend or earn: *a modest contribution/expenditure/fee/gain/investment/outlay/profit/sum*; buildings that are not very expensive or grand: *a modest house/flat/villa.* □ *modest premises*; and the size of something: *a modest size/amount/quantity/scale/share/proportion.*
Word family **modestly** adverb: *She pointed out modestly.* □ *modestly priced goods.* □ *Revenue grew modestly last quarter.* **modesty** noun: *He accepted the award with characteristic modesty.*

modify *verb*
1 to change something slightly, especially in order to make it more suitable for a particular purpose: *Patients are taught how to modify their diet.* □ *We found it cheaper to modify existing equipment rather than buy new.* **2** to make your behaviour, attitude, or language less extreme, especially in order to avoid offending someone: *The social worker at first aimed to get Mrs Robinson to modify her behaviour, without success.*

Usage **modify** or **adjust**? See **adjust**.
Word family **modification** noun the act or process of changing something in order to correct or improve it or make it more acceptable; a change that is made: *Considerable modification of the existing system is needed.* □ *It might be necessary to make a few slight modifications to the design.*

momentous *adjective*
(especially of events and occasions) very important or serious, especially because there may be important results: *At the same time, momentous events were taking place in Russia.* □ *a period of momentous changes in East-West relations.* □ *a momentous decision.*
Word family **momentously** adverb: *More momentously, it goes right to the heart of the national consciousness.* **momentousness** noun: *the momentousness of the occasion.*

momentum *noun*
1 the impetus and driving force gained by the development of a process or course of events: *The investigation gathered momentum.* **2** the force gained by a moving object: *The vehicle gained momentum as the road dipped.*

monitor *verb*
1 to observe and check the progress or quality of something over a period of time; to keep under systematic review: *Equipment was installed to monitor air quality.* □ *each student's progress is closely monitored over the term.* **2** to maintain regular surveillance over: *He was a man of routine and it was easy for an enemy to monitor his movements.*
Usage As a noun, *monitor* has various senses including: 'an instrument used to check something' (*a heart monitor*), 'a display screen from a computer or camera', and 'a person whose job is to check something is done fairly and honestly, especially in a foreign country' (*UN monitors declared the referendum fair*).

morale *noun*
the amount of confidence and enthusiasm that a person or group has at a particular time: *Morale amongst the players is very high at the moment.*
Usage **morale** or **spirits**? Both *morale* and *spirits* are usually described as either high or low and verbs used to describe someone's *morale* or *spirits* often involve movement up or down: *to lift/raise someone's morale/spirits.* □ *someone's spirits lift/raise/soar.* □ *The*

competition will boost children's morale and self-esteem. □ We sang songs to keep our spirits up. □ My spirits sank at the thought of starting all over again.

mosaic *noun*
1 a combination of diverse elements forming a more or less coherent whole: *The painting is a rich mosaic of light, colour, and form.* □ *A mosaic of fields, rivers, and woods lay below us.* 2 a picture or pattern produced by arranging together small variously coloured pieces of hard material such as stone, tile, or glass: *a mosaic on the floor.* 3 decorative work of this kind: *The walls and vaults are decorated by marble and mosaic.* 4 a colourful and variegated pattern: *The bird's plumage was a mosaic of slate-grey, blue, and brown.*

motif *noun*
1 a small, simple picture of something that is used once, or repeated in different places or parts of something: *the colourful hand-painted motifs that adorn narrowboats.* 2 a design used as a decoration: *The rug was decorated with a simple flower motif.* 3 a subject, idea, or phrase that is repeated and developed in a work of literature or piece of music: *Alienation is a central motif in her novels.* □ *The equation of humans and hyenas becomes a recurrent motif in the book.*

motivate *verb*
1 to make someone want to do something, especially something that involves hard work or effort: *She's very good at motivating her students.* □ *The plan is designed to motivate employees to work more efficiently.* 2 to be the reason why someone decides to do something or behave in a particular way: *He is motivated entirely by self-interest.* □ *What motivates people to carry out such attacks?*
Word family **motivated** adjective: *a highly motivated student* (= one who is very interested and works hard). **motivation** noun the reason why someone does something or behaves in a particular way; something that makes someone want to be successful: *I soon understood his motivation in inviting me.* □ *He's intelligent enough but he lacks motivation.*

motivational adjective: *an important motivational factor.*

multifaceted *adjective*
1 having many sides: *the diamond's multifaceted surface.* 2 having many different aspects or features: *his extraordinary and multifaceted career.*

multi-purpose *adjective*
that can be used for several different purposes: *Just one multi-purpose cleaner should be enough for the whole house.* □ *The school includes twelve classrooms, a multi-purpose hall, a dining room, and offices.*
Usage **multi-purpose** or **all-purpose**? See **all-purpose**.

mutual *adjective*
1 (of a feeling or action) experienced or done by each of two or more parties towards the other or others: *a partnership based on mutual respect and understanding.* □ *My father hated him from the start and the feeling was mutual.* 2 (of two or more people) having the same specified relationship to each other: *They cooperated as potentially mutual beneficiaries of the settlement.* 3 held in common by two or more parties: *We were introduced by a mutual friend.*
Usage Traditionally it has long been held that the only correct use of *mutual* is in describing a reciprocal relationship: *mutual respect*, for example, means that the parties involved feel respect for each other. The other use of *mutual* meaning 'held in common', as in *mutual friend*, is held to be incorrect. The latter use has a long and respectable history, however. It was first recorded in Shakespeare and has since appeared in the writing of Sir Walter Scott, George Eliot, and, most famously, in the title of Dickens' novel *Our Mutual Friend*. It is now generally accepted as part of standard English.
Word family **mutually exclusive** not able to exist or be true at the same time as something else: *It's tempting for children to see 'reading' and 'pleasure' as mutually exclusive.* □ *The two options are not mutually exclusive* (= you can have them both).

Nn

natural *adjective*
1 (of behaviour, qualities, or feelings) part of the character that a person or animal was born with: *Hunting is one of a cat's natural instincts.* □ *His natural gifts as a preacher meant he was in great demand.* □ *It's only natural to worry about your children.* **2** (of a person) having an innate skill or quality: *He was a natural leader/teacher.* **3** (of a skill or quality) coming instinctively to a person; innate: *Laura's natural adaptability enabled her to settle quickly.* **4** (of a person or their behaviour) relaxed and unaffected; spontaneous: *He replied with just a little too much nonchalance to sound natural.* **5** entirely to be expected: *Ken was a natural choice for chairman.* **6** having had a minimum of processing or preservative treatment: *natural food.* □ *Our nutritional products are completely natural.*
Usage **natural** or **innate**? See **innate**.
Word family **naturally** *adverb*: *She was naturally gifted when it came to music.*

neat *adjective*
1 (of a person) liking to keep things in order; careful about your appearance: *She was a very efficient, neat woman.* □ *The children are always neat and tidy.* □ *By nature he was clean and tidy.* **2** carefully done or arranged with everything in the correct place or the correct order: *She was wearing a neat black suit.* □ *You've got very neat handwriting!* □ *This hairstyle is easy to keep neat and tidy.*
Usage **neat**, **tidy**, or **orderly**? *Neat* is the most general of these words and can describe someone's appearance, a place, or an arrangement of things such as a *row* or *pile*; *tidy* usually describes a place such as a *room* or *desk*; *orderly* usually describes the way things are arranged in rows or piles.
Word family **neatly** *adverb*: *The tools were neatly arranged on the bench.*

negligible *adjective*
so small or unimportant that it is not worth considering: *The cost was negligible.* □ *Tests found only a negligible amount of the chemical in the product.*
Usage When you use *negligible*, you mean that an amount of the thing described exists or is present, but that there is not enough of it to have an effect.
Word family **negligibly** *adverb*: *a negligibly small probability of repeated occurrence.*

negotiate *verb*
1 to try to reach an agreement or to settle a dispute by formal discussion: *The government will not negotiate with terrorists.* □ *We are negotiating the release of the prisoners.* □ *They have refused to negotiate on this issue.* □ *Her financial adviser is negotiating on her behalf.* **2** to arrange or agree the details of something, e.g. a contract or a deal, by formal discussion: *Rents are individually negotiated between landlord and tenant.* □ *We successfully negotiated the release of the hostages.*
Word family **negotiable** *adjective*: *The price is negotiable.* **negotiation** *noun*: *peace/trade/ wage negotiations.* □ *They begin another round of negotiations today.* **negotiator** *noun* a person who is involved in formal political or financial discussions, especially as a job: *The chief union negotiator indicated that they would reject the pay award.* □ *She has an image as a tough negotiator.*

nestle *verb*
to be located in a position that is protected, sheltered, or partly hidden: *The little town nestles snugly at the foot of the hill.* □ *a delightful little village nestling on the banks of the river by the castle.*

notable *adjective*
deserving to be noticed or to receive attention because it is unusual, important, or

interesting: *The town is notable for its ancient harbour.* □ *It is notable that only 15% of senior managers are women.* □ *With a few notable exceptions, everyone gave something.*
Word family **notably** adverb: *The house had many drawbacks, most notably its price.*

nucleus *noun*

the central part of something around which other parts are situated or collected: *These paintings will form the nucleus of a new collection.* □ *It was this cluster of houses which formed the nucleus of the village.*
Usage The word *nucleus* is most often used to talk about the most important part of a place or exhibition, or the most important people within a group.

nurture *verb, noun*

verb **1** to care for and encourage the growth or development of: *He was nurtured by his parents in a close-knit family.* □ *My father nurtured my love of art.* **2** to cherish a hope, belief, or ambition: *For a long time she had nurtured the dream of buying a shop.* □ *noun* the process of nurturing someone or something: *the nurture of children.* □ *the nurture of musical talent.*
Usage The words *nurture* and *nature* are often contrasted, *nurture* being the upbringing, education, and environment contrasted with *nature* as the inborn or hereditary characteristics as an influence on or determining personality.

n

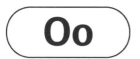

Oo

objective *adjective, noun*
adjective not influenced by personal opinions or feelings, but considering only the facts: *There's little objective evidence to suggest that he is guilty.* □ *It's hard for parents to be objective about their own children.* □ *noun* something that you are trying to achieve: *What is the main objective of this project?* □ *You must set realistic aims and objectives for yourself.*
Usage **objective**, **goal**, or **target**? See **target**.
Usage The opposite of *objective* is *subjective*, 'based on your own ideas and opinions rather than facts and therefore sometimes unfair': *a highly subjective point of view.* □ *Everyone's opinion is bound to be subjective.*
Word family **objectively** adverb: *Try to weigh up the issues as objectively as you can.*
objectivity noun: *The survey's claims to scientific objectivity are highly dubious.*

observant *adjective*
quick to notice things: *Observant walkers may see red deer along this stretch of the roads.*
Word family **observantly** adverb: *'You don't look too happy,' she said, observantly.*

observe *verb*
1 to see or notice someone or something: *Have you observed any changes lately?* □ *He was observed entering the bank.* **2** to watch someone or something carefully, especially to learn more about them: *The patients were observed over a period of several months.* □ *He observes keenly, but says little.* **3** to say or write what you have noticed about a situation: *'You look tired,' she observed.* **4** to act according to a law, agreement, or custom: *Will the rebels observe the ceasefire?* □ *We observed a two-minute silence for the victims of the bombing.*
Usage **observation**, **comment**, or **remark**? See **comment**.
Word family **observation** noun **1** the act of watching someone or something carefully for a period of time, especially to find something out: *Most of the information was collected by*

direct observation of the animals' behaviour. **2** a comment, especially one based on something you have seen, heard, or read: *He began by making a few general observations about the report.*

operational *adjective*
1 ready to be used; in use: *The new airport should be fully operational by the end of the year.* **2** relating to the routine functioning of an organization: *operational costs.* **3** relating to active operations of the armed forces, police, or emergency services: *an operational fighter squadron.*
Usage The word *operational* is very often used in the phrase *fully operational*.
Word family **operationally** adverb: *The forces are trained and equipped but are not necessarily operationally ready.*

opportune *adjective*
1 (of a time) at which a particular action or event occurs, especially conveniently or appropriately: *The offer couldn't have come at a more opportune moment.* **2** done or occurring at a favourable or useful time; well timed: *the opportune use of humour to lower tension.*
Usage **opportune**, **auspicious**, or **timely**? *Opportune* is used mainly to denote a favourable time or moment for doing something: *I waited for an opportune moment to discuss the idea.* When applied to actions or events occurring at favourable moments, it can suggest the role of chance in producing a happy outcome: *An opportune visit from the manager allowed him to air his views. Auspicious* is used where all the circumstances are conducive to the success of a new undertaking, and it is used typically to describe a point in time: *He is waiting for the most auspicious moment to call an election.* It is often used precisely when circumstances are not conducive to success, especially when referring to the start of something: *He did not*

make the most auspicious of starts to the season. A *timely* action or event occurs at a moment when it can make the greatest difference to a situation: *The assassins were stopped only by the timely intervention of a patrol.* A *timely* reminder is given when it is much needed, if not overdue.

opportunity *noun*
1 a favourable time or set of circumstances when a particular situation makes it possible to do or achieve something: *You'll have the opportunity to ask questions at the end.* □ *I'd like to take this opportunity to thank my colleagues for their support.* **2** a career opening; a chance for employment or promotion: *There are more job opportunities in the south.* □ *Our company promotes equal opportunities for women* (= women are given the same jobs, pay, etc. as men). □ *career opportunities in our New York headquarters.* □ *There'll be plenty of opportunities to relax once the work is done.*

optimism *noun*
a feeling that good things will happen and that something will be successful; a tendency to have this feeling: *He returned with renewed optimism about the future.*
Usage The word *optimism* is often used in business or political contexts, when business managers or politicians express a belief that their company or policies will be successful.
Word family **optimistic** *adjective* expecting good things to happen or something to be successful: *She's not very optimistic about the outcome of the talks.* □ *They are cautiously optimistic that the reforms will take place.*
optimistically *adverb*: *He spoke optimistically about better relations between the two countries.*

optimum *adjective, noun*
adjective being the best possible; producing the best possible results: *We aim for optimum efficiency in all our operations.* □ *noun* (**the optimum**) the best possible condition: *For efficient fuel consumption a speed of 60 mph is about the optimum.*
Word family **optimal** *adjective* being the most favourable: *seeking the optimal solution.*

option *noun*
something that you can choose to have or do; the freedom to choose what you do: *As I see*

it, we have two options. □ *We are currently studying all the options available.*
Usage **option**, **alternative**, or **choice**?
See **alternative**.
Word family **optional** *adjective* that you can choose to do or have if you want to: *Certain classes are compulsory; others are optional.* □ *This model comes with a number of optional extras* (= things you can choose to have but which you pay extra for).

orderly *adjective*
1 arranged in a neat and logical way: *The vegetables were placed in orderly rows.* **2** doing things in a careful and logical way: *Public policy changes can be made in an orderly and rational manner.*
Usage **orderly**, **neat**, or **tidy**? See **neat**.
Word family **orderliness** *noun*

organize *verb*
1 to make arrangements or preparations for an event or activity: *Social programmes are organized by the school.* **2** to arrange in a systematic way: *The book is organized in nine thematic chapters.*
Word family **organization** *noun* **1** an organized group of people with a particular purpose, e.g. a business: *There need to be changes throughout the organization.* □ *Voluntary organizations working with the homeless are against the proposal.* **2** the action of organizing something: *They blamed the government for the poor organization of the election.* **3** a systematic arrangement or approach: *She's highly intelligent but lacks organization.* **organizational** *adjective*: *We are seeking a more effective organizational framework in which decisions can be made.*
organized *adjective* (of a person) able to plan their life and work well and efficiently: *The chairman is one of the most organized people I know.* **organizer** *noun* a person who arranges for something to happen or be provided: *Police had several meetings with the organizers of the race to discuss safety.*

original *adjective*
having or showing new, different, and interesting ideas: *The film is challenging and highly original.* □ *This work is the product of a highly original mind.*
Usage **original**, **imaginative**, **ingenious**, **innovative**, or **inventive**? See **inventive**.

O

Word family *originality* noun the ability to have interesting new ideas; the quality of being new and interesting in a way that is different from anything that has existed before: *His originality as a painter lies in his representation of light.* *originally* adverb in a novel and inventive way: *the suggestions so originally and persuasively outlined.*

outdo *verb*

to be better than someone or something in action or performance: *The men tried to outdo each other in their generosity.* □ *Not to be outdone, Vicky and Laura reached the same standard.*
Usage *outdo*, *excel*, or *surpass*? See **excel**.

outgoing *adjective*

liking to meet people, enjoying their company and being friendly towards them; socially confident: *She was always cheerful and outgoing.* □ *I think the role needs a more outgoing personality.*
Usage The adjective *outgoing* also means 'leaving a job or position': *the outgoing prime minister;* or 'going out or away from a place': *incoming and outgoing telephone calls.* As a noun, *outgoings* are the money that is spent regularly.

outline *noun*

a description of the main facts or points involved in something: *This is a brief outline of the events.* □ *The article describes in outline the main findings of the research.*
Usage *outline*, *overview*, or *summary*? An *outline* can be written or given before the full version is produced or worked out: *You should draw up an outline for the essay before you start*

writing. □ *The outline agreement about the country's transition to full democracy still has to be discussed at a multi-party forum.* An *overview* is similar to an *outline*, but the emphasis is more on the fact that someone wants to look for general trends across a wide area, rather than that the details are still to be worked out. A *summary* is always written or made after the full version of a text, discussion, etc. has been written or recorded; it may be read after, before, or instead of reading the full text.

outstanding *adjective*

extremely good: *She's one of their most outstanding young players.* □ *The valley has been designated an Area of Outstanding Natural Beauty.*
Usage The word *outstanding* is used especially about how well someone does something or how good someone is at something. Other meanings of the word *outstanding* are 'clearly noticeable': *the most outstanding decorative element of the mausoleum*; and 'not yet dealt with or paid': *outstanding debts.* □ *How much work is still outstanding?*
Word family *outstandingly* adverb: *The team has been outstandingly successful.*

overview *noun*

a description or understanding of the main facts or points involved in something: *The second chapter will provide an overview of the issues involved.* □ *My main concern is to get an overview of the main environmental problems facing the area.*
Usage *overview*, *outline*, or *summary*? See **outline**.

o

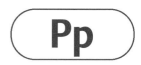

Pp

painstaking *adjective*
needing or giving a lot of care, effort, and attention to detail: *The event had been planned with painstaking attention to detail.*
Word family **painstakingly** adverb: *a historic site that has been painstakingly restored to its original appearance.*

palpable *adjective*
(of a feeling or atmosphere) so intense that you seem to experience it as a physical sensation: *a palpable sense of loss.*
Usage The word *palpable* also means 'able to be touched or felt': *a palpable bump at the bridge of the nose.*
Word family **palpably** adverb: *Such a claim is palpably absurd.*

panache *noun*
flamboyant confidence of style or manner: *He entertained London society with great panache.*

panorama *noun*
1 a view of a wide area of land: *There is a wonderful panorama of the mountains from the hotel.* 2 a complete and comprehensive survey or presentation of a subject: *a panorama of black history in dance and song.*
Word family **panoramic** adjective: *Stop in the tearoom and enjoy a panoramic view of the valley and mountains.*

paradigm *noun*
a typical example, pattern, or model of something: *Society's paradigm of the 'ideal woman'.*
Usage You should take care in using the phrase *paradigm shift*, meaning 'a fundamental change in approach or underlying assumptions', because some people consider it jargon.

paragon *noun*
a person or thing regarded as a perfect example of a particular quality: *It would have*

taken a paragon of virtue not to feel viciously jealous.

parameter *noun*
something that marks the limits of what you are considering or how something can be done: *We need to define the parameters of this debate.* □ *We had to work within the parameters that had already been established.*
Usage The word *parameter* is usually used in the plural.

par excellence *adjective*
better than all the others of the same kind; being a very good example of something: *She turned out to be an organizer par excellence.*
Usage This phrase, which comes from French, is pronounced par **ek**-suh-lonss.

participate *verb*
to choose to be involved in an activity or event: *She didn't participate in the discussion.* □ *We want to encourage students to participate fully in the running of the college.*
Word family **participant** noun a person who is taking part in an activity or event: *Staff are to be active participants in the decision-making process.* **participation** noun the act of taking part in an activity or event: *It's a show with lots of audience participation.* □ *A back injury prevented active participation in any sports for a while.*

partner *noun*
1 one of the people who owns a business and shares the profits: *He has recently been made a junior partner in the family business.* 2 a person that you are doing an activity with, such as dancing or playing a game: *Choose a partner for the next activity.*
Word family **partnership** noun 1 a relationship between two people, organizations, etc. in which the two work together for a result that is good for both of them; the state of having this relationship: *the*

school's partnership with parents. □ a partnership between the United States and Europe. **2** a business owned by two or more people who share the profits: *a junior member of the partnership.*

passionate *adjective*
having or showing strong feelings of enthusiasm for something or belief in something: *She is passionate about her work.* □ *She was a passionate defender of civil liberties.*
Usage The word *passionate* is used especially to talk about someone's beliefs and commitment as well as people themselves who strongly support someone or something: *a passionate speech/sincerity/attachment/belief/ commitment/conviction.* □ *a passionate supporter/defender of something.*
Word family **passionately** *adverb*: *She believes passionately in education and hard work.*

pastoral *adjective*
1 relating to or denoting a teacher's responsibility for the general well-being of pupils or students: *Does the school operate a pastoral and counselling system?* **2** (in the Christian Church) concerning or appropriate to the giving of spiritual guidance: *pastoral and doctrinal issues.* □ *clergy doing pastoral work.*
Usage The above senses derive from the sense of *pastor* as a shepherd; the word *pastoral* is also used to mean 'associated with country life': *The view was pastoral, with rolling fields and grazing sheep.*

pathos *noun*
(in writing, speech, and plays) the power of a performance, description, etc. to produce feelings of sadness and sympathy: *The actor injects his customary humour and pathos into the role.*
Usage The word *pathos* should not be confused with *bathos*, which is used (especially in a literary work) to refer to an effect of anticlimax created by an unintentional lapse in mood from the sublime to the trivial or ridiculous: *His epic poem has passages of almost embarrassing bathos.*

pattern *noun, verb*
noun **1** the regular way in which something happens or is done: *changing patterns of behaviour/work/weather.* □ *The murders all seem to follow a (similar) pattern* (= happen in the same way). □ *There is no set pattern for*

these meetings. **2** an excellent example of something such as a system that other people should copy: *He set the pattern for subsequent study.* □ *verb* (**pattern on/after**) to use something as a model for something else: *The clothing is patterned on athletes' wear.*
Usage *pattern* or *model*? See **model**.

peacemaker *noun*
a person who tries to persuade people or countries to stop arguing or fighting and to make peace: *She always acted as a peacemaker to help prevent further conflict.*

penchant *noun*
a strong or habitual liking for something or tendency to do something: *He has a penchant for adopting stray dogs.* □ *the company's penchant for system integration.*
Usage The word *penchant* is pronounced **pon**-shon.

perceptive *adjective*
having or showing the ability to make or understand things quickly, especially things that are not obvious: *It was very perceptive of you to notice that.* □ *The article gives a perceptive analysis of the way bureaucracies work.*
Word family **perceptively** *adverb*: *He writes perceptively about Gandhi's weaknesses.*

perfect *adjective*
1 having all the required elements or qualities: *She tried to be the perfect wife.* **2** free from any flaws or defects; as good as possible; excellent: *an E-type Jaguar in perfect condition.* □ *Conditions were perfect for walking.* **3** exactly right; ideal: *the perfect Christmas present for golfers everywhere.*
Word family **perfection** *noun* **1** the state of being perfect: *All the food was cooked to perfection.* **2** the action of making perfect: *the perfection of new mechanisms of economic management.* **perfectly** *adverb*: *The arrangements worked out perfectly.*

permit *verb*
1 to allow someone to do something; to allow something to happen: *The banks were not permitted to invest overseas.* □ *The rules of the club do not permit it.* □ *Permit me to make a suggestion.* **2** to enable something: *We hope to visit the cathedral, if time permits.* □ *I'll come tomorrow, weather permitting* (= if the weather is fine).

Usage As a verb, the stress is on the second syllable: per-**mit**. As a noun, meaning an official document allowing someone to do something (*a work permit*), the stress is on the first syllable: **per**-mit.

Usage **permission**, **authorization**, or **consent**? See **authorization**.

Word family **permission** noun the fact of being allowed to do something by someone who has the authority or right to decide: *I asked permission to photograph the house.* □ *Who gave permission for you to do this?*

persevere *verb*

to continue trying to do or achieve something in difficult circumstances: *Despite a number of setbacks, they persevered in their attempts to fly around the world in a balloon.* □ *You have to persevere with difficult students.*

Usage **perseverance** or **persistence**? People show *perseverance* in the face of difficult circumstances, usually created by situations outside anyone's control, such as illness, bad economic conditions, or just bad luck. *Persistence* is necessary when other people create difficulties, either by refusing to help or by actively trying to stop you.

Word family **perseverance** noun the fact of continuing to try to achieve a particular aim in spite of failure or difficulties: *They showed great perseverance in the face of difficulty.*

persist *verb*

to continue trying to do or achieve something in difficult circumstances, or in spite of opposition, in a way that can seem unreasonable: *Why do you persist in blaming yourself for what happened?* □ *He persisted with his questioning.* □ *'So, did you agree or not?' he persisted.*

Usage **persistence** or **perseverance**? See **persevere**.

Word family **persistence** noun the fact of continuing to try to do something in spite of difficulties, especially when other people are against you and think that you are being annoying or unreasonable: *His persistence was finally rewarded when the insurance company agreed to pay for the damage.* □ *It was her sheer persistence that wore them down in the end.*

persistent *adjective* continuing to do something in spite of difficulties, especially when other people are against you and think that you are being annoying or unreasonable: *She can be very persistent when she wants*

something. **persistently** adverb: *They have persistently denied claims of illegal dealing.*

personable *adjective*

(especially of a man) pleasant in appearance, character, or behaviour: *Her assistant seemed a very personable young man.*

Usage The word *personable* is used especially to describe your impression of someone that you do not know well.

personality *noun*

1 a person's qualities and features that combine to form an individual's distinctive character and make them different from other people: *The children all have very different personalities.* □ *His wife has a strong personality.* □ *There are likely to be tensions and personality clashes in any social group.* **2** the qualities of a person's character that make them interesting and attractive to other people; lively, engaging qualities: *In his plays, his characters always have lots of personality.*

Usage The word *personality* is used especially to talk about the way someone behaves in the company of other people, for example whether they are lively or quiet, confident or shy, cheerful or bad-tempered.

perspective *noun*

a particular attitude towards an issue or problem; a particular way of thinking about something: *Try to approach the problem from a different perspective.* □ *We need to take a global perspective on the environment.*

Usage The word *perspective* is also used to mean 'a true understanding of the relative importance of things; a sense of proportion': *We must keep a sense of perspective about what he's done.* □ *Though the figures are shocking, they need to be put into perspective.*

persuade *verb*

1 to make someone agree to do something by giving them good reasons for doing it: *Can you persuade him to come?* □ *Please try and persuade her.* □ *He was fairly easily persuaded.* □ *I allowed myself to be persuaded into entering the competition.* **2** to make someone believe that something is true, especially by what you say: *No one was persuaded by his argument.* □ *It has been difficult to persuade people that we have no political objectives.*

Usage **persuade**, **convince**, or **induce**? See **convince**.

Word family *persuasion* noun: *After a little gentle persuasion, he agreed to come.* □ *She has great powers of persuasion.*

persuasive *adjective*
(of an argument, reason, etc. or a person) able to persuade someone to believe or do something: *Advertising relies heavily on the persuasive power of imagery.* □ *an informative and persuasive speech.*
Word family *persuasively* adverb: *They argue persuasively in favour of a total ban on handguns.* **persuasiveness** noun: *assess the persuasiveness of the evidence.*

phase *noun, verb*
noun a period in a process of change or development: *We are now entering a critical phase of the campaign.* □ *His anxiety about the work was just a passing phase.* □ *Most teenagers go through a difficult phase.* □ *verb* **1** (**be phased**) to carry out in gradual stages: *The work is being phased over a number of years.* **2** (**phase in/out**) to introduce into/withdraw from use in gradual stages: *Our armed forces policy was to be phased in over ten years.*
Usage *phase* or *stage*? A *phase* is always a period of time with a beginning and an end; you can *enter*, *go through*, or *finish* a *phase* and you can talk about what happens *during* a *phase* and how long it will last. The word *phase* is used especially to talk about planned stages of a project or the different emotional stages of a person's life. The word *stage* can be used in the same way, but it can also be used to talk about a particular state or moment within a longer period of time; something can be *at a particular stage*, but not *at a phase*.

phenomenal *adjective*
very great or impressive: *There was a phenomenal response to the appeal.* □ *He has a phenomenal memory for facts and figures.* □ *Exports have been phenomenal this year.*
Word family *phenomenally* adverb: *phenomenally successful.*

phlegmatic *adjective*
(of a person) having an unemotional and stolidly calm disposition: *the phlegmatic British character.* □ *a phlegmatic attitude to every crisis.*
Word family *phlegmatically* adverb: *He's taken it phlegmatically and is even making a joke about it.*

picturesque *adjective*
(of a place or building) visually attractive, especially in a quaint or pretty style: *ruined abbeys and picturesque villages.* □ *This picturesque setting is perfect for a relaxing holiday.*
Word family *picturesquely* adverb: *a place content to bask picturesquely in rural timelessness.* □ *These sturdy wooden boats mingle picturesquely alongside the quay.* **picturesqueness** noun

pinpoint *verb*
to find or locate exactly: *It is difficult to pinpoint the source of his life's inspiration.* □ *to pinpoint the cause of the trouble.*
Usage As an adjective, the word *pinpoint* means 'absolutely precise; to the finest degree': *This weapon fired shells with pinpoint accuracy* or 'tiny': *a pinpoint hole.* As a noun, a *pinpoint* refers to a tiny dot or point: *a pinpoint of light from a torch.*

pioneer *noun, verb*
noun a person who is among the first to do something or to study and develop a particular area of knowledge or culture that other people then continue to develop: *He is known as a pioneer in veterinary surgery.* □ *She later became a pioneer of education for women.* □ *verb* to be one of the first people to do, discover, or use something new: *He pioneered the sale of car insurance through high-street shops.* □ *This is a new technique, pioneered by surgeons in a London hospital.*
Usage *Pioneers* were originally the first people to go to a particular area in order to live and work there: *Early pioneers settled on both sides of the Maple River.* The verb *pioneer* is used in scientific contexts. People typically *pioneer* a *treatment*, *new approach*, or *technique.* It is often used in the passive, to talk about where a treatment or technique was first developed: *This technique was pioneered by a Swiss doctor in the 1930s.*

pivotal *adjective*
extremely important because a particular situation or activity depends on it: *The Foreign Secretary has played a pivotal role in European affairs.* □ *Accountancy, law, and economics are pivotal to a successful career in any financial services area.*
Usage The word *pivotal* is used especially to describe the part that someone or something

plays in a particular situation; it is not used to describe items or actions that are simply extremely important: *essential* (not: *pivotal*) *services/supplies/repairs.* □ *It is vital* (not: *pivotal*) *that we get this right.*
Word family **pivotally** adverb: *Discussion is a pivotally important part of the implementation of the proposals.*

platform noun
1 an opportunity to voice your views or initiate action: *The forum will provide a platform for discussion of communication issues.* **2** the declared policy of a political party or group: *seeking election on a platform of low taxes.* □ *She campaigned on a platform of zero tolerance towards racist behaviour.*
Usage These figurative senses derive from the senses meaning 'a raised floor or stage used by public speakers or performers' and 'a raised structure along the side of a railway track where passengers get on and off trains at a station'.

pleasurable adjective
that you enjoy; pleasing: *She had the pleasurable sensation of being swept off her feet.* □ *Dining becomes a pleasurable experience in our chic new restaurant.*
Usage **pleasurable** or **enjoyable**? *Pleasurable* is a more formal word than *enjoyable* and is used especially to describe physical pleasures and feelings.
Word family **pleasurably** adverb: *a pleasurably varied trek.*

plentiful adjective
existing in or yielding great quantities; abundant: *Coal is cheap and plentiful.*
Word family **plentifully** adverb: *Evidence is plentifully available.* **plentifulness** noun: *The plentifulness of labour and capital.*

plethora noun
an excess of something: *The plethora of choices available is enough to make you wish you were colour-blind.* □ *a plethora of newspaper opinion polls.*
Usage A *plethora* is not simply an abundance of something, but rather an overabundance, as in: *The bill had to struggle through a plethora of committees and subcommittees.* In phrases such as *a plethora of play spaces and equipment*, the looser meaning of 'abundance' is often not considered good style.

poignant adjective
having a strong effect on your feelings, especially in a way that makes you feel sad: *It was the city's street children who provided some of the most poignant images.* □ *Her face was a poignant reminder of the passing of time.*
Usage The derived noun *poignancy* is used much more frequently than the variant *poignance.*
Word family **poignancy** noun: *The film ends with a chase that resonates with unexpected poignancy.* **poignantly** adverb: *The documentary poignantly captures the variety and conflict of feelings that followed the war.*

pointed adjective
(of a remark or look) expressing criticism in a direct and unambiguous way: *The report inspired a pointed critique.* □ *She gave a pointed glare.*
Word family **pointedly** adverb: *He looked pointedly at her.* **pointedness** noun: *The text is written in careful prose, belying the pointedness of its conclusions.*

polished adjective
1 accomplished and skilful: *his polished performance in the film.* **2** refined, sophisticated, or elegant: *He was polished and charming.* □ *polished manners.*

political adjective
of or relating to the state, the government, or the public affairs of a country: *a period of political and economic stability.*
Usage **politic** or **political**? The word *politic* means (of an action) 'seeming sensible and judicious in the circumstances': *I did not think it politic to express my reservations.* The word *political* means 'relating to the government or public affairs of a country': *in a period of economic and political stability*; 'related to politics'; or 'concerned with power or status within an organization rather than matters of principle': *Snooker is paying the price for years of political infighting.* The adverb that is derived from *politic* is *politicly*, but this is found very rarely; the adverb derived from *political* is used much more frequently: *a politically motivated decision.* Note the different stress patterns of these two words: *politic* is stressed on the first syllable; *political* on the second.

p

popular *adjective*

1 (of people, things, or activities) liked or enjoyed by a large number of people: *He was a hugely popular singer.* □ *This is one of our most popular designs.* □ *These policies are unlikely to prove popular with middle-class voters.* **2** (of ideas, beliefs, or opinions) shared by a large number of people: *By popular demand, the tour has been extended by two weeks.* □ *Contrary to popular belief, women cause fewer road accidents than men.*
3 connected with ordinary people in society in general: *They won the largest share of the popular vote.* □ *The regime was overthrown by a popular uprising.*

Usage **popular** or **public**? In many cases you can use either word: *public/popular pressure/ awareness/opinion. Popular* usually describes something, such as an idea or action, which comes from ordinary people: *popular support.* □ *a popular movement/uprising. Public* is more general and can also describe things which are for, about, or involve everyone: *public health.* □ *the public interest.*

Word family **popularity** noun: *Their music still enjoys widespread popularity among teenagers.* **popularly** adverb: *a popularly held belief.* □ *a popularly elected government.*

portfolio *noun*

a range of products or services offered by an organization, especially when considered as a business asset: *an unrivalled portfolio of quality brands.*

Usage The more literal senses of the word *portfolio* include 'a thin, flat case for carrying drawings, maps, etc.'; 'a set of pieces of creative work intended to demonstrate a person's ability'; and 'a range of investments held by a person or organization'. A *portfolio* is also the position and duties of a government minister: *He took on the foreign-affairs portfolio.* The word is used as an adjective before a noun to refer to an employment pattern which involves a succession of short-term contracts and part-time work, rather than the more traditional model of a single job for life: *Portfolio careers allow women to balance work with family commitments.*

portrait *noun*

a detailed description or dramatic presentation of someone or something in a book, film, etc.: *Her first film was a stunning portrait of life in the sugar plantations of her native Martinique.* □ *The book paints a vivid portrait of contemporary Italy.*

Usage A *portrait* is also a painting, drawing, or photograph of a person, especially of the head and shoulders: *Vermeer's 'Portrait of the artist in his studio'.* □ *She had her portrait painted.* A *self-portrait* is a painting that you do of yourself.

Usage **portrait** or **portrayal**? A *portrait* is the description, play, or film itself. The *portrayal* of someone or something is the way someone or something is shown in words or pictures.

portray *verb*

to show someone or something in a picture or describe someone or something in a piece of writing; to present someone or something in a particular way, especially when this does not give a complete or accurate impression of what they are like: *His war poetry vividly portrays life in the trenches.* □ *Throughout the trial, he portrayed himself as the victim.*

Usage **portrayal** or **portrait**? See **portrait**.

Word family **portrayal** noun the act of showing or describing someone or something, especially a person or group of people, in a picture, book, film, etc.; the particular way in which this is done: *The article examines the portrayal of gay men in the media.* □ *He is best known for his chilling portrayal of Hannibal Lecter.*

positive *adjective*

1 (of the effect of someone or something on someone or something) good or useful: *Local residents made a very positive contribution to the debate.* **2** thinking about what is good in a situation; confident and hopeful about the future: *She tried to be more positive about her new job.* □ *On the positive side, profits have increased.* **3** expressing agreement, approval, or support for someone or something: *Most of his remarks were positive, but there were a few criticisms.* □ *You should try to be a bit more positive about your students.* **4** giving clear and definite proof or information: *We have no positive evidence that she was involved.*

Word family **positively** adverb **1** in a positive way: *She was portrayed very positively in the movie.* □ *Her attacker has been positively identified by the police.* **2** used to emphasize that something is the case, even though it may seem surprising or unlikely: *Some of the diets may be positively dangerous.*

potential *noun, adjective*
noun the possibility of something happening or being developed or used; qualities that exist in someone or something and can be developed: *She has great potential as an artist.* □ *All children should be encouraged to realize their full potential.* □ *adjective* expected to develop into something or to be developed in the future: *First we need to identify actual and potential problems.* □ *What are the potential benefits of these proposals?*
Usage People and things generally *have* or *show* potential when they have qualities that can be developed. When they use these qualities successfully, they *fulfil, reach,* or *realize* their *potential.* The adjective *potential* is used in several main ways: to talk about people who might buy a product or use a service: *a potential audience/buyer/client/consumer/customer*; to talk about things that might go wrong: *a potential complication/danger/disaster/drawback/embarrassment/hazard/pitfall/risk/threat*; and to talk about things that people might gain from: *a potential advantage/benefit/improvement/saving.*
Usage **potential** or **prospective**? Both these words can be used to talk about people who are expected to become buyers, employees, etc. However, *prospective* is used more to talk about a person who has already shown some interest in a product or service; *potential* is used more to talk about people in general who could be targeted by a company's advertising, for example.
Word family **potentially** adverb: *a potentially dangerous situation.*

powerful *adjective*
1 (of people or groups) having a lot of power to control and influence people and events: *He is one of the most powerful directors in Hollywood.* □ *This extremist movement has become increasingly powerful in recent years.* □ *Why are there still so few women in politically powerful positions?* 2 having a strong effect on people's feelings or thoughts: *His photomontages are powerful anti-war images.*
Usage The word *powerful* is used to describe someone who has power, especially because of their position, and is able to use it to control people and events. Leaders, politicians, and top business people are often described as *powerful.*

Word family **powerfully** adverb: *His skills contributed powerfully to a recasting of the nation's politics.* **powerfulness** noun: *the greatness and powerfulness of society.*

practicable *adjective*
1 able to be done or put into practice successfully: *The measures will be put into effect as soon as is reasonably practicable.* □ *It was not reasonably practicable to call her as a witness.* 2 able to be used; useful: *Signal processing can let you transform a signal into a practicable form.*
Usage **practicable** or **practical**? Practicable describes 'that which can be done or put into practice successfully' whereas *practical* is used more generally. A *practicable option* is one that is possible or feasible; a *practical option* implies a choice that is realistic and sensible and will probably be effective.
Word family **practicability** noun: *The practicability of taking precautions can be significant.* **practicably** adverb: *as soon as practicably possible.*

practical *adjective*
1 connected with real situations rather than with ideas or theories: *practical advice/help/support.* □ *practical applications of the research.* □ *The candidate should have practical experience of agriculture.* 2 suitable for a particular purpose; realistic; economical; likely to be effective or successful: *strategies that are practical for small businesses.* □ *It was difficult to find a practical solution to the problem.* 3 solving problems in a sensible way: *Let's be practical and work out the cost first.*
Usage **practical** or **practicable**? See **practicable**.
Usage In senses 2 and 3, the word *practical* is used to describe ideas, courses of action, and ways of doing things: *a practical alternative/approach/measure/method/option/possibility/proposition.*
Word family **practicality** noun the quality or state of being practical: *There are still major doubts about the practicality of the proposal.* **practically** adverb: *It sounds like a good idea but I don't think it will work practically.*

pragmatic *adjective*
solving problems in a sensible way rather than by having fixed ideas or theories: *We take a pragmatic approach to management problems.*

P

Usage Being *pragmatic* often means finding solutions which do not follow traditional practices. *Pragmatic* is usually used to describe a course of action: *a pragmatic response/solution/approach/attitude.*
Word family pragmatically adverb: *The company responded pragmatically to local conditions.* **pragmatism** noun a way of solving problems and dealing with situations that is based on what is practically possible rather than on ideas and theories: *The new government needs pragmatism, not some vague ideology.*

praiseworthy *adjective*
deserving approval and admiration: *the government's praiseworthy efforts.*
Word family praiseworthily adverb **praiseworthiness** noun

precious *adjective*
(of an object, substance, or resource) of great value; not to be wasted or treated carelessly: *a precious Chinese vase, valued at half a million pounds.* □ *precious memories of our time together.* □ *My time is precious.*
Usage You should take care when using this word as it is also used in informal contexts to express the speaker's contempt for someone or something greatly valued by another person: *You and your precious schedule - you've got to lighten up!*; for emphasis, often in an ironic context: *A precious lot you know about dogs!*; and in a derogatory way to mean 'affectedly concerned with elegant or refined behaviour, language, or manners': *his exaggerated, precious manner.*
Word family preciously adverb **preciousness** noun **precious stone** noun a highly attractive and valuable piece of mineral, used especially in jewellery; a gemstone.

precise *adjective*
giving all the details clearly and correctly; based on correct and careful measurement or judgement: *Please give precise details about your previous experience.* □ *It measures 3.4 metres, to be precise.*
Usage The word *precise* is also used to emphasize that something happens at a particular time or in a particular way: *Doctors found it hard to establish the precise nature of her illness.*
Usage precise, **accurate**, or **exact**? See **accurate**.

Word family precisely adverb: *That's precisely what I mean.* □ *The meeting starts at 2 o'clock precisely.* **precision** noun: *Her writing is imaginative but lacks precision.*

predominant *adjective*
most obvious or noticeable; main or strongest: *A predominant feature of his work is the use of natural materials.* □ *Yellow is the predominant colour this spring in the fashion world.*
Word family predominantly adverb: *Ours is a predominantly Buddhist country.* □ *It is predominantly a coastal bird.*

pre-eminent *adjective*
surpassing all others; very distinguished in some way: *the world's pre-eminent expert on asbestos.*
Word family pre-eminence noun: *the technological pre-eminence of industrialized countries.* **pre-eminently** adverb above all; in particular: *The 19th century was pre-eminently the Railway Age.*

preferable *adjective*
more desirable or suitable: *Lower interest rates were preferable to higher ones.*
Word family preferably adverb ideally; if possible: *He would like a place of his own, preferably outside the town.*

preference *noun*
1 a greater interest in or desire for someone or something than someone or something else: *It's a matter of personal preference.* □ *Many people expressed a strong preference for the original plan.* □ *Let's make a list of possible speakers, in order of preference.* **2** a thing that is liked better or best: *They are undertaking a study of consumer preferences.* □ *Tastes and preferences vary from individual to individual.*
Usage preference or **favourite**? Your *favourites* are the things you like best, and that you have, do, listen to, etc. often; your *preferences* are the things that you would rather have or do if you can choose.
Word family preferential adjective of or involving preference or partiality; constituting a favour or privilege: *Preferential interest rates may be offered to employees.* □ *Regular blood donors do not receive preferential treatment.*

preferred *adjective*
that most people think is the best: *The company has not yet identified a preferred*

candidate for the job. □ *a preferred method/ option.*

premise *noun*
(*formal*) a statement or idea that forms the basis for a reasonable theory: *The basic premise of this argument is deeply flawed.* □ *the fundamental premise of the report.*
Usage In logic, a *premise* is a previous statement or proposition from which another is inferred or follows as a conclusion: *If the premise is true, then the conclusion must be true.* The word *premise* is also sometimes used as a verb to mean 'to base an argument, theory, or undertaking on': *The reforms were premised on our findings*, or 'to state or presuppose something as a premise': *One school of thought premised that the cosmos is indestructible.*

premium *noun*
1 an amount to be paid for a contract of insurance. **2** a sum added to an ordinary price or charge: *Customers are reluctant to pay a premium for organic fruit.* **3** a sum added to interest or wages; bonus. **4** something given as a reward, prize, or incentive: *The Society of Arts awarded him a premium.*
Usage The word *premium* is also used as an adjective to mean 'relating to or denoting a commodity or product of superior quality and therefore a higher price': *premium lagers.*
Word family **at a premium 1** scarce and in demand: *Space was at a premium.* **2** above the usual or nominal price: *Touts sell the tickets at a premium.* **put** (or **place**) **a premium on** to regard or treat as particularly valuable or important: *He put a premium on peace and stability.*

prerogative *noun*
a privilege or right that distinguishes a person or group: *The administration has the prerogative to appoint a successor as it sees fit.* □ *Owning a motor car used to be the prerogative of the rich.*

presence *noun*
the quality of making a strong impression on other people by the way you look, talk, or behave: *She has a strong voice but absolutely no stage presence.* □ *He had a commanding presence in meetings.* □ *Richard was not a big man but his presence was overwhelming.*
Usage The word *presence* is also used to refer to a person or thing that exists or is present in

a place but is not seen: *The monks became aware of a strange presence*; and a group of people, especially soldiers or police, stationed in a particular place: *The USA maintains a presence in the Indian Ocean region.*

presentable *adjective*
clean, smart, or decent enough to be seen in public: *I did my best to make myself look presentable.* □ *Where once it was dilapidated, it is now a presentable little ground.*

presentation *noun*
1 the manner or style in which something is given, offered, or displayed: *The presentation of foods is designed to stimulate your appetite.* **2** a meeting at which something, especially a new idea, product, or piece of work, is shown to a group of people; the act of doing this: *The sales manager will give a presentation on the new products.* □ *Candidates have to give a short presentation on a subject of their choice.*
Word family **presentational** adjective: *improve your presentational skills.*

prestige *noun*
the widespread respect and admiration that someone or something has because of their social position or what they have done: *The post carried great prestige within the civil service.* □ *The jobs are accorded different levels of prestige.*
Word family **prestigious** adjective respected and admired as very important or of very high quality: *The Gold Cup is one of the most prestigious events in the racing calendar.* □ *It's the city's most prestigious and exclusive hotel.* **prestigiously** adverb: *a prestigiously talented individual.*

prevalent *adjective*
that exists or is very common at a particular time or in a particular place: *Temporary working is most prevalent among people in service occupations.* □ *Our diet contributes to the high levels of heart disease prevalent in this country.*
Word family **prevalence** noun: *the prevalence of smoking among teenagers.* **prevalently** adverb: *the botanical species used most prevalently in Chinese medicine.*

primacy *noun*
the fact of being primary, pre-eminent, or more or most important: *London's primacy as*

p

a financial centre. □ *the primacy of industry over agriculture.*

primary *adjective*

1 of chief importance; principal: *The government's primary aim is to see significant reductions in unemployment.* **2** earliest in time or order of development: *The country was in the primary stage of socialism.* **3** not derived from, caused by, or based on anything else: *The research involved the use of primary source materials in national and local archives.*
Usage **primary** or **prime**? In many cases you can use either word: *your prime/primary concern/purpose/aim/object/objective/task.* □ *to be of prime/primary importance.* However, *prime* is used in some fixed phrases where *primary* cannot be used: *the prime attraction/contender/suspect.*
Word family **primarily** adverb for the most part; mainly: *Around 80 per cent of personal computers are used primarily for word processing.*

prime *adjective*

1 most important; to be considered first: *A nurse's prime concern is the well-being of the patient.* □ *The care of the environment is of prime importance.* □ *He's the police's prime suspect in this case.* **2** of the best quality: *Use only prime cuts (= pieces) of beef.* □ *a prime location in the centre of town.*
Usage **prime** or **primary**? See **primary**.
Usage As a noun, the word *prime* means 'a state of time of greatest strength, vigour, or success in a person's life': *You're in the prime of life.* □ *He wasn't elderly, but clearly past his prime.*

principal *adjective*

most important: *New roads will link the principal cities.* □ *Tourist revenue is now our principal source of wealth.* □ *My principal concern is to get the job done fast.*
Usage **principal**, **central**, **key**, or **major**? See **central**.
Usage The words *principal* and *principle* are pronounced in the same way but they do not have the same meaning. *Principal* is normally an adjective meaning 'main or most important': *one of the country's principal cities.* *Principle* is normally used as a noun meaning 'a fundamental basis of a system of thought or belief': *This is one of the basic principles of democracy.* *Principal* can also be a noun, where

it is used to refer to the most senior or most important person in an organization or other group: *the deputy principal.*

priority *noun*

something that you think is more important than other things and should be dealt with first; the condition of being more important than someone else and therefore coming or being dealt with first: *a high/low priority.* □ *Education is a top priority.* □ *You need to get your priorities right (= decide what is important to you).* □ *Club members will be given priority.* □ *Her family takes priority over her work.* □ *List the tasks in order of priority.*
Word family **prioritization** noun: *Prioritization of customer requirements is more important than market research.* **prioritize** verb **1** to designate or treat something as more important than other things: *The department has failed to prioritize safety within the oil industry.* **2** to determine the order for dealing with a series of items or tasks according to their relative importance: *Age affects the way people prioritize their goals.* □ *Do you enjoy a challenge - are you able to prioritize?*

privilege *noun*

1 a special right or advantage granted or available to a particular person or group: *Education is a right, not a privilege.* **2** an opportunity to do something regarded as a special honour: *She had the privilege of giving the opening lecture.*
Usage The noun *privilege* is also used in a disapproving way to refer to the rights and advantages that only rich and powerful people have: *a young man of wealth and privilege.*
Word family **privileged** adjective **1** having been granted a special honour: *I felt I had been privileged to compete in such a race.* **2** (sometimes disapproving) having a special right or advantage because you come from a rich family: *She comes from a privileged background.* **3** (of information) legally protected from being made public: *The ombudsman's reports are privileged.*

proactive *adjective*

(of a person or action) creating or controlling a situation rather than just responding to it after it has happened: *Employers must take a proactive approach to equal pay.*

Usage Do not overuse this word as some people consider it jargon.
Word family **proactively** adverb: *proactively prevent behavioural problems in the classroom.*

probity noun
the quality of being completely honest and having strong moral principles: *financial probity.* □ *They have very high standards of probity.*

prodigious adjective
remarkably or impressively great in extent, size, or degree: *The stove consumed a prodigious amount of fuel.* □ *Her memory was prodigious.*
Word family **prodigiously** adverb: *a prodigiously talented dancer.* **prodigiousness** noun: *Prodigiousness can mar a writer's skill.*

prodigy noun
1 a person, especially a young one, endowed with exceptional qualities or abilities: *a Russian pianist who was a child prodigy in his day.* **2** an impressive or outstanding example of a particular quality: *Germany seemed a prodigy of industrial discipline.* □ *the technological prodigy of the millennium.*

productive adjective
making goods or growing crops, especially in large quantities; achieving a lot: *highly productive farming land/manufacturing methods.* □ *productive farmers/workers.* □ *My time spent in the library was very productive.*
Word family **productively** adverb: *We need to use the land more productively.* □ *It's important to spend your time productively.* **productivity** noun the rate at which a company, country, or worker produces goods; the amount produced compared with the amount of time, work, and money needed to produce it: *Wage rates depend on levels of productivity.* □ *If you want to stay in this job you'll need to get your productivity up.*

professional noun, adjective
noun a person qualified in a paid occupation, especially one that involves prolonged training and a formal qualification: *professionals such as lawyers and surveyors.* □ *adjective* **1** having or showing the skill appropriate to a person who is a professional person; competent or skilled: *Their music is both memorable and professional.* □ *He dealt with the problem in a highly professional way.*

2 worthy of or appropriate to a professional person: *his professional expertise.*
Usage You should take care when using the word *professional* because it is also sometimes used in an informal and derogatory way to refer to a person who persistently makes a feature of a particular activity or attribute: *a professional gloom-monger.*
Word family **professionalism** noun **1** the competence or skill expected of a professional: *The key to quality and efficiency is professionalism.* **2** the practising of an activity, especially a sport, by professional rather than amateur players: *the trend towards professionalism.*

proficient adjective
able to do something well because of training and practice: *I was proficient at my job.* □ *She's proficient in several languages.* □ *With practice, you should become proficient within six months.*
Word family **proficiency** noun the ability to do something well because of training and practice: *The exercise is aimed at developing proficiency.* □ *A high level of oral proficiency in English is required for the job.* **proficiently** adverb: *She can speak Chinese proficiently.*

profile noun, verb
noun **1** a description of someone or something that gives useful information: *We first build up a detailed profile of our customers and their requirements.* □ *His psychological profile is revealing.* **2** the general impression that someone or something gives to the public and the amount of attention they receive: *The deal will certainly raise the company's international profile.* □ *verb* to give or write a description of someone or something that gives the most important information: *His career is profiled in this month's journal.*
Usage The word *profile* is used in several phrases: *This issue has had a high profile* (= a lot of public attention) *in recent months.* □ *I advised her to keep a low profile* (= not to attract attention) *for the next few days.*

profitable adjective
1 (of a business or activity) yielding profit or financial gain: *She runs a highly profitable business.* □ *It is usually more profitable to sell direct to the public.* **2** beneficial; useful: *He'd had a profitable day.*

P

Word family profitability noun: Downsizing is one way to increase profitability. **profitably** adverb: This is no way to run a business profitably.

profound *adjective*

1 (of a state, quality, or emotion) very great or intense: *profound social changes.* □ *profound feelings of disquiet.* **2** (of a person or statement) having or showing great knowledge or insight: *a profound philosopher.* **3** needing a lot of study or thought: *expressing profound truths in simple language.*

Word family profoundly adverb: *a profoundly disturbing experience.* **profundity** noun **1** deep insight; great depth of knowledge or thought: *the simplicity and profundity of the message.* **2** great depth or intensity of a state, quality, or emotion: *the profundity of her misery.*

programme *noun, verb*

noun **1** a set of related measures, events, or activities with a particular long-term aim: *the British nuclear power programme.* **2** a planned series of future events, items, or performances: *a weekly programme of films.* □ *The programme includes Dvorak's New World Symphony.* **3** a course of study or training, especially at a college or university: *Take a look at our new history and language programmes.* □ *We especially encourage those from minorities to apply for our degree programmes.* □ *We urge as many people as possible to enrol on our management training programme.* □ *verb* **1** to arrange according to a plan or schedule: *We learn how to programme our own lives consciously.* **2** to schedule an item within a framework: *The next stage of the treaty is programmed for next year.* □ *The station does not programme enough contemporary works.*

Usage In American English, this word is spelt *program*. In both British and American English, *program* is the spelling for the series of coded software instructions to control the operation of a computer or other machine.

progress *noun, verb*

noun the process of improving or developing, or of getting nearer to achieving or completing something: *We have made great progress in controlling inflation.* □ *Technological progress is changing the demand for labour.* □ *Work on the new offices is now in progress.* □ *They asked for a progress report on the*

project. □ *verb* to improve or develop over a period of time; to make progress: *The course allows students to progress at their own speed.* □ *Work on the new road is progressing slowly.*

Usage *Progress* is often used as a positive way of talking about technological changes, particularly when there are other people who feel that the changes are having a damaging effect on society.

Usage As a noun, *progress* is pronounced **proh**-gress; as a verb, pruh-**gress**.

Word family progression noun the process of developing gradually from one stage or state to another: *The medication halts the rapid progression of the disease.* **progressive** adjective in favour of new ideas, modern methods, and change: *progressive schools.* □ *Are you in favour of progressive teaching methods?*

project *noun, verb*

noun a planned piece of work that is designed to find information about something, to produce something new, or to improve something: *He's working on a research project in the department of social sciences.* □ *We want to set up a project to computerize the library system.* □ *verb* **1** to estimate or forecast something on the basis of present trends: *Substantial growth is projected over the next five years.* **2** to plan a scheme: *a projected exhibition of contemporary art.* **3** to present a particular image or impression: *He strives to project an image of youth.*

Usage As a noun, *project* is pronounced **pro**-jekt; as a verb, pruh-**jekt**.

Word family projection noun: *population projection is essential for planning.* □ *the legal profession's projection of an image of altruism.*

prolific *adjective*

1 (of an artist, writer, etc.) producing many works etc.: *a prolific author.* □ *He was noted for his prolific output - ten books a year was normal.* □ *a prolific goal-scorer.* □ *one of the most prolific periods in her career.* **2** existing in large numbers: *a pop star with a prolific following of teenage fans.*

Word family prolifically adverb: *to write prolifically.* □ *animals that breed prolifically.*

prominent *adjective*

1 important or well known: *A number of prominent politicians made public statements supporting the change.* □ *He played a prominent part in the campaign.* □ *She was prominent in*

p

the fashion industry. **2** particularly noticeable: *The statue occupies a prominent position in the Sculpture Garden.*

Usage The word *prominent* is often used to talk about people in politics and business.

Word family **prominence** noun the state of being important, well known, or noticeable: *She came to prominence as an artist in the 1990s.* □ *The issue was given great prominence in the press.* **prominently** adverb: *Teenagers featured prominently in international competitions.*

promise *noun, verb*

noun **1** a statement that tells someone that you will definitely do or not do something: *I try not to make promises that I can't keep.* □ *She had obviously forgotten her promise to call me.* **2** a sign that someone or something will be successful: *Her work shows great promise.* □ *Their future was full of promise.* □ *verb* to tell someone that you will definitely do or not do something, or that something will definitely happen: *I'll see what I can do but I can't promise anything.* □ *You promised me that you'd be home early tonight.*

Usage *promise* or *guarantee*? See **guarantee**.

Word family **promising** adjective showing signs of being good or successful: *At that time, I had a promising career in TV.* □ *The weather doesn't look very promising.*

promote *verb*

1 to help something to happen or develop; to support or actively encourage a cause, venture, or aim: *These measures are designed to promote economic growth.* □ *Basketball stars from the US have helped promote the sport in Italy and Spain.* □ *The church tries to promote racial harmony.* **2** to publicize a product or celebrity: *She's over in America, promoting her new book.*

Word family **promoter** noun a person who tries to persuade others about the value or importance of something: *She is a leading promoter of European integration.* **promotion** noun: *a society for the promotion of religious tolerance.* □ *We're doing a special promotion of Chilean wines.*

prompt *adjective, verb*

adjective done without delay: *Prompt action was required as the fire spread.* □ *Prompt payment of the invoice would be appreciated.*

□ *verb* **1** to cause something to start or happen, especially discussion, questioning, or criticism of something: *The news prompted speculation that prices will rise further.* □ *His speech prompted an angry outburst from the crowd.* **2** (especially of an event or experience) to be the reason why someone decides to do something: *What prompted you to choose this area?* □ *I understand your views and the reasons which prompted you to write.*

Usage Things that can be *prompted* include *debate*, *speculation*, *allegations*, and *criticism*.

Word family **promptly** adverb: *She read the letter and promptly burst into tears.*

propensity *noun*

(*formal*) a tendency to a particular kind of behaviour: *There is an increased propensity for people to live alone.* □ *They all knew about his propensity for violence.*

propose *verb*

1 to tell people about a plan or idea for them to think about and decide on; to tell people about a plan or idea at a formal meeting and ask them to vote on it; to suggest an explanation of something for people to consider: *The measures have been proposed as a way of improving standards.* □ *He proposed changing the name of the company.* □ *It was proposed that the president be elected for a period of two years.* **2** to intend to do something in the future: *What do you propose to do now?* □ *How do you propose getting home?*

Word family **proposal** noun an idea or plan that someone formally suggests should be considered; the act of doing this: *I welcome the proposal to reduce taxes for the low-paid.* □ *His proposal that the system be changed was rejected.*

proposition *noun*

1 an idea or plan that is suggested, especially in business: *I'd like to put a business proposition to you.* □ *He was trying to make it look like an attractive proposition.* **2** (*formal*) a statement that expresses an opinion, especially one used as the basis of an argument: *Her argument is based on the proposition that power corrupts.*

Usage You should take care when using the word *proposition*, as in informal usage it is used as a verb to mean 'to make a suggestion of sexual intercourse to someone with whom one is not sexually involved, especially in an unsubtle or offensive way': *She had been*

P

propositioned at the party by a subeditor with bad breath.

prospect *noun*

1 the possibility that something might happen, especially something good: *There is no immediate prospect of peace.* □ *A place in the semi-finals is in prospect* (= likely to happen). **2** an idea of what might or will happen in the future: *Travelling alone around the world is a daunting prospect.* □ *The prospect of becoming a father filled him with alarm.* **3** the chances of being successful, especially in your career: *they want a reasonable salary and good career prospects.* □ *At 25 he was an unemployed musician with no prospects.* **4** a person regarded as likely to be successful: *He was seen as a leading medal prospect for the Olympics.*

prospective *adjective*

1 expected to happen soon: *They are worried about prospective changes in the law.* **2** expected to do or become something: *I had a phone call from a prospective client today.* Usage **prospective** or **potential**? See **potential**. Usage The word *prospective* is mainly used to talk about people: *a prospective buyer/client/customer/applicant/candidate/employee/employer/husband/wife/parent.*

prosper *verb*

(of a person, business, or economy) to develop in a successful way; to be successful, especially financially: *The economy prospered under his administration.* □ *The railway prospered from the new mining traffic.* Usage **prosperity** or **affluence**? *Affluence* is often used to contrast rich people or societies with poor ones, in a way that suggests that it is not always a good thing: *the city's mixture of private affluence and public squalor.* The word *prosperity* is not used in this way; it is always seen as a good thing and is something that you can wish for other people: *Please drink to the health and prosperity of the bride and groom.* Word family **prosperity** *noun* the state of being financially successful and able to enjoy a good standard of living: *The future prosperity of the region depends on economic growth.* □ *The country is enjoying a period of peace and prosperity.* **prosperous** *adjective* rich and successful: *These countries became prosperous*

through trade, not aid. □ *The 1990s were prosperous years for the company.*

provide *verb*

1 to make something available for someone to use: *The hospital has a commitment to provide the best possible medical care.* □ *Please answer questions in the space provided.* □ *The report was not expected to provide any answers.* **2** (**provide for**) to give someone the things that they need to live, such as food, money, and clothing: *Local authorities must do more to provide for children in need.* □ *He provided for her in his will.* **3** (**provide for**) to make preparations to deal with something that might happen in the future: *It is impossible to provide for every eventuality.* Usage **provide** or **give**? The word *provide* is more formal than *give*, used especially in written English. *Provide* is often used when something is being made available to people in general, or to someone who is not mentioned; *give* is more often used when something is being made available to a particular person: *The hospital aims to provide the best possible medical care.* □ *We want to give you the best possible care.*

provision *noun*

1 preparations that you make for something that might or will happen in the future: *You need to make adequate provision for your retirement.* □ *The company had made provisions against falls in land prices.* **2** the act of providing or supplying something for use: *new contracts for the provision of services.* **3** a condition or arrangement in a legal document: *The Act contains detailed provisions for appeal against the court's decision.*

provoke *verb*

to cause a particular feeling or reaction, especially a negative one, sometimes deliberately: *The announcement provoked a storm of protest.* □ *The article was intended to provoke discussion.* □ *provoke controversy/criticism/hostility/outrage/jealousy/resentment.* Usage The word *provoke* also means 'to say or do something that you know will annoy someone so that they react in an angry way': *She had been trying to provoke her sister into an argument.* □ *She laughed aloud, which provoked him to fury.* □ *Be careful what you say - he's easily provoked.*

Word family **provocation** noun: *The crime was committed under provocation.* □ *You should remain calm and not respond to provocation.*

prudent *adjective*
sensible and careful when making decisions, avoiding unnecessary risks: *She has always been a prudent businesswoman.*
Usage The word *prudence* is used especially in financial contexts.
Word family **prudence** noun being sensible and careful when you make judgements and decisions; avoiding unnecessary risks: *As a matter of prudence, agreement on these issues should be reached at an early stage in the partnership.* □ *Maybe you'll exercise a little more financial prudence next time.* **prudently** adverb

pure *adjective*
1 not mixed with anything else; with nothing added: *These shirts are 100% pure cotton.* □ *Classical dance in its purest form requires symmetry and balance.* **2** complete and not mixed with anything else: *They met by pure chance.* □ *She laughed with pure joy.* □ *It was a pure accident. I'm not blaming anybody.*
Usage Other senses of the word *pure* include 'free of contamination': *pure drinking water*; 'innocent or morally good': *His motives were pure*; and 'theoretical rather than practical or applied': *Are you studying pure or applied mathematics?*

Word family **purely** adverb: *I saw the letter purely by chance.* □ *She took the job purely and simply for the money.*

purpose *noun*
1 the reason for which something is done; what something is supposed to achieve; what someone is trying to achieve: *The main purpose of the campaign is to raise money.* □ *A meeting was called for the purpose of appointing a new treasurer.* □ *The experiments serve no useful purpose.* □ *The building is used for religious purposes.* **2** the feeling that there is a definite aim in what you do and that it is important and valuable to you: *Volunteer work gives her life a sense of purpose.* □ *He has enormous confidence and strength of purpose.*
Usage **purpose** or **aim**? See **aim**.
Usage The phrase *for . . . purposes* is used when you are talking about what is needed in a particular situation: *These gifts count as income for tax purposes.* □ *For the purposes of this study, the three groups have been combined.*
Word family **purposeful** adjective acting with a clear aim and with determination: *She looked purposeful and determined.* □ *He approached each task in the same purposeful manner.* **purposefully** adverb: *Edward strode purposefully towards the door.*

P

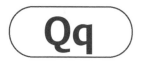

Qq

qualify *verb*

1 to meet the necessary standard or conditions to be entitled to do or receive something: *It's the best chance in years for the team to qualify for a major tournament.* **2** to provide someone with the skills and knowledge they need to do something: *The training should qualify you for a better job.* □ *The test qualifies you to drive heavy vehicles.* □ *Are you qualified to administer drugs?* **3** to add something to a previous statement to make the meaning less strong or less general: *I want to qualify what I said earlier - I didn't mean he couldn't do the job, only that he would need supervision.*

Usage The word *qualify* is usually used to talk about the result of a particular course, programme, test, or examination. Students usually receive a certificate to show that they are qualified to do a particular job.

Word family **qualification** *noun* **1** the passing of an exam or the official completion of a course. **2** the action of qualifying or the fact of becoming qualified: *England need to beat Poland to ensure qualification for the World Cup finals.* **3** a quality that makes someone suitable for a job or activity; an official requirement. **4** a statement that restricts the meaning of another: *I accept his theories, but not without certain qualifications.* □ *The plan was approved without qualification.*

quality *noun*

1 the standard of how good or bad something is, especially when compared with something similar: *Most of the goods on offer are of very poor quality.* □ *Use the highest quality ingredients you can find.* □ *Their quality of life improved dramatically when they moved to the US.* **2** a high standard: *We aim to provide quality at reasonable prices.* □ *Get it right, even if it takes time; it's quality not quantity that*

matters. **3** a part of a person's character, especially a good one such as the ability to do something or a good way of behaving; a feature of a thing, especially one that is good and makes it different from something else: *personal qualities such as honesty and generosity.* □ *It's hard to find people with the right qualities for the job.* □ *He showed great energy and leadership qualities.* □ *The ancient city of Assisi has a wonderful magical quality.*

Usage In informal English, especially in advertising and selling, the word *quality* means 'of a high quality': *We specialize in quality furniture.* □ *We offer a quality service to all customers.*

Word family **quality control** *noun* a system of maintaining quality in manufactured products by testing a sample to see if it meets the required standard. **quality time** *noun* time spent in giving your full attention to your child or partner, in order to strengthen the relationship.

quantify *verb*

to describe or express something as an amount or number: *The risks to health are difficult to quantify.* □ *It is impossible to quantify the extent of the black economy.*

Word family **quantifiable** *adjective*: *Few of the reports provided quantifiable data.* **quantification** *noun*: *a request to supply a quantification of the losses incurred.*

quintessential *adjective*

being the most typical or perfect example of someone or something: *He was the quintessential tough guy—strong, silent, and self-contained.*

Word family **quintessentially** *adverb*: *a sense of humour that is quintessentially British.* □ *handmade soba noodles, a quintessentially Japanese food.*

Rr

radical *adjective*

1 (of changes or differences) concerning the most central and important parts of something; thorough and complete: *There have been demands for radical reform of the law.* □ *This document marks a radical departure from earlier recommendations.* **2** (of ideas) new, different, and likely to have a great effect; (of people or their opinions) in favour of thorough and complete political or social change: *He proposed a radical solution to the problem.* □ *the radical wing of the party.* □ *radical politicians/students/writers.*
Word family **radically** *adverb*: *The new methods are radically different from the old.* □ *Attitudes have changed radically.*

ramification *noun*

a consequence of an action or event, especially when complex or unwelcome: *The political ramifications of shutting the factory would be immense.* □ *Any change is bound to have legal ramifications.*
Usage A *ramification* is also a subdivision of a complex structure or process perceived as comparable to a tree's branches: *an extended family with its ramifications of neighbouring in-laws.*

range *noun, verb*

noun **1** the limits between which something varies: *Most of the students are in the 17–20 age range.* □ *The students in Class 4 have a very wide range of abilities.* □ *It's difficult to find a house in our price range* (= that we can afford). □ *This was outside the range of his experience.* **2** a set of several different types of a particular thing: *The hotel offers a wide range of facilities and services.* □ *There is a full range of activities for children.* □ *This material is available in a huge range of colours.* **3** the scope or extent of a person's or thing's abilities or capacity: *He has shown his range in a number of roles.* □ *verb* (of a group of similar things) to include a variety of amounts, levels, sizes, or

points of view, between two particular amounts, levels, etc.; to include a variety of different things in addition to those mentioned: *The disease ranges widely in severity.* □ *Estimates of the damage range between $1 million and $5 million.* □ *The opinions they expressed ranged right across the political spectrum.* □ *She has had a number of different jobs, ranging from chef to swimming instructor.*
Usage The word *range* is often used in business and marketing in phrases such as *offer a large/wide/full range of something.*
Usage *range* or *variety*? *Range* emphasizes the (often large) number of things available; *variety* emphasizes the amount of difference between the types of a particular thing.

rapid *adjective*

happening in a short period of time; done or happening very quickly: *There has been a rapid rise in sales.* □ *The patient made a rapid recovery.*
Usage The word *rapid* is most often used to describe the speed with which something changes: *The disease is spreading at a rapid rate.*
Word family **rapidity** *noun*: *These changes happen with extreme rapidity.* **rapidly** *adverb*: *Crime figures are rising rapidly.*

rapport *noun*

a friendly relationship in which people like and understand each other: *Honesty is essential if there is to be a good rapport between patient and therapist.* □ *There was little rapport between the two women.*
Usage The word *rapport* is used to describe a personal relationship between individuals that is based on understanding and liking each other. A *rapport* may need to be *established* but you can also have an *instant rapport* with someone, which just happens without effort. The word is pronounced rap-**por**.

rational *adjective*

1 (of behaviour or a way of thinking) based on reason and facts rather than emotions: *There's no rational explanation for his actions.* □ *In some ways their behaviour is perfectly rational.* **2** able to think clearly and make decisions based on reason rather than emotions: *Human beings are essentially rational.*

Word family **rationality** *noun* a way of thinking or behaving that is based on logical thought rather than on emotions and feelings: *The concept of scientific rationality is crucial to modern thinking.* **rationally** *adverb*: *Scientific training helps you to think rationally.* □ *She remained calm and rationally thought out a plan.*

realism *noun*

a way of accepting and dealing with situations as they really are without being influenced by your emotions or by false hopes: *There was a new mood of realism among the leaders at the peace talks.*

Usage The word *realistic* is often used to talk about what you can hope to achieve in business or at work: *a realistic alternative/demand/estimate/goal/hope/option/plan/solution/target.*

Word family **realistic** *adjective* **1** accepting in a sensible way what it is actually possible to do or achieve in a particular situation: *This report takes a much more realistic view of the situation.* □ *We have to be realistic about our chances of winning.* □ *It is not realistic to expect people to spend so much money.* **2** sensible and appropriate; that can be achieved: *We must set realistic goals.* □ *If you want to retain good employees, you have to pay a realistic salary.* **3** representing things as they are in real life: *We try to make these training courses as realistic as possible.* **realistically** *adverb*: *Realistically there is little prospect of a ceasefire.* □ *How many can you realistically hope to sell?*

reality *noun*

the true situation and the problems that actually exist in life, in contrast to how you would like life to be: *You're out of touch with reality.* □ *Outwardly she seemed confident but in reality she felt extremely nervous.* □ *the harsh realities of life in a farming community.* □ *Slowly the reality of the situation dawned on him.*

realize *verb*

to understand or become aware of a particular fact or situation: *I didn't realize (that) you were so unhappy.* □ *I don't think you realize how important this is.* □ *We make assumptions all the time without realizing it.*

Usage To *realize* something can mean to become aware of it, as well as to be aware of it: *As soon as I walked in the room I realized something was wrong.* □ *Suddenly I realized what he meant.* Even if the process of becoming aware takes any time, even a short time, you can use *realize*: *I soon/quickly/gradually/slowly realized what he meant.*

Word family **realization** *noun* the process of becoming aware of something: *The realization of what she had done suddenly hit her.* □ *the gradual realization that they were losing the war.*

realm *noun*

an area of activity, interest, or knowledge: *Questions of consciousness lie outside the realm of physics.* □ *At the end of the speech he seemed to be moving into the realms of fantasy.*

Usage The word *realm* is often used to draw attention to the boundaries between one area of interest and another: things are *within/outside/beyond the realms of something* or people *enter/move into the realms of something.*

reason *noun, verb*

noun **1** why something has happened or someone has done something; a fact that makes it right or fair to do something: *I'd like to know the reason why you're so late.* □ *He said no but he didn't give a reason.* □ *For reasons of security, the door is kept locked.* **2** a way of thinking that is sensible and logical: *I can't get her to listen to reason.* □ *I'm willing to do anything—within reason—to get my case heard.* □ *verb* to form a judgement about something by considering the facts and using your power to think in a logical way: *They reasoned, correctly, that the enemy would not attempt an attack at night.*

Usage Some people object to a construction like *The reason why I decided not to phone* on the grounds that what follows *the reason* should express a statement, using *that*, not imply a question with a *why*: *The reason that I decided not to phone* (or, more informally, *The reason I decided not to phone*). An objection is also made to the construction *The reason . . . is because*, as in *The reason I didn't phone is because my mother had been ill.* The objection is made on the grounds that either *because* or *the reason* is redundant; it is better to use the word *that* instead (*The reason I didn't phone is that ...*) or to rephrase altogether (*I didn't phone because ...*). Nevertheless, both the above usages are well established and, though more elegant phrasing can be found, they are generally accepted in standard English.

Word family **reasoned** *adjective* (of an argument or opinion) presented in a logical way that shows careful thought: *They refused the appeal without offering any reasoned argument*. **reasoning** *noun* the process of thinking about something in a logical way; ideas or opinions that are based on this process: *Could you please explain the reasoning behind this decision?* □ *It was difficult to follow his line of reasoning*.

reasonable *adjective*
1 practical, sensible, and treating people in an appropriate and equal way: *It is reasonable to assume that she knew beforehand that this would happen*. □ *It seems a perfectly reasonable request to make*. **2** acceptable and appropriate in a particular situation: *The furniture is in reasonable condition*. □ *You must submit your claim within a reasonable time*. **3** (of prices) not too expensive: *We sell good-quality food at reasonable prices*. **4** fairly good, but not very good: *Most people here have a reasonable standard of living*.

Word family **reasonably** *adverb* to some degree but not very: *He couldn't reasonably be expected to pay back the loan all at once*. □ *The instructions are reasonably straightforward*. □ *The hostages had been reasonably well cared for*.

receptive *adjective*
willing to consider or accept new suggestions and ideas: *a receptive audience*. □ *The institution was receptive to new ideas*.

Word family **receptively** *adverb*: *He looked at me receptively*. **receptiveness**, **receptivity** *noun*: *Among young people there is a far greater receptivity to fresh thinking*.

recognize *verb*
1 to identify or know someone or something from having come across them before: *Pat is very good at recognizing wild flowers*. **2** to accept or acknowledge the existence, validity, or legality of: *He was recognized as an international authority on postage stamps*. **3** to

show official appreciation of: *His work was recognized by an honorary degree from Glasgow University*.

Word family **recognition** *noun*: *Methods of production have improved out of all recognition*. □ *She received the award in recognition of her courageous human rights work*. **recognizable** *adjective*: *instantly recognizable postwar suburbs*.

recommend *verb*
1 to tell someone that something is good or useful, or that someone would be suitable for a particular job etc.; to make someone or something seem attractive or good: *Can you recommend a good hotel?* □ *I recommend the book to all my students*. □ *The hotel's new restaurant comes highly recommended*. □ *The system has much to recommend it*. **2** to tell someone what you think they should do in a particular situation; to say what you think the price or level of something should be: *I recommend that he see a lawyer*. □ *He recommended reading the book before seeing the movie*. □ *It is dangerous to exceed the recommended dose*.

Usage If you *recommend* someone or something, it usually means that you have personal experience of the person or thing you are recommending. For example, you would only be able to recommend a person for a job if you knew them personally, and you could only recommend a book to someone if you had actually read it yourself.

Usage **recommend** or **advise**? *Advise* is a stronger word than *recommend* and is often used when the person giving the advice is in a senior position or a position of authority: *Police are advising fans without tickets to stay away. I advise you ...* can suggest that you are trying to be helpful and is less likely to cause offence. *Recommend* is often used with more positive advice to tell someone about possible benefits and *advise* with more negative advice to warn someone about possible dangers: *He recommended reading the book before seeing the film*. □ *I would advise against going out on your own*.

Word family **recommendation** *noun* **1** an idea or plan that a person or group officially suggests concerning the best thing to do, especially one contained in a report: *The committee made recommendations to the board on teachers' pay and conditions*. □ *The major recommendation is for a change in the*

r

law. **2** the act of telling someone that something is good or useful or that someone would be suitable for a particular job etc.; a formal letter or statement that someone would be suitable for a particular job: *We chose the hotel on their recommendation.* □ *It's best to find a builder through personal recommendation.*

recruit *noun, verb*

noun a person who has recently joined the armed forces or the police; a person who joins a company or organization: *Army recruits are all trained in first aid.* □ *They are stepping up attempts to attract recruits to the nursing profession.* □ *verb* to find new people to join a company, an organization, or the armed forces: *The police are trying to recruit more officers from ethnic minorities.* □ *They recruited several new members to the club.*

refine *verb*

to improve something by making small changes, in particular make an idea, theory, or method more subtle and accurate: *Our methods have been gradually refined over the years.* □ *They would constantly refine their designs until they were almost perfect.*
Usage This sense of the word *refine* is a figurative extension of the sense 'to make a substance pure by taking other substances out of it, especially as part of an industrial process': *The process of refining oil produces several useful chemicals.*
Word family *refined* adjective elegant and cultured in appearance, manner, or taste: *Her voice was very low and refined.* **refinement** noun: *This gross figure needs considerable refinement.* □ *recent refinements to production techniques.*

refreshing *adjective*

1 serving to refresh or reinvigorate someone: *a refreshing drink.* □ *The morning air was so refreshing.* **2** welcome or stimulating because new or different: *It makes a refreshing change to be able to write about something pleasant.* □ *Her directness is refreshing.*
Word family *refreshingly* adverb: *a refreshingly different concept.* □ *Refreshingly, the party's current spokesman is very frank.*

reinforce *verb*

to make something such as a feeling or idea stronger: *The actions of the leaders reinforced*

fears and suspicions so that war became unavoidable.
Word family *reinforcement* noun: *a reinforcement of the traditional male–female relationship.*

relate *verb*

1 to show or make a connection between things: *I found it difficult to relate the two ideas in my mind.* □ *In future, pay increases will be related to productivity.* **2** (**relate to**) to be connected with someone or something; to refer to someone or something: *We shall discuss the problem as it relates to our specific case.* □ *The second paragraph relates to the situation in Scotland.*
Usage *relate*, *associate*, or *connect*? See **associate**.
Usage The word *relate* is often used in business texts, describing how one thing will change according to how much something else changes: *performance-related pay.* □ *income-related benefits.* □ *an earnings-related pension scheme.*
Word family *related* adjective connected with someone or something in some way: *Much of the crime in this area is related to drug abuse.* □ *These two problems are closely related.* □ *He was suffering from a stress-related illness.*
relation noun the way in which two or more things are connected: *The fee they are offering bears no relation to the amount of work involved.* □ *Its brain is small in relation to* (= compared with) *its body.* □ *(formal) I have some comments to make in relation to* (= concerning) *this matter.* □ *The study shows a close relation between poverty and ill health.*

relative *adjective*

considered according to its position or connection with something else; considered and judged by being compared with something else; that exists or has a particular quality only when compared with something else: *the position of the sun relative to the earth.* □ *You must consider the relative merits of the two plans.* □ *They now live in relative comfort* (= compared with how they lived before).
Usage The use of *relatively*, as in *It was relatively successful*, has been criticized on the grounds that there is no explicit comparison being made and that another word, such as *quite* or *rather*, would therefore be more appropriate. But even if no explicit comparison is being made, *relatively* is often

used in this way and has become generally acceptable in standard English.
Word family **relatively** adverb: *At first glance the poem seems to be relatively straightforward.* □ *The colleges had become, relatively speaking, short of funds.*

relaxed *adjective*

(of a place) calm and informal: *It's a family-run hotel with a relaxed atmosphere.*
Usage The word *relaxed* also means 'not anxious or worried': *I had to learn to be more relaxed about things.* □ *She appeared relaxed and confident before the match* and 'not caring too much about discipline or making people follow rules': *I take a fairly relaxed attitude towards what the children wear to school.*

relevant *adjective*

closely connected to the subject or situation that you are discussing or thinking about; having ideas that are useful or valuable to people in their lives and work: *I don't think that question is relevant.* □ *They are looking for someone with relevant experience in childcare.*
Word family **relevance** noun: *I don't see the relevance of your question.* □ *It's a classic play of contemporary relevance.* **relevantly** adverb: *She has experience in teaching and, more relevantly, in industry.*

reliable *adjective*

1 (of a person or thing) that can be trusted to do something well; that you can rely on: *We are looking for someone who is reliable and hardworking.* □ *My car's not as reliable as it used to be.* □ *There is no reliable supply of electricity or running water.* **2** (of information or a source of information) that is likely to be correct or true: *These tests are a reliable indicator of future performance.* □ *Prosecution lawyers tried to show that she was not a reliable witness.*
Word family **reliability** noun: *The incident cast doubt on her motives and reliability.* □ *The reliability of these results has been questioned.* **reliably** adverb: *You need to show that you can work reliably and be trusted to handle responsibility.* □ *I am reliably informed* (= told by someone who knows the facts) *that the company is being sold.*

relish *verb, noun*

verb to get great pleasure from an activity or experience or the thought of doing something: *I always relish a good debate.*
□ *I don't relish the prospect of getting up early tomorrow.* □ *noun* great enjoyment; a pleasant feeling of looking forward to something: *He was waiting with relish for her promised visit.*
Usage A *relish* is also a tangy or spicy sauce or pickle.

remarkable *adjective*

unusual or surprising in a way that causes people to take notice: *She was a truly remarkable woman.* □ *The interior of the house was remarkable for its beauty.* □ *It was remarkable that the body had not been found sooner.*
Word family **remarkably** adverb: *She looked remarkably fit for an eighty-year-old.*

renaissance *noun*

a revival of or renewed interest in something: *Cinema-going is enjoying something of a renaissance.*
Usage This usage alludes to the *Renaissance*, the revival of art and literature under the influence of classical models in the 14th–16th century.

renowned *adjective*

famous and respected: *We asked for advice from the renowned legal expert, Sam Pincher.* □ *It is renowned as one of the region's best restaurants.* □ *She is renowned for her patience.*
Usage **renowned**, **celebrated**, **famous**, or **well-known**? See **celebrate**.
Usage A person who is *renowned* is respected because they do their job very well, or because they have a special skill or ability. A place that is *renowned* is respected because it provides a service of a very high standard.

represent *verb*

1 to be something; to be the result of something; to amount to: *This contract represents 20% of the company's annual revenue.* □ *These results represent a major breakthrough in AIDS research.* □ *The peace plan represents* (= is the result of) *weeks of negotiation.* **2** to be an example or expression of an idea, quality, or opinion: *The project represents all that is good in the community.* □ *Those comments do not represent the views of us all.* □ *The artist uses doves to represent peace.* **3** to show someone or something, especially in a picture; to present someone or something in a particular way, especially when this may not be fair: *The results are*

r

represented in figure 3 below. □ *The risks were represented as negligible.*
Usage **represent**, **embody**, or **symbolize**? See **embody**.
Word family **representation** noun something that shows or describes something; the act of presenting someone or something in a particular way: *The snake swallowing its tail is a representation of infinity.* □ *the negative representation of single mothers in the media.*

representative *adjective*
typical of a particular group of people; containing or including examples of all the different types of people or things in a large group: *The paper-thin models in magazines are not representative of most women.* □ *We interviewed a representative sample of teachers.*
Usage Something that is *representative* of someone or something is typical of a group of people or things and therefore useful as a source of information about them: *a representative sample.*
Word family **representativeness** noun: *the representativeness of the sample/results.*

reputable *adjective*
honest and known to provide a good service: *Buy your car from a reputable dealer.*
Usage The word *reputable* is usually used about companies and people involved in business or trade.
Word family **reputably** adverb

reputation *noun*
the opinion that people have about what someone or something is like, based on what has happened in the past and what they have been told: *The restaurant has an excellent reputation.* □ *He had staked his reputation on the success of the play.* □ *The weather in England is living up to its reputation* (= is exactly as expected).

resilience *noun*
(in people and things) the ability not to be affected or to recover quickly after something unpleasant, such as a shock, injury, or disadvantage: *This comeback says much for the resilience of the team.* □ *The industry has developed a resilience to the dips the national economy may take.*
Word family **resilient** adjective: *He'll get over it—young people are amazingly resilient.*

resolute *adjective*
having or showing great determination to keep to a plan or decision that you have made: *She became even more resolute in her opposition to the plan.* □ *Her voice sounded calm and resolute.*
Word family **resolutely** adverb: *They remain resolutely opposed to the idea.*

resolve *verb, noun*
verb **1** to find a satisfactory solution to a problem or argument: *Where can ordinary people get help with resolving family problems?* □ *The matter has never really been satisfactorily resolved.* **2** to make a firm decision to do something; to reach a decision in a meeting etc. by means of a formal vote: *She resolved that she would never see him again.* □ *The Supreme Council resolved to resume control over the press.* □ noun strong determination to do something that you believe to be right: *The difficulties in her way merely strengthened her resolve.* □ *He did not weaken in his resolve.*
Word family **resolution** noun the act of solving or settling a problem or dispute: *The government is pressing for an early resolution of the hostage crisis.* □ *Hopes for a peaceful resolution to the conflict were fading.*

resonance *noun*
the ability to evoke or suggest images, memories, and emotions; strong appeal: *The concepts lose their emotional resonance.* □ *His approach has a surprising resonance with today's citizens.*

resonate *verb*
to evoke or suggest images, memories, and emotions; to appeal strongly: *The words resonate with so many different meanings.* □ *The idea has a charm that resonates with a sense of simplicity.* □ *The proposal failed to resonate with voters.*
Usage This sense of the word is a figurative extension of the verb's basic meaning 'to make a deep, clear sound that continues for a long time, especially the sound made by a voice or musical instrument; (of a place) to be filled with sound or make a sound continue longer': *Her voice resonated through the theatre.* □ *The body of the violin acts as a resonating chamber and makes the sound louder.*

retain

resource *noun, verb*

noun **1** (**resources**) a stock or supply of materials or assets that can be drawn on when required: *Local authorities complained that they lacked resources.* **2** (**resources**) a country's means of supporting itself or becoming wealthier, as represented by its minerals, land, and other assets: *the exploitation of minerals and other natural resources.* □ *We do not have the resources* (= money) *to update our computer software.* □ *We agreed to pool our resources.* **3** a source of help or information: *The database could be used as a teaching resource.* **4** a strategy adopted in a difficult situation: *Sometimes anger is the only resource left in a situation like this.* **5** (**resources**) personal qualities that help you to cope in a difficult situation: *We had been left very much to our own resources.* □ *verb* to provide someone or something with resources: *a strategy which ensures that primary health care workers are adequately resourced.*

Usage The phrase *human resources* refers to people's skills and abilities, seen as something a company or organization can make use of: *She's responsible for making the best use of human resources.* □ *She works in the human resources department.*

resourceful *adjective*

having the ability to find quick and clever ways to overcome difficulties: *He proved how resourceful he was by organizing the help of local firefighters.*
Word family *resourcefully* adverb *resourcefulness* noun

resplendent *adjective*

attractive and impressive through being richly colourful or sumptuous: *She was resplendent in a sea-green dress.*
Word family *resplendence* noun: *The actual vestments better illustrate the resplendence of the liturgical service.* *resplendently* adverb: *resplendently dressed in silver-grey uniforms.*

responsible *adjective*

1 having a duty to do something, or having control over or care for something or someone: *the Cabinet Minister responsible for Education.* **2** being the cause of something and so able to be blamed or credited for it: *Gooch was responsible for 198 of his side's 542 runs.* **3** (of a job or position) involving

important duties or decisions or control over others: *She holds a responsible position in marketing.* **4** (**responsible to**) having to report to a senior person; answerable to: *responsible to the president.* **5** capable of being trusted: *Clare has a mature and responsible attitude to work.*
Word family *responsibility* noun **1** the state or fact of having a duty to deal with something or of having control over someone: *In his new role, he has overall responsibility for personnel matters.* **2** the state or fact of being accountable or to blame for something: *The group has claimed responsibility for a string of murders.* **3** the opportunity or ability to act independently and take decisions without authorization: *We would expect individuals lower down the organization to take on more responsibility.* **4** (often *responsibilities*) a thing which you are required to do as part of a job, role, or legal obligation: *He will take over the responsibilities of Overseas Director.* **5** a moral obligation to behave correctly: *Individuals have a responsibility to control their personal behaviour.* *responsibly* adverb: *act responsibly.*

responsive *adjective*

1 reacting quickly and positively: *a flexible service that is responsive to changing social and economic patterns.* **2** responding readily and with interest or enthusiasm: *our most enthusiastic and responsive students.*
Word family *responsively* adverb: *listen responsively.* *responsiveness* noun: *responsiveness to students' needs.*

restrained *adjective*

(especially to describe a person's actions or behaviour) showing calm control rather than emotion: *a restrained approach/attitude.*
Usage *restrained* or *controlled*? The word *restrained* is used more to talk about people being polite, and not shouting or getting too excited about things: *restrained optimism/passion.* The word *controlled* is usually used to describe a person or their behaviour when they are able to stop themselves from panicking or getting angry (or showing their anger): *controlled panic/aggression/anger/fury.*

retain *verb*

1 to continue to have; to keep possession of: *Built in 1830, the house retains many of its original features.* **2** not to abolish, discard, or

reveal

3 to keep in your memory: *I retained a few French words and phrases.* **4** to keep engaged in your service: *He has been retained as a freelance.*
Word family **retention** noun: *recruitment and retention of school governors.*

reveal *verb*

1 to make previously unknown or secret information known to others: *For operational reasons, the police cannot reveal his whereabouts.* **2** to cause or allow to be seen: *The data can be used to reveal a good deal about the composition of Anglo-Norman households.*
Usage You should take care when using the adjective *revealing* as this word can also refer to an item of clothing that allows more of the wearer's body to be seen than is usual: *a very revealing dress.*
Word family **revealing** adjective making interesting or significant information known, especially about a person's attitude or character: *a revealing radio interview.* **revelation** noun: *Seeing them play at international level was a revelation.*

revel *verb*

(**revel in**) to enjoy an activity or experience very much: *He revelled in the freedom he was allowed.*
Usage The verb *revel* also means 'to engage in lively and noisy festivities, especially those which involve drinking and dancing'. As a plural noun, the word *revels* is used to refer to 'lively and noisy festivities, especially those which involve drinking and dancing'.

review *noun, verb*

noun **1** a formal assessment or examination of something with the possibility or intention of instituting change if necessary: *a comprehensive review of UK defence policy.* □ *All areas of the company will come under review.* **2** a critical appraisal of a book, play, exhibition, etc. published in a newspaper or magazine: *a film review.* **3** a survey or evaluation of a particular subject: *a review of recent developments in multicultural education.* **4** a retrospective survey or report on past events: *the Director General's end-of-year review.* □ *verb* **1** to examine or assess formally with the possibility or intention of instituting change if necessary: *The Home Secretary was*

called on to review Britain's gun laws. **2** to write a critical appraisal of a book, play, film, etc. for publication in a newspaper or magazine: *I reviewed his first novel.* **3** to survey or evaluate a particular subject: *In the next chapter we review a number of recent empirical studies.* **4** to make a retrospective assessment or survey of past events: *Ministers will meet to review progress on conventional arms negotiations in March.*
Usage The word *review* is often used to talk about a report that considers all the research and writing on a subject or events over a period of time, and gives an opinion about the current situation or state of knowledge.

revisit *verb*

to consider a situation again from a different perspective: *The council will have to revisit the issue at a general meeting this summer.*

revitalize *verb*

to give new life and vitality to: *a package of tax cuts designed to revitalize the economy.*
Word family **revitalization** noun: *plans for revitalization of the city centre.*

revive *verb*

1 to restore interest in or the popularity of: *This style was revived in the 1990s.* **2** to improve the condition of something.
Word family **revival** noun an improvement in the condition, strength, or popularity of something: *an economic revival.* □ *a revival of the fortunes of the party.* □ *Cross-country skiing is enjoying a revival.*

revolutionary *adjective*

involving a great or complete change; connected with political revolution: *It was a time of rapid and revolutionary change.* □ *At the time this idea was revolutionary.* □ *a revolutionary new drug.*

reward *noun, verb*

noun something that you are given because you have done something good or worked hard: *You deserve a reward for being so helpful.* □ *The company is now reaping the rewards of their investments.* □ *Winning the match was just reward for the effort the team made.* □ *verb* to give a reward to someone to show appreciation of their service, qualities, or achievements: *She was rewarded for her efforts with a cash bonus.* □ *Our patience was finally rewarded.*

Usage *rewarding*, *fulfilling*, or *satisfying*?
Almost any experience, important or very brief, can be *satisfying*. *Rewarding* and *fulfilling* are used more for longer, more serious activities, such as jobs or careers: *What is the most satisfying moment in your career so far?* □ *All in all, it's been an extremely rewarding/ fulfilling career.* *Satisfying* and *fulfilling* are used more to talk about your personal satisfaction or happiness; *rewarding* is used more to talk about your feeling of doing something important and being useful to others.
Word family *rewarding* adjective (of an experience or activity) that makes you happy because you think it is useful or important: *Nursing can be a very rewarding career.*

rightful *adjective*
1 having a legitimate right to property, position, or status: *the rightful owner of the jewels.* 2 legitimately claimed; fitting: *They are determined to take their rightful place in a new South Africa.*
Word family *rightfully* adverb: *denied a job that was rightfully his.*

rigorous *adjective*
very thorough, especially when studying or testing something or dealing with a problem: *Few people have gone into the topic in such rigorous detail.* □ *The second team adopted a much more rigorous approach to the problem.*
Usage In American English, the word *rigour* is spelt *rigor*.
Word family *rigorously* adverb: *Each product is rigorously tested before being put on sale.* *rigour* noun: *academic rigour.*

robust *adjective*
forceful and uncompromising; down to earth, realistic, or pragmatic: *Britain's top military officer last night issued a robust defence of the government's cuts programme.*
Word family *robustly* adverb: *robustly tackle criminal activity.* **robustness** noun

role *noun*
1 the function or position that someone has or is expected to have in an organization, in society, or in a relationship: *This report examines the role of the teacher in the classroom.* 2 the degree to which someone or something is involved in a situation or activity and the effect that they have on it: *He stressed the role of diet in preventing disease.* □ *The media play a major role in influencing people's opinions.* □ *Regional managers have a crucial role in developing a strategic framework.* 3 a character that an actor plays in a play or film: *It is one of the greatest roles she has played.* □ *Who is in the leading role* (= the most important one)?
Usage *role* or *part*? The word *part* is used mainly in phrases: *have a part to play.* □ *have/ play a part in something.* □ *have/play/take no part in/of something.* □ *take part* (*in something*). The word *role* is slightly more formal, and common in business and economic contexts. It is used especially with adjectives like *key*, *important*, *essential*, *crucial*, *central*, *fundamental*, *major*, *pivotal*, *prominent*, and *primary*.
Word family *role model* noun a person that you admire and try to copy: *We need positive role models for young people to aspire to.*

romance *noun*
1 a feeling of excitement and mystery associated with love: *I had a thirst for romance.* 2 a quality or feeling of mystery, excitement, and remoteness from everyday life: *the beauty and romance of the night.* □ *the romance of the Orient Express.*
Word family *romantic* adjective: *a romantic candlelit dinner.* □ *a romantic attitude to the past.* □ *some romantic dream of country peace.* **romantic** noun a person who is very imaginative and emotional, and who has ideas and hopes that may not be realistic: *She's an incurable romantic.* □ *He was a romantic at heart and longed for adventure.*

Ss

safeguard *noun, verb*
noun an action or law that is designed to protect people from harm, risk, or danger: *The measures have been introduced as a safeguard against fraud.* □ *Stronger legal safeguards are needed to protect the consumer.* □ *verb* to protect something from loss, harm, or damage: *It is hoped that the new order will safeguard jobs at the plant.* □ *The leaflet explains how to safeguard against dangers in the home.*

salient *adjective*
most noticeable or important: *It succinctly covered all the salient points of the case.* □ *The salient points stuck clearly in her mind.*
Word family salience *noun*: *the moral salience of nationhood.* **saliently** *adverb*: *most saliently, we turn to ...*

sample *noun, verb*
noun a small part or quantity intended to show what the whole is like: *Samples of the water contained pesticide.* □ *The interviews were given to a random sample of students.* □ *verb* **1** to test part of something or question part of a group of people in order to find out what the rest is like: *The survey was done using a group of 100 children randomly sampled from the school population.* **2** to experience something briefly to see what it is like: *Our children sampled the hotel's disco.*

sanctuary *noun*
a place or state of refuge, safety, or protection: *Patients in need of emotional and psychological support can find sanctuary in a private room separate from the ward.* □ *They fled to Kabul where they were offered sanctuary.*
Usage The original sense of the word *sanctuary* was *sanctuarium*, meaning 'a church or other sacred place where a fugitive was immune from arrest'.

sanguine *adjective*
cheerfully optimistic: *They are not sanguine about the prospect.* □ *He is sanguine about the remorseless advance of information.*
Usage The word *sanguine* is often used where there is a lack of hope: *It is too soon to be sanguine, the board says.*

satisfy *verb*
1 to fulfil a desire or need: *Social services are trying to satisfy the needs of so many different groups.* **2** to provide someone with adequate information or proof so that they are convinced about something: *People need to be satisfied that the environmental assessments are accurate.* **3** to meet someone's expectations, needs, or desires: *I have never been satisfied with my job.* □ *Wealth has failed to satisfy.* **4** to adequately meet or comply with a condition, obligation, or demand: *The whole team is working flat out to satisfy demand.*
Usage **satisfying**, **fulfilling**, or **rewarding**? See **rewarding**.
Word family satisfaction *noun* fulfilment of your wishes, expectations, or needs, or the pleasure derived from this: *I looked round with satisfaction.* □ *managing directors seeking greater job satisfaction.* **satisfactory** *adjective* good enough for a particular purpose: *Their work is satisfactory but not outstanding.* □ *You haven't yet given us a satisfactory explanation.* **satisfied** *adjective* contented; pleased: *satisfied customers.* □ *She was very satisfied with the results.* **satisfying** *adjective* giving fulfilment or the pleasure associated with this: *The work proved to be more satisfying than being a solicitor.*

savour *verb*
to enjoy the full taste or flavour of something, especially by eating or drinking it slowly; obtain great pleasure from an experience or feeling: *He ate his meal slowly, savouring every mouthful.* □ *Come and savour the amazing*

diversity and ingenuity of artistic talent in this exhibition.
Usage In American English, the word is spelt *savor*.

scene *noun*
a view that you see, especially one with people or animals moving about and doing things: *It was a delightful rural scene.*
Word family **scenery** *noun* the natural features of an area, such as mountains, valleys, rivers, and forests, especially when these are attractive to look at: *Alpine scenery.* □ *We stopped on the mountain pass to admire the scenery.* **scenic** *adjective* having beautiful natural scenery: *Loch Lomond is an area of scenic beauty.* □ *We took the scenic route* (= using country roads, not the motorway) *back to the hotel.*

scent *noun*
a light, pleasant smell: *The air was filled with the scent of lavender.*
Usage **scent**, **aroma**, or **fragrance**?
See **aroma**.
Word family **scented** *adjective*: *scented soap.*

scope *noun*
1 the opportunity or ability to do or achieve something: *Her job offers very little scope for creativity.* □ *There is clearly scope for development in the future.* **2** the range of things that a subject, organization, or activity deals with: *These issues were outside the scope of the article.* □ *The police are broadening the scope of their investigation.*

scrupulous *adjective*
very careful to be honest and do what is morally right: *She has a reputation for scrupulous honesty.* □ *He is scrupulous in all his business dealings.*
Word family **scrupulously** *adverb*: *All court proceedings need to be scrupulously fair to each side.*

scrutinize *verb*
to look at or examine someone or something carefully: *The statement was carefully scrutinized before publication.*
Word family **scrutiny** *noun* careful and thorough examination: *Her argument doesn't really stand up to scrutiny.* □ *Foreign policy has come under close scrutiny recently.*

seamless *adjective*
smooth and without obvious joins: *a seamless service between health and social care.* □ *a seamless transition from university to a career in industry.* □ *a seamless mesh of hip-hop, space rock, and violin.*
Word family **seamlessly** *adverb*: *blend/flow/ merge seamlessly.*

secluded *adjective*
private or having little contact with other people, especially when you find this pleasant: *a secluded beach.* □ *to lead a secluded life.*
Usage The word *seclusion* has a strong sense of being far away from other people and so protected from being disturbed.
Word family **seclusion** *noun*: *For the long summer vacation, I prefer the relative seclusion of the countryside.*

secret *noun*
1 something that is not yet fully understood or that is difficult to understand; a mystery: *They hope to unlock the secrets of the universe.* **2** a valid but not commonly known or recognized method of achieving or maintaining something: *The secret of a happy marriage is compromise.*
Usage The noun *secret* is also sometimes used in marketing to refer to something mysterious, strange, and intriguing: *The book explains the secrets of the English language.*

secure *adjective, verb*
adjective **1** not subject to threat; certain to remain or continue safe and unharmed: *They are working to ensure that their market share remains secure against competition.* **2** feeling safe, stable, and free from fear or anxiety: *Everyone needs to have a home and to feel secure and wanted.* **3** protected against attack or other criminal activity: *The official said that no airport could be totally secure.* **4** (of a place of detention) having provisions against the escape of inmates: *a secure unit for young offenders.* □ *verb* **1** to protect against threats; to make safe: *The government is concerned to secure the economy against too much foreign ownership.* **2** to succeed in obtaining, especially with difficulty: *The division secured a major contract.* **3** to make a door or container hard to open; to fasten or lock: *Doors are likely to be well secured at night.*

S

Usage Financially, to *secure* a loan is to guarantee it by having the right to take possession of property or goods if the borrower is unable to repay the money, and *security* is something that is promised as a guarantee that a loan will be repaid.
Word family **securely** *adverb*: *store information securely.* **security** *noun* **1** the state of being free from danger or threat: *The system is designed to provide maximum security against toxic spills.* □ *job security.* **2** the safety of a state or organization against criminal activity such as terrorism, theft, or espionage: *a matter of national security.* **3** procedures followed or measures taken to ensure such safety: *Amid tight security, the presidents met in the Colombian resort.* **4** the state of feeling safe, stable, and free from fear or anxiety: *He could give the emotional security she needed.*

select *verb, adjective*

verb to choose someone or something, usually according to a system, from a group of people or things: *He hasn't been selected for the team.* □ *All our hotels have been carefully selected for the excellent value they provide.* □ *a randomly selected sample of 23 schools.* □ *adjective* (of a society, club, or place) used only by people who have a lot of money and/ or a high social position: *They live in a very select area.* □ *It is a select restaurant with fine Italian food.*
Usage The word *selection* is used especially in marketing: *Despite its size, the resort offers a wide selection of tourist attractions and beaches.*
Word family **selection** *noun* **1** the process of choosing someone or something, usually according to a system, from a group of people or things: *The final team selection will be made tomorrow.* □ *What are their selection criteria?* **2** a number of people or things that have been chosen from a larger group: *A selection of readers' comments are published below.* **3** the number or range of different things to choose from: *The showroom has a vast selection of kitchens.*

self-confident *adjective*

having confidence in yourself and your abilities: *a self-confident child.*
Usage **self-confident** or **confident**? *Confident* can describe a person or what they do; *self-confident* only describes a person. Other

adjectives with similar meanings include: *self-assured, positive,* and *assertive.*
Word family **self-confidence** *noun*: *She took care to build up his self-confidence by involving him in the planning.* **self-confidently** *adverb*: *He drove too fast and too self-confidently.*

self-contained *adjective*

able to operate or exist without outside help or influence: *The village was an isolated and self-contained community.* □ *Each chapter is self-contained and can be studied in isolation.*

self-control *noun*

the ability to remain calm and not show your emotions even though you are feeling angry or excited: *It took all his self-control not to shout at them.* □ *She struggled to keep her self-control.*
Usage **self-control** or **restraint**? *Self-control* is an ability that people have as part of their character. You can have *self-control* or you can keep or lose it on a particular occasion. *Restraint* is less a part of someone's character and more a matter of their behaviour; you can exercise or show *restraint,* but it is not something that you have, keep, or lose.
Word family **self-controlled** *adjective*: *He was always mature, self-controlled, and reasonable.*

self-discipline *noun*

the ability to make yourself do something, especially something difficult or unpleasant: *It takes a lot of self-discipline to go jogging in winter.*
Word family **self-disciplined** *adjective*: *I've learnt that being self-disciplined is critical to success.*

selfless *adjective*

concerned more with the needs and wishes of others than with your own; unselfish: *an act of selfless devotion.*
Word family **selflessly** *adverb*: *act selflessly on behalf of the oppressed.* **selflessness** *noun*: *display remarkable courage and selflessness during the rescue.*

self-motivated *adjective*

motivated to do or achieve something because of your own enthusiasm or interest, without needing pressure from others: *She's a very independent self-motivated individual.*
Word family **self-motivation** *noun*: *have a high degree of self-motivation.*

self-respect *noun*
pride and confidence in yourself; feeling that you are behaving with honour and dignity.
Usage You should use the word *self-respecting* with care as it is sometimes used humorously to refer to a person who merits a particular role or name: *No self-respecting editor would include such an article.*
Word family **self-respecting** adjective having self-respect: *proud, self-respecting mountain villagers.*

self-starter *noun*
a person who is sufficiently motivated or ambitious to start a new career or business or to pursue further education without the help of others: *He was the self-starter who worked his way up from messenger boy to account executive.*
Word family **self-starting** adjective: *self-starting entrepreneurs.*

seminal *adjective*
(e.g. of a work or event) strongly influencing later developments: *his seminal work on chaos theory.* □ *their seminal contribution to cancer research.*
Word family **seminally** adverb: *a seminally important film.*

sensational *adjective*
causing great surprise, excitement, or interest: *Police have uncovered sensational new evidence.* □ *It was the most sensational 24 hours of the jockey's career.*
Usage The word *sensational* can also be used to refer to an account or publication that presents information in a way that is intended to provoke public interest and excitement, at the expense of accuracy: *cheap sensational periodicals.* In informal usage, *sensational* means 'very good indeed', 'very impressive or attractive': *You look sensational in that dress!*
Word family **sensationally** adverb: *The trial ended sensationally.*

sensitive *adjective*
1 quick to detect or respond to slight changes, signals, or influences: *The new method of protein detection was more sensitive than earlier ones.* □ *Spiders are sensitive to vibrations on their web.* **2** easily damaged, injured, or distressed by slight changes: *The community called for improved protection of wildlife in environmentally sensitive areas.*
3 (of a person or a person's behaviour) having

or displaying a quick and delicate appreciation of others' feelings: *I pay tribute to the Minister for his sensitive handling of the bill.* **4** easily offended or upset: *I suppose I shouldn't be so sensitive.* **5** kept secret or with restrictions on disclosure to avoid endangering security: *He was suspected of passing sensitive information to other countries.*
Word family **sensitively** adverb: *deal with someone sensitively.* **sensitivity** noun: *a total lack of common decency and sensitivity.* □ *The only rules that matter are practical ones that respect local sensitivities.*

sentiment *noun*
1 a feeling or opinion, especially one based on emotions: *This is a sentiment that I totally agree with.* □ *Nationalist sentiment spread quickly, especially in the cities.* **2** (sometimes disapproving) feelings of pity, romantic love, or sadness which may be too strong or not appropriate: *There is no room for sentiment in business.* □ *There was no fatherly affection, no display of sentiment.*
Word family **sentimental** adjective: *She kept the letters for sentimental reasons.* □ *The ring wasn't worth much but it had great sentimental value.* □ (disapproving) *a slushy, sentimental love story.* □ *He's not the sort of man who gets sentimental about old friendships.*
sentimentally adverb: *a programme that sentimentally explores quaint examples of family life.*

serendipity *noun*
the occurrence and development of events by chance in a happy or beneficial way: *Technical innovations may be the result of pure serendipity.* □ *a fortunate stroke of serendipity.*
Usage The word *serendipity* was coined by Horace Walpole in 1754 and was suggested by *The Three Princes of Serendip*, the title of a fairy tale in which the heroes 'were always making discoveries, by accidents and sagacity, of things they were not in quest of'.
Word family **serendipitous** adjective: *Their diligent efforts were coupled with the joy of serendipitous discovery.* **serendipitously** adverb: *My introduction to the virtuoso happened serendipitously.*

serene *adjective*
calm, peaceful, and untroubled; tranquil: *Her eyes were closed and she looked very serene.*

Word family **serenely** adverb: smile/flow/glide serenely. **serenity** noun: an oasis of serenity amidst the bustling city.

serious adjective

1 (of a subject, state, or activity) demanding careful consideration or application: Marriage is a serious matter. **2** (of thought or discussion) careful or profound: We give serious consideration to safety recommendations. **3** significant or worrying because of possible danger or risk; not slight or negligible: She escaped serious injury. □ Haydn was Mozart's only serious rival. **4** (of a person) solemn or thoughtful in character or manner: Her face grew serious. **5** (of music, literature, or other art forms) requiring deep reflection and inviting a considered response: He bridges the gap between serious and popular music. Usage In informal contexts, the word serious also means 'substantial in terms of size, number, or quality': He suddenly had serious money to spend.
Word family **seriously** adverb: The amount of fat you eat can seriously affect your health. □ Three men are seriously ill in hospital. **seriousness** noun

share noun, verb

noun **1** one part of something that is divided between two or more people; a part which someone has in a particular activity that involves several people; an amount of something that is thought to be normal or acceptable for one person: How much was your share of the winnings? □ Next year we hope to have a bigger share of the market. □ I'm hoping for a share in the profits. □ We all did our share of the work. **2** an amount regarded as normal or acceptable: The new system had more than its fair share of problems. □ verb **1** to have or use something at the same time as someone else; to give some of what you have to someone else or let someone else use something that is yours; to separate something into parts so that two or more people can have a part of it: She shares a house with three other students. □ The conference is a good place to share information and exchange ideas. **2** to work together with other people in an equal way to make work or responsibilities easier: Don't try to do everything yourself: you will need to share the load with your partner.

Usage Words that are used with the verb share in sense **2** include work, load, burden, and responsibilities.

showcase verb

verb to exhibit; to display: The albums showcase his production skills. □ He is currently touring Britain, showcasing his work in several exhibitions.
Usage This usage as a verb is a figurative extension of the original noun sense of showcase 'a glass case used for displaying articles in a shop or museum' and later 'a place or occasion for presenting something favourably to general attention': The gallery will provide a showcase for Scotland's young photographers.

shrewd adjective

clever and good at making judgements about a situation; showing good judgement and likely to be right: My mother was a shrewd judge of character. □ I could take a pretty shrewd guess at who had sent the letter. □ She had a shrewd idea of what their motives were.
Word family **shrewdly** adverb: As he shrewdly observed . . . **shrewdness** noun: business/ financial shrewdness.

significant adjective

large or important enough to have an effect or be noticed: There are no significant differences between the two groups of students. □ The results of the experiment are not statistically significant. □ These views are held by a significant proportion of the population.
Usage **significant** or **important**? See **important**.
Word family **significance** noun: Tourism is of considerable significance in this area. **significantly** adverb: High calcium concentrations in drinking water have been correlated with a significantly reduced risk of developing breast cancer.

silhouette noun, verb

noun the dark outline or shape of a person or object that you see against a light background; the shape of a person's body or an object: The trees were black silhouettes against the pale sky. □ The mountains stood out in silhouette. □ verb (**be silhouetted**) to cast or show someone or something as a dark shape and outline against a lighter background: The castle was silhouetted against the sky.

S

Usage The word *silhouette* derives from the 18th-century French author and politician, Étienne de Silhouette.

simulate *verb*

to create particular conditions that exist in real life using computers or models, usually for study or training purposes: *Computer software can be used to simulate conditions on the sea bed.* □ *Role play is a way of simulating real-life situations.*
Word family **simulation** noun: *a computer simulation of how the planet functions.* □ *An important part of training is role play and the simulation of court cases.*

sincere *adjective*

1 free from pretence or deceit; proceeding from genuine feelings: *They offer their sincere thanks to Paul.* **2** saying what you really feel or believe; not dishonest or hypocritical: *He seemed sincere enough when he said he wanted to help.*
Usage **sincere** or **genuine**? See **genuine**.
Usage The phrase *yours sincerely* is a formula used to end a letter, typically a formal one in which the recipient is addressed by name.
Word family **sincerely** adverb: *I sincerely believe that this is the right decision.* **sincerity** noun: *I can say in all sincerity that I knew nothing of these plans.*

single-minded *adjective*

only thinking about one particular aim or goal because you are determined to achieve something: *She is very single-minded about her career.* □ *He spent his life in the single-minded pursuit of wealth and power.*
Usage The word *single-minded* is occasionally used with disapproval, suggesting that the person does not care about what other people think: *the single-minded pursuit of profit.*
Word family **single-mindedly** adverb: *They devoted themselves single-mindedly to helping other people.*

skill *noun*

1 the ability to do something well because of training and practice: *The job requires skill and an eye for detail.* □ *She is a negotiator of considerable skill.* **2** something that someone is able to do well, especially when this has been acquired through practice: *We need people with practical skills like carpentry.* □ *The*

course focuses on management skills and customer service.
Usage The word *skill* or *skills* often comes after a noun that describes a particular type of ability: *communication/leadership/management/computer skills*. *Skills* are usually a result of experience and training.
Word family **skilful** adjective (of a person) good at doing something, especially something that needs a particular ability or special training; (of an action) done with skill: *As Foreign Secretary he proved to be a skilful diplomat.* □ *Everyone admired her skilful handling of the matter.* **skilfully** adverb: *a skilfully crafted masterpiece.* **skilled** (of a person) having enough ability, experience, and knowledge to be able to do a particular job or activity well; (of a job) needing special abilities or training: *We need more skilled engineers.*

sleek *adjective*

1 (of an object) having an elegant, streamlined shape or design: *His sleek black car slid through the traffic.* □ *Here you can view the sleekest designs.* **2** (of a person) having a wealthy and well-groomed appearance: *a sleek and ambitious junior Minister.* **3** (of hair, fur, or skin) smooth and glossy: *He was tall, with sleek, dark hair.* **4** (of a person or animal) having smooth, glossy skin, hair, or fur, often taken as a sign of physical fitness: *a sleek black cat.*
Usage The adjective *sleek* can also mean 'ingratiating': *She gave Guy a sleek smile to underline her words.*
Word family **sleekly** adverb: *a sleekly designed iPod player.* **sleekness** noun: *The new furniture range focuses on sleekness and simplicity.*

smart *adjective*

1 (of people) looking clean and neat; wearing fashionable and/or formal clothes; (of clothes etc.) clean, neat, and looking new and attractive: *You look very smart in that suit.* □ *They wear smart blue uniforms.* **2** connected with rich fashionable people: *The restaurant has a smart new décor.* **3** quick at learning and understanding things; showing the ability to make good business or personal decisions: *She's smarter than her brother.* □ *If you're smart, you'll take my advice.* □ *That was a smart career move.*
Usage Sense 3 is used in informal contexts. The adjective *smart* is also used to refer to a

device that has been programmed so as to be capable of independent action: *hi-tech smart weapons.* A *smart card* is a plastic card with a built-in microprocessor, used typically to perform financial transactions.
Word family **smartly** adverb: *smartly dressed.* **smartness** noun

smooth *adjective*
1 completely flat and even, without any lumps, holes, or rough areas: *The water was as smooth as glass.* □ *Use a paint that gives a smooth, silky finish.* 2 (of an action, event, or process) without problems or difficulties: *The group's expansion into the US market was not quite so smooth.*
Usage You should take care when using the word *smooth* because it can be used with disapproval to refer to a person who has a confident and pleasant manner which may get them what they want, but who actually should not be trusted: *He was a smooth talker who seemed to be able to persuade anyone to buy his rip-off radios.*
Word family **smoothly** adverb: *The ceremony went smoothly.* **smoothness** noun

snug *adjective*
warm, comfortable, and protected, especially from the cold: *I spent the afternoon snug and warm in bed.* □ *It had rained during the night but our tents were snug and dry.* □ *sitting in a snug café while it rained outside.*
Word family **snugly** adverb: *The baby nestled snugly in his rescuer's arms.*

sociable *adjective*
enjoying spending time with other people: *She's a sociable child who'll talk to anyone.* □ *I'm not feeling very sociable this evening.* □ *We had a very sociable weekend* (= we did a lot of things with other people).
Usage *Sociable* is an approving term and can describe someone's character, behaviour, or mood; its opposite is *unsociable* which is a disapproving term.
Word family **sociability** noun: *the sociability of working together.* **sociably** adverb: *chat sociably.*

society *noun*
1 the total number of people living together in a more or less ordered community: *drugs, crime, and other dangers to society.* 2 the community of people living in a particular country or region and having shared customs,

laws, and organizations: *the ethnic diversity of British society.* □ *modern industrial societies.*
3 an organization or club formed for a particular purpose or activity: *the Royal Society for the Protection of Birds.*
Usage The word *society* is also used to refer to a group of people who are fashionable, wealthy, and influential, regarded as forming a distinct group in a community: *She was a poor girl who married into New York society.*

solidarity *noun*
support by one person or group for another because they share feelings, opinions, or aims: *Demonstrations were held as a gesture of solidarity with the hunger strikers.*
Usage The word *solidarity* is a term used especially in the context of strikes and industrial relations.

solve *verb*
1 to find the solution to a problem or explanation for something that is difficult to understand or explain: *We were given clues to help us solve the puzzle.* □ *The mystery has not yet been completely solved.* 2 to find a way of dealing with a problem or difficult situation: *You can't solve all your difficulties by running away.* □ *Unemployment will not be solved by offering low-paid jobs in call centres.*
Usage Words with a similar meaning to *solution* include *answer, result, resolution, way out, remedy,* and *key.*
Word family **solution** noun a way of solving a problem or dealing with a difficult situation; the act of solving a problem: *Do you have a better solution?* □ *Will this lead to a peaceful solution of the conflict?*

soothe *verb*
1 to gently calm a person or their feelings: *A shot of brandy might soothe his nerves.* 2 to reduce pain or discomfort in part of the body: *To soothe the skin try chamomile or thyme.* □ *It contains a mild anaesthetic to soothe the pain.*
Word family **soothing** adjective: *soothing music.* **soothingly** adverb: *'There's no need to worry,' he said soothingly.*

sophisticated *adjective*
1 (of a machine, system, or technique) highly developed and complex: *sophisticated production techniques.* 2 having a lot of experience of the world and knowing about fashion, culture, and other things that people think are socially important: *Ben did his best to*

S

look sophisticated. □ *Students have more sophisticated tastes nowadays.*
Word family **sophistication** noun: *Despite his jeans, there was still an air of sophistication about him.*

soul *noun*

1 the spiritual element of a person, believed to be immortal: *Painting is the art of reaching the soul through the eyes.* **2** a person's moral or emotional nature: *In the depths of her soul, she knew he would betray her.* **3** emotional or intellectual energy or power: *Their performance lacked soul.* **4** a person regarded as a perfect example of a particular quality: *She's the soul of discretion.* **5** an individual person: *I'll never tell a soul.*
Usage *Soul music* is a kind of music which incorporates elements of gospel music and rhythm and blues, popularized by black Americans.
Word family **soulful** adjective: *She gave him a soulful glance.* **soulless** adjective: **1** lacking character and individuality: *soulless post-war apartments.* **2** (of an activity) dull and uninspiring: *soulless non-productive work.* **3** lacking human feelings: *Two soulless eyes were watching her.*

sound *adjective*

1 based on reason, sense, or judgement: *sound advice for healthy living.* □ *The scientific concept is sound.* **2** in good condition; not damaged, injured, or diseased: *Your heart is as sound as a young man's.* **3** competent, reliable, or holding acceptable views: *He's a bit stuffy, but he's very sound on his law.* **4** financially secure: *She got her business on a sound footing for the first time.*
Word family **soundly** adverb **soundness** noun

source *noun, verb*

noun **1** a place, person, or thing from which something comes or can be obtained: *Mackerel is a good source of fish oil.* **2** a person who provides information: *Military sources announced a reduction in strategic nuclear weapons.* **3** a book or document used to provide evidence in research: *A historian will need to use both primary and secondary sources.* □ *verb* **1** to obtain from a particular source: *Each type of coffee is sourced from one country.* **2** to find out where something can be obtained: *She was called upon to source a supply of carpet.*

special *adjective*

1 better, greater, or otherwise different from what is usual: *They always made a special effort at Christmas.* **2** exceptionally good or precious: *She's a very special person.* **3** belonging specifically to a particular person or place: *We want to preserve our town's special character.* **4** designed or organized for a particular person, purpose, or occasion: *We will return by special coaches.*
Usage There is some overlap in the uses of *especially* and *specially*. In the broadest terms, both words mean 'particularly' and the preference for one word over the other is linked with particular conventions of use rather than with any deep difference in meaning. For example, there is little to choose between *written especially for Jonathan* and *written specially for Jonathan* and neither is more correct than the other. On the other hand, in sentences such as *He despised them all, especially Sylvester*, substitution of *specially* is found in informal uses but should not be used in written English, while in *The car was specially made for the occasion*, substitution of *especially* is somewhat unusual. Overall, *especially* is by far the commoner of the two.
Word family **specially** adverb for a special purpose: *a new coat and hat bought specially for the occasion.* **specialness** noun: *the specialness of certain friendships.*

specialism *noun*

an area of study or work that someone officially gives most of their attention to, especially in the context of a course of study or a particular company: *He's doing a business degree with a specialism in computing.* □ *Dr Crane's specialism is tropical diseases.*
Word family **specialist** noun a person who is an expert in a particular area of work or study; a doctor who is an expert in a particular area of medicine: *He's a noted specialist in his field.* □ *I was sent to see a specialist at the local hospital.* □ *a cancer/ear/eye/heart specialist.* **specialist** adjective: *You need some specialist advice.* **specialize** verb: *He specialized in criminal law.* □ *Many students prefer not to specialize too soon.*

speciality *noun*

1 a pursuit, area of study, or skill to which someone has devoted much time and effort and in which they are expert: *His speciality was watercolours.* **2** a product, especially a type of

food, which a person or region is famous for making well: *This wine is a speciality of southern Australia.*
Usage In American English and medical contexts, the variant *specialty* is common: *Funding was agreed for specialties such as psychiatry and anaesthesia.*

specific *adjective*
1 clearly defined or identified: *Savings were made by increasing the electricity supply only until it met specific development needs.*
2 precise and clear in making statements or issuing instructions: *When ordering goods, please be specific.* **3** belonging or relating uniquely to a particular subject: *Information needs are often very specific to companies and individuals.*
Usage The word *specific* is frequently used to ask someone to be more exact, or to complain that someone has not been precise.
Word family **specifically** adverb: *a magazine aimed specifically at working women.* **specificity** *noun*

specify *verb*
to give exact details of something such as a measurement, a time, or instructions: *Forms must be returned by the specified date.* □ *The contract clearly specifies who can operate the machinery.* □ *The regulations specify that calculators may not be used in the examination.*
Word family **specification** noun: *the technical specifications of the new model.* □ *The house has been built exactly to our specifications.*

spectacular *adjective*
1 (especially of scenery or a performance) extremely beautiful and impressive: *The coastal road has spectacular scenery.* □ *In the evening, there will be a spectacular display of fireworks.* **2** (of an achievement or skill) very impressive: *Rooney scored a spectacular goal.* □ *They were absolutely delighted with the show's spectacular success.*
Usage An achievement or skill that is *unspectacular* is not exciting or special: *He had a steady but unspectacular career.*
Word family **spectacularly** adverb: *It had been a spectacularly successful season.*

spectrum *noun*
a complete or wide range of related ideas, opinions, or qualities: *We shall hear views from across the political spectrum.* □ *The policy has*

the support of a broad spectrum of opinion. □ *to the left and right of the political spectrum.*
Usage This figurative sense derives from *spectrum*, meaning 'the band of colours produced by separating light into elements with different wavelengths, e.g. in a rainbow'.

spellbinding *adjective*
holding the complete attention of someone as though by magic; fascinating: *a spellbinding tale of her life in the Far East.*
Word family **spellbound** adjective: *The singer held the audience spellbound.*

sphere *noun*
an area of activity, interest, or expertise; a section of society or an aspect of life distinguished and unified by a particular characteristic: *political reforms to match those in the economic sphere.* □ *This area was formerly within the sphere of influence of the US.*

spirit *noun*
1 the typical or dominant character, quality, or mood: *They shared her spirit of adventure.*
2 (**spirits**) a person's mood: *The warm weather lifted everyone's spirits after the winter.*
3 courage, energy, and determination: *His visitors admired his spirit and good temper.*
4 the real meaning of something as opposed to its strict interpretation (*the letter*): *The rule had been broken in spirit if not in letter.* **5** the part of a person that consists of their character and feelings rather than their body, often believed to survive after their body is dead: *We seek a harmony between body and spirit.*
Usage **spirits** or **morale**? See **morale**.
Usage The word *spirit* is used especially to talk about how people are feeling, their attitudes, and their behaviour at a particular period in time: *The spirit of the 70s/the age/the times/the Enlightenment.*

splendid *adjective*
magnificent; very impressive: *a splendid view of Windsor Castle.* □ *His robes were splendid.*
Usage The *splendours* of something, especially a place, are its beautiful and impressive features: *the splendours of Rome* (= its fine buildings etc.).
Word family **splendidly** adverb: *a splendidly ornate style.* **splendour** noun grand and impressive beauty, especially of places and buildings: *The room has a view of Rheims Cathedral, in all its splendour.*

stabilize *verb*
to make or become stable: *His condition appears to have stabilized.* □ *an emergency programme designed to stabilize the economy.*
Word family **stabilization** noun: *drastic stabilization measures.*

stable *adjective*
1 not likely to change or fail; firmly established: *a stable relationship.* □ *Prices have remained relatively stable.* **2** (of a person) sane and sensible; not easily upset or disturbed: *The officer concerned is mentally and emotionally stable.*
Usage The word *stable* is used especially to talk about people's personal and home life: *a stable mind/relationship/family/home*; the economic, political, or social situation: *a stable situation/environment/government/population* □ *stable employment*; or the condition of a patient who has been very ill, but who is not getting worse.
Word family **stability** noun: *There are fears for the political stability of the area.* **stably** adverb

stage *noun*
1 a state or period that someone or something passes through while developing or making progress; a separate part that a process is divided into: *The product is at the design stage.* □ *The children are at different stages of development.* □ *At one stage it looked as though they would win.* □ *The pay increase will be introduced in stages* (= not all at once). □ *We can take the argument one stage further.* **2** an area of activity where important things happen, especially in politics: *Germany is playing a leading role on the world stage.*
Usage **stage** or **phase**? See **phase**.
Word family **staged** adjective: *staged pay increases.*

stakeholder *noun, adjective*
noun a person with an interest or concern in something, especially a business: *consultation with stakeholders across institutional boundaries.* □ adjective referring to a type of organization or system in which all the members or participants are seen as having an interest in its success: *a stakeholder economy.*
Usage You should take care in using this word because some people consider it jargon.

stamina *noun*
(in people) the physical or mental ability to continue doing something difficult or tiring for long periods of time: *She didn't have the stamina to complete the course.* □ *Rowing is ideal for building stamina.* □ *Their secret is stamina not speed.*

standard *noun, adjective*
noun **1** a level of quality or attainment: *Their restaurant offers a high standard of service.* □ *the government's ambition to raise standards in schools.* □ *Half of the beaches fail to comply with European standards.* □ *Their tap water was not up to standard* (= not good enough). **2** an idea or thing used as a measure, norm, or model in comparative evaluations: *The wages are low by today's standards.* □ *The system had become an industry standard.* **3** (**standards**) principles of behaviour informed by notions of honour and decency: *a decline in moral standards.* □ adjective **1** used or accepted as normal or average: *the standard rate of income tax.* □ *It is standard practice in museums to register objects as they are acquired.* **2** (of a size, measure, design, etc.) such as is regularly used or produced; not special or exceptional: *All these doors come in a range of standard sizes.* **3** (of a work, repertoire, or writer) viewed as authoritative or of permanent value and so widely read or performed: *His essays on the interpretation of reality became a standard text.*

state *verb*
to express something definitely or clearly in speech or writing: *The report stated that more than 51% of voters failed to participate.* □ *People will be invited to state their views.*
Usage The word *statement* is also used to refer to an action, possession, etc. that is a clear expression of an opinion: *Today owning a football club has become a fashion statement for the wealthy.*
Word family **statement** noun **1** a definite or clear expression of something in speech or writing: *Do you agree with this statement?* □ *This is correct as a statement of fact.* **2** an official account of facts, views, or plans, especially one for release to the media: *The ministers issued a joint statement calling for negotiations.*

stature *noun*
the importance and respect that a person or group has because of their ability and achievements: *The orchestra has grown in*

stature. □ *The election result enhanced the party's stature.*

status *noun*
1 high rank or social position; the level of importance or respect that is given to something: *The job brings with it status and a high income.* □ *This reflects the high status accorded to science in our culture.* □ *In the teaching of literature, Shakespeare is given a special status.* **2** the social or professional position of someone or something in relation to others, based on the amount of respect they get from other people: *The only jobs on offer were of low status and badly paid.* □ *How do people perceive the status of the full-time mother?*
Word family **status symbol** noun a possession that is taken to indicate a person's wealth or high social or professional status.

statutory *adjective*
required, permitted, or enacted by statute: *statutory controls over prices.* □ *When you buy goods, you have certain statutory rights.*
Usage In informal contexts, the word *statutory* also means 'having come to be required or expected through being done or made regularly': *the statutory Christmas phone call to his mother.*

steadfast *adjective*
resolutely or dutifully firm and unwavering: *steadfast loyalty.*
Word family **steadfastly** adverb: *steadfastly refuse to comment.* **steadfastness** noun: *steadfastness of purpose.*

steady *adjective*
1 (of a person) sensible, reliable, and self-restrained: *a solid, steady young man.*
2 regular, even, and continuous in development, frequency, or intensity: *a steady decline in the national birth rate.* □ *Sales remain steady.* **3** not faltering or wavering; controlled: *a steady gaze.* □ *She tried to keep her voice steady.* **4** firmly fixed, supported, or balanced; not shaking or moving: *The lighter the camera, the harder it is to hold steady.* **5** not changing; regular and established: *I thought I'd better get a steady job.*
Word family **steadily** adverb: *The company's exports have been increasing steadily.* □ *The situation got steadily worse.* **steadiness** noun: *We are encouraged by the steadiness of software sales.*

stellar *adjective*
exceptionally good; outstanding: *His restaurant has received stellar ratings in the guides.* □ *highlights of his stellar career.*
Usage In informal usage, the word *stellar* means 'featuring or having the quality of a very talented or successful performer or performers': *A stellar cast had been assembled.*

stimulate *verb*
to make something develop or to encourage something, such as growth, interest, discussions, feelings, or ideas: *A newspaper article can be used to stimulate discussion among students.* □ *Any increase in industrial activity will stimulate demand for electricity.* □ *The first workshop is intended to stimulate ideas.*
Word family **stimulating** adjective full of interesting or exciting ideas; making people feel enthusiastic: *Thank you for a most stimulating discussion.* □ *She was a very stimulating teacher who got the best out of her students.*

stimulus *noun*
something that helps or encourages someone or something to start or to develop better or more quickly: *Books provide children with ideas and a stimulus for play.* □ *He stressed the value of public investment as a stimulus to growth.*
Usage The plural form of *stimulus* is *stimuli.*
Usage **stimulus** or **impetus**? See **impetus.**

stirring *adjective*
causing strong feelings, especially feelings of excitement: *a stirring performance of Beethoven's 5th Symphony.* □ *stirring memories of past victories.*
Word family **stirringly** adverb: *stirringly beautiful clouds.*

stoical *adjective*
enduring pain and hardship without showing your feelings or complaining: *He taught a stoical acceptance of suffering.*
Word family **stoically** adverb: *defend stoically.*

straightforward *adjective*
1 easy to do or to understand; not complicated: *a straightforward process.* □ *It's quite straightforward to get here.* **2** (of a person or their behaviour) honest and open; not trying to trick someone or hide something: *She's nice: very straightforward and easy to get on with.*

S

Usage *straightforward* or *simple*? These two words are very similar in meaning and use. Words that combine with either include *question, answer, case, matter, method, procedure*, and *exercise*. Something that is *straightforward* may not be quite as basic as something that is *simple* but it causes no problems because there is nothing unusual or unexpected about it.

Word family **straightforwardly** *adverb*: *Let me put it more straightforwardly.* **straightforwardness** *noun*

strand *noun*

one of the different parts of something, especially an idea, plan, or story: *There are three main strands to the policy.* □ *The author draws the different strands of the plot together in the final chapter.*

Usage The word *strand* is used to refer to an element that forms part of a complex whole: *Marxist theories evolved from different strands of social analysis.*

strategy *noun*

a plan of action or policy designed to achieve a major or overall aim: *time to develop a coherent economic strategy.* □ *shifts in marketing strategy.*

Usage **strategy** or **tactics**? Both these words denote approaches adopted after reasoning about the best way to achieve aims. In military usage, *strategy* denotes the overall planning of operations, while *tactics* applies to the deployment of troops in battle, contributing towards the achievement of a larger *strategy*. More generally, *strategy* denotes planning, usually long-term, towards a major goal: *rethinking sales strategy* □ *The Tourist Board has launched a major review of its strategy for tourism*, while *tactics* refers to the adoption of plans in response to a more immediate problem: *The player should be free to concentrate on the tactics of the game.* Usage The word *strategy* should not be confused with *stratagem* which refers to a plan or scheme, especially one used to outwit an opponent or achieve a purpose: *a series of devious stratagems.*

Word family **strategic** *adjective* 1 relating to the identification of long-term or overall aims and interests and the means of achieving them: *Strategic planning for the organization is the responsibility of top management.* 2 carefully designed or planned to serve a

particular purpose or advantage: *Alarms are positioned at strategic points around the room.* 3 relating to the gaining of overall or long-term especially military advantage: *Newark Castle was of strategic importance.* □ *a hazard to British strategic and commercial interests.* **strategically** *adverb*: *a strategically placed depot.*

strength *noun*

1 (in people) the quality of being brave and determined in a difficult situation: *You have shown great strength of character.* □ *During his ordeal he was able to draw strength from his faith.* 2 a quality or ability that someone or something has that gives them an advantage: *The ability to keep calm is one of her many strengths.* □ *Consider all the strengths and weaknesses of the argument.*

Usage The word *strengthen* can mean 'to make someone or something stronger in any way': physically, emotionally, morally, politically, or financially.

Word family **strengthen** *verb* to make or become stronger: *The wind had strengthened overnight.* □ *Her position in the party has strengthened in recent weeks.* □ *Repairs are necessary to strengthen the bridge.*

striking *adjective*

1 attracting attention by reason of being unusual, extreme, or prominent: *The murder bore a striking similarity to an earlier shooting.* □ *It is striking that no research into the problem is being carried out.* 2 dramatically good-looking or beautiful: *She is naturally striking.* □ *a striking landscape.*

Word family **strikingly** *adverb*: *strikingly different styles.*

strong *adjective*

1 (of an argument or case) likely to succeed because of sound reasoning or convincing evidence: *There is a strong argument for decentralization.* 2 possessing skills and qualities that create a likelihood of success: *The competition was too strong.* 3 powerfully affecting the mind, senses, or emotions: *His imagery made a strong impression on the critics.* 4 able to perform a specified action well and powerfully: *He was not a strong swimmer.* 5 (of a person's character) showing determination, self-control, and good judgement: *Only a strong will enabled him to survive.* 6 in a secure financial position: *The company's business*

S

remains strong. **7** offering security and advantage: *The company was in a strong position to negotiate a deal.* **8** (of a belief or feeling) intense and firmly held. **9** (of a relationship) lasting and remaining deep despite difficulties. **10** (of something seen or heard) not soft or muted; clear or prominent: *She should wear strong colours.*

Word family **strongly** adverb: *strongly believe/disagree/influence.*

structure *noun*

1 the way in which the parts of something are connected together, arranged, or organized, especially when there are a number of different parts or levels: *the structure of the building/human body.* □ *a career/salary/tax structure.* □ *the grammatical structures of a language.* □ *Students study the structure of human societies throughout history.* **2** the state of being well organized or planned with all the parts linked together: *In terms of structure the novel has several flaws.* □ *Children need structure in their lives.*

Word family **structural** adjective of or relating to the arrangement of and relationships between the parts or elements of a complex whole: *There have been structural changes in the industry.* **structurally** adverb

study *noun, verb*

noun **1** the devotion of time and attention to acquiring knowledge on an academic subject, especially by means of books: *the study of English.* □ *an application to continue full-time study.* **2** an academic book or article on a particular topic: *a study of Jane Austen's novels.* **3** (**studies**) used in the title of an academic subject: *undergraduate courses in transport studies.* **4** a detailed investigation and analysis of a subject or situation: *a study of a sample of 5,000 children.* □ *the study of global problems.* **5** (**study in**) a thing or person that is an embodiment or good example of something: *He perched on the edge of the bed, a study in confusion and misery.* □ *verb* **1** to devote time and attention to acquiring knowledge on an academic subject, especially by means of books: *students studying A-level drama.* **2** to investigate and analyse a subject or situation in detail: *He has been studying badgers for many years.* **3** to look at closely in order to observe or read: *She bent her head to study the plans.*

stunning *adjective*

1 extremely surprising or shocking: *The election result was a stunning blow for the party.* □ *The team is celebrating a stunning victory.* **2** extremely beautiful or attractive: *You look absolutely stunning!*

Usage The word *stunning* in these senses tends to be used in informal contexts.

Word family **stunningly** adverb: *stunningly beautiful/attractive.*

style *noun, verb*

noun **1** the quality of doing something well, with ease, control, and good judgement, in a way that is pleasing to see; the quality of being attractive and made to a high standard of design: *She does everything with style and grace.* □ *The hotel has been redecorated but it's lost a lot of its style.* □ *a sophisticated nightspot with style and taste.* **2** a manner of doing something: *different styles of management.* **3** a distinctive appearance, typically determined by the principles according to which something is designed: *The pillars are no exception to the general style.* □ *verb* **1** to design or make in a particular form: *The yacht is well proportioned and conservatively styled.* **2** to designate with a particular name, description, or title: *The official is styled principal and vice-chancellor of the university.*

Usage The word *style* ('the way or form in which something is presented') is sometimes contrasted with *substance* ('its subject matter or content'): *There is a difference in style and substance between the president of a university with a religious mission ministering the truth to a congregation of faculty and students, and the president of a modern research university administering to the faculty and staff.*

Word family **stylish** adjective having or displaying a good sense of style; fashionably elegant: *These are elegant and stylish performances.* □ *a stylish and innovative range of jewellery.*

substance *noun*

1 the quality of being important, valid, or significant: *He had yet to accomplish anything of substance.* **2** the most important or essential part of something; the real or essential meaning: *the substance of the trade agreement.*

Usage **substantial** or **substantive**? Something that is *substantial* is of considerable size or importance: *a substantial decrease in output.*

Substantive is a more formal word; something that is *substantive* is real, actual, or essential: *The following are the substantive issues . . .*
Usage See **style**.
Word family substantial adjective of considerable importance, size, or worth: *a substantial amount of cash.* **substantially** adverb to a great or significant extent: *Profits grew substantially.* □ *substantially higher pension costs.* **substantiate** verb to provide evidence to support or prove the truth of: *They found nothing to substantiate the allegations.*

substantive *adjective*
having a firm basis in reality and so important, meaningful, or considerable: *There is no substantive evidence for the efficacy of these drugs.*
Usage substantive or **substantial**? See **substance**.
Word family substantively adverb: *deal substantively with the matter of illegal immigration.*

subtle *adjective*
1 (especially of a change or distinction) so delicate or precise as to be difficult to analyse or describe: *His language expresses rich and subtle meanings.* **2** (of a mixture or effect) delicately complex and understated: *subtle lighting.* **3** making use of clever and indirect methods to achieve something: *He tried a more subtle approach.*
Word family subtlety noun: *the textural subtlety of Degas.* □ *the subtleties of English grammar.* **subtly** adverb

succeed *verb*
1 to achieve something that you have been trying to do or get; to have the result or effect that was intended: *He succeeded in getting a place at art school.* □ *Our plan succeeded.* **2** to be successful in your career, earning money, power, and/or respect: *You will have to work hard if you are to succeed.* □ *She doesn't have the ruthlessness to succeed in business.*
Word family success noun **1** the art of succeeding: *I didn't have much success in finding a job.* □ *commercial/economic/electoral success.* **2** a person or thing that has achieved a good result and been successful: *We had one or two outstanding successes.* □ *She wasn't a success as a teacher.* □ *He was determined to make a success of the business.* **successful**

adjective **1** achieving your aims or what was intended: *The successful candidate will be responsible for a large research project.* □ *The experiment was entirely successful.* □ *He had been successful at every job he had done.* **2** making a lot of money, especially by being popular: *The play was very successful on Broadway.* □ *She has had a long and successful career in television.* **successfully** adverb: *The operation was successfully completed.*

succinct *adjective*
(of a comment or piece of writing) expressed clearly and using few words: *Keep your answers as succinct as possible.*
Word family succinctly adverb: *You put that very succinctly.* **succinctness** noun: *I like the clarity and succinctness of this definition.*

suitable *adjective*
acceptable or correct for a particular purpose, person, or situation: *The exercise-with-answer-key format makes the book suitable for self-study.* □ *I don't think he's a suitable partner for her.*
Usage suitable or **appropriate**? How *suitable* or *appropriate* someone or something is is a matter of judgement and it depends on what is acceptable to other people. The word *suitable* is used when something is correct for a particular purpose, but *appropriate* is only used about people or situations. In American English *suitable* is only used in formal or official language; in everyday spoken or written American English, *appropriate* or *right* is used.
Word family suitability noun: *the suitability of the property.* **suitably** adverb: *suitably qualified candidates.*

suite *noun*
a set of things belonging together, e.g. a set of computer programs with a uniform design and the ability to share data: *a suite of graphical environments and applications.* □ *The existing stakeholder pension will become part of the suite of new products.*

superlative *adjective*
of the highest quality or degree: *He is without doubt a superlative photographer.*
Usage In grammar, *superlative* is used to describe an adjective or adverb that expresses the highest or a very high degree of a quality, e.g. *bravest, fastest, most fiercely.*

Word family **superlatively** adverb: *He was superlatively fit.* **superlativeness** noun

supplement noun, verb

noun **1** something which completes or enhances something else when added to it: *The handout is a supplement to the official manual.* **2** a substance taken to remedy the deficiencies in a person's diet: *multivitamin supplements.* **3** a separate section, especially a colour magazine, added to a newspaper or periodical. **4** an additional charge payable for an extra service or facility: *The single room supplement is £5 per night.* □ verb to add an extra element or amount to: *She took the job to supplement her husband's income.*
Usage This word should not be confused with **complement**.
Word family **supplementary** adjective completing or enhancing something: *The centre's work was to be seen as supplementary to orthodox treatment and not a substitute for it.*

supply verb, noun

verb **1** to make something needed or wanted available to someone; to provide: *The farm supplies apples to cider makers.* □ *They struggled to supply the besieged island with aircraft.* **2** to be a source of something needed: *eat foods which supply a significant amount of dietary fibre.* **3** to be adequate to satisfy a requirement or demand: *The two reservoirs supply about 1% of the city's needs.* □ noun **1** a stock of a resource from which a person or place can be provided with the necessary amount: *There were fears that the drought would affect the town's water supply.* **2** the action of providing what is needed or wanted: *The deal involved the supply of forty fighter aircraft.*

support verb, noun

verb **1** to give assistance to, especially financially; to enable to function or act: *The government gives £2,500 million a year to support the activities of the voluntary sector.* **2** to approve and encourage: *The proposal was supported by many delegates.* **3** to suggest the truth of; to corroborate: *The studies support our findings.* **4** to give comfort and emotional help to: *I like to visit her to support her.* **5** to be actively interested in and concerned for the success of a particular sports team. **6** to produce enough food and water for; to be

capable of sustaining: *The land had lost its capacity to support life.* **7** to be capable of fulfilling a role adequately: *Tutors gain practical experience which helps them support their tutoring role.* **8** (of a computer or operating system) to allow the use or operation of a program, language, or device: *The new versions do not support the graphical user interface standard.* □ noun **1** material assistance: *He urged that military support be sent to protect humanitarian convoys.* **2** approval and encouragement: *The policies of reform enjoy widespread support.* **3** comfort and emotional help offered to someone in distress: *She's been through a bad time and needs our support.* **4** technical help given to the user of a computer or other product.
Word family **in support of 1** giving assistance to: *documents in support of my application.* **2** showing approval of: *The paper printed many letters in support of the government.* **3** attempting to promote or obtain: *a strike in support of an 8.5% pay rise.* **supporter** noun **1** a person who approves of and encourages someone or something, e.g. a public figure, a movement or party, or a policy: *Labour supporters.* **2** a person who is actively interested in and wishes success for a particular sports team. **supportive** adjective providing encouragement or emotional help: *The staff are extremely supportive of each other.* **supportively** adverb **supportiveness** noun

survey verb, noun

verb **1** to examine and give a general description of something: *This chapter briefly surveys the current state of European politics.* **2** to investigate the opinions or experience of a group of people by asking them questions: *95% of patients surveyed were satisfied with the health service.* **3** to investigate behaviour or opinions by questioning a group of people: *The investigator surveyed the attitudes and beliefs held by residents.* □ noun **1** a general study, examination, or description of someone or something: *they are carrying out a survey of small businesses in London.* □ *The author provides a survey of the relevant literature.* **2** an investigation of the opinions or experience of a group of people, based on a series of questions.

sustain verb

1 to make something continue for some time at the same level: *We were experiencing a* period of sustained economic growth. □ She managed to sustain everyone's interest until the end of her speech. □ His health will no longer enable him to sustain the heavy burdens of office. **2** to strengthen or support physically or mentally: This thought had sustained him throughout the years.

Usage **sustain** or **maintain**? In some cases you can use either word: to sustain/maintain a balance/a pretence/people's interests/life. The word sustain is used more to talk about keeping something at a higher than usual level for a long but not unlimited period: How long can this level of growth be sustained? The word maintain is used especially to talk about keeping something at its usual level for an unlimited period of time: They believe that the role of the state is to maintain the status quo, rather than to promote major economic and social change.

Word family **sustainability** noun **sustainably** adverb **sustainable** adjective **1** able to be maintained at a certain rate or level: sustainable economic growth. **2** (especially of development, exploitation, or agriculture) conserving an ecological balance by avoiding depletion of natural resources: sustainable development.

symbiosis noun

(formal) a mutually beneficial relationship between different people or groups: a perfect mother and daughter symbiosis. □ Western society's failure to recognize the symbiosis between population growth and environmental degradation.

Usage In biology, the word symbiosis refers to the interaction between two different organisms living in close physical association, typically to the advantage of both.

Word family **symbiotic** adjective: a symbiotic relationship between car distributors and dealers. **symbiotically** adverb: The fine art tradition today does not live symbiotically with design.

symbol noun

1 a thing that represents or stands for something else, especially a material object representing something abstract: The limousine was another symbol of his wealth and authority. **2** a mark or character used as a conventional representation of an object, function, or process; a shape or sign used to

represent something such as an organization, e.g. a red cross.

Usage **symbolize**, **embody**, or **represent**? See **embody**.

Word family **symbolic** adjective **1** serving as a symbol; involving the use of symbols or symbolism: a repeating design symbolic of eternity. □ the symbolic meaning of motifs and designs. **2** significant purely in terms of what is being represented or implied: The release of the dissident was an important symbolic gesture. □ The new regulations are largely symbolic (= they will not have any real effect). **symbolically** adverb: a symbolically significant gesture. **symbolize** verb to be a symbol of; to represent by means of symbols: The use of light and dark symbolizes good and evil. □ He came to symbolize his country's struggle for independence.

sympathy noun

1 feelings of pity and sorrow for someone else's misfortune: They had great sympathy for the flood victims. **2** understanding between people; common feeling: The special sympathy between the two boys was obvious to all. **3** (**sympathies**) support in the form of shared feelings or opinions: His sympathies lay with his constituents. **4** agreement with or approval of an opinion or aim; favourable attitude: I have some sympathy for this view.

Word family **in sympathy** relating harmoniously to something else; in keeping: repairs had to be in sympathy with the original structure. **sympathetic** adjective **1** feeling, showing, or expressing sympathy: He was sympathetic towards staff with family problems. **2** showing approval of or favour towards an idea or action: He was sympathetic to evolutionary ideas. **3** (of a structure) designed in a sensitive or fitting way: buildings that were sympathetic to their surroundings. **sympathetically** adverb: nod/smile sympathetically. **sympathize** verb **1** to feel or express sympathy: It is easy to understand and sympathize with his predicament. **2** to agree with a sentiment or opinion: They sympathize with critiques of traditional theory.

symphony noun

something regarded, usually favourably, as a composition of different elements: Autumn is a symphony of texture and pattern. □ The tulips bloomed in a brilliant symphony of colours.

S

Usage In music, a *symphony* is an elaborate composition for full orchestra, typically in four movements, at least one of which is traditionally in sonata form.
Word family **symphonic** *adjective*

synergy *noun*
the interaction or cooperation of two or more organizations, substances, or other agents to produce a combined effect greater than the sum of their separate effects: *the synergy between artist and record company.*
Usage The word *synergy* is sometimes popularly explained as 2+2 = 5.

synthesis *noun*
the combination of components or elements to form a connected whole: *the synthesis of intellect and emotion in his work.* □ *The ideology represented a synthesis of certain ideas.*
Word family **synthesize** *verb* to combine a number of things into a coherent whole:
Pupils should synthesize the data they have gathered.

system *noun*
1 a set of principles or procedures according to which something is done; a particular way of doing something, especially one that involves a planned and fixed series of actions that you follow each time: *This is a highly effective system for storing data.* □ *Once your systems are in place you can concentrate on the main focus of your business.* **2** orderliness; method: *There was no system at all in the company.* **3** a set of things working together as parts of a mechanism or an interconnecting network: *the state railway system.*
Word family **systematic** *adjective* done or acting according to a fixed plan or system; methodical: *a systematic search of the whole city.* **systematically** *adverb*: *The topic has never been systematically studied.*

S

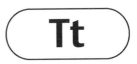

Tt

tackle *verb*

1 to make determined efforts to deal with a problem or difficult task: *Police have launched an initiative to tackle rising crime.* **2** to initiate discussion with someone about a disputed or sensitive issue: *A young man tackled him over why the council had spent money on a swimming pool.*

Usage As a noun the word *tackle* is used to refer to the equipment required for a task or sport: *fishing tackle.* You should take care when using this word, because in British vulgar slang *tackle* is a man's genitals.

tact *noun*

the ability to deal with people in difficult situations without upsetting or offending them: *Settling the dispute required great tact and diplomacy.* □ *She is not exactly known for her tact.*

Usage *tactful* or *diplomatic*? See **diplomatic**.

Usage Using *tact* often involves not saying particular things that you know will upset or offend a particular person (because, for example, of something that has happened to them). Someone who introduces subjects that will embarrass or offend a particular person can be considered *tactless*.

Word family **tactful** *adjective*: *That wasn't a very tactful thing to say!* **tactfully** *adverb*: *approach the subject as tactfully as possible.*

tactic *noun*

the particular method that you use to achieve something: *The manager discussed tactics with his team.* □ *Confrontation is not always the best tactic.* □ *This was just the latest in a series of delaying tactics.*

Usage *tactics* or *strategy*? See **strategy**.

Word family **tactical** *adjective* (of a person or their actions) showing skilful planning; aiming at an end beyond the immediate action: *In a tactical retreat, she moved into a hotel with her daughters.* **tactically** *adverb*

tailor *verb*

to make or adapt something for a particular purpose or person: *Special programmes of study are tailored to the needs of specific groups.* □ *Most travel agents are prepared to tailor travel arrangements to meet individual requirements.*

Word family **tailor-made** *adjective* made for someone or something in particular, and therefore very suitable: *We can offer you a tailor-made financial package to suit your needs.*

talent *noun*

natural ability or skill: *He possesses more talent than any other player.* □ *She displayed a talent for garden design.*

Usage *talent* or *gift*? *Talent* is used more often than *gift* in spoken English. It can also be used to talk about people's abilities in the arts, but it is commonly used to talk about business skills: *a talent for business/computing/ diplomacy/leadership/figures/governing/ management/organization. Gift* is often used in more literary contexts, especially to talk about people's ability in the arts, as well as in relationships and helping people: *a gift for drawing/painting/writing/drama/improvisation/ languages/music.* □ *a gift for friendship/ teaching/humour/calming people down/ bringing people together/healing.*

Usage *talented* or *gifted*? People who are *talented* are usually good at a particular thing such as music or sport. People who are *gifted* may be good at a particular thing or just very intelligent: *academically gifted. Gifted* is often used about children or young people because you do not need to have a lot of experience in something to be *gifted* at it.

Usage You should take care when using this word, as in informal contexts *talent* can mean 'people regarded as sexually attractive or as prospective sexual partners': *Most Saturday nights I have this urge to go on the hunt for new talent.*

Word family **talented** adjective having a natural ability to do something well, especially something connected with art, music, literature, drama, or sport: *We're looking for talented young designers to join our team.* □ *The kids at this school are all exceptionally talented in some way.*

tangible adjective

1 perceptible by touch: *The atmosphere of neglect and abandonment was almost tangible.* **2** clear and definite; real: *The emphasis is now on tangible results.*

Word family **tangibly** adverb: *What would be tangibly different with a new president?*

target noun, verb

noun a result that you try to achieve: *Set yourself targets that you can reasonably hope to achieve.* □ *We're aiming to meet a target date of April 2012.* □ *Write a plan that sets out your business goals and targets.* □ *The new sports complex is on target to open in June.* □ *Our target audience* (= the particular audience that the programme is aimed at) *is men aged between 18 and 35.* □ *What's the target market for this product?* □ *They exceeded their sales target.* □ *verb* to try to help or influence a particular group of people, especially by offering a product or service designed for them: *The booklet is targeted at people approaching retirement.* □ *We target our services towards specific groups of people.*

Usage **target**, **objective**, or **goal**? A *target* is usually officially recorded in some way, for example by an employer or by a government committee. It is often specific, and in the form of figures, such as a number of sales or exam passes, or a date. People often set their own *objectives*: these are things that they wish to achieve, often as part of a project or a talk they are giving. *Goals* are often long-term, and relate to people's life and career plans or the long-term plans of a company or organization.

task force noun

a group of people who are chosen to deal with a particular problem, usually by a government: *She is expected to lead a task force on health care reform.* □ *The government has set up a task force to monitor the implementation of the new recycling schemes.*

Usage Originally, a *task force* was an armed force organized for a special operation. You

should take care not to overuse this description merely to refer to the work of a committee.

tasteful adjective

showing good judgement as to quality, appearance, or appropriate behaviour: *The décor throughout the hotel is simple and tasteful.*

Word family **tastefully** adverb: *tastefully decorated/furnished.* **tastefulness** noun: *the importance of comfort and tastefulness.*

technique noun

1 skill or ability in a particular field: *He has excellent technique.* □ *an established athlete with a very good technique.* **2** a particular way of doing something, especially one that involves a special skill or that you need to learn and practise: *The artist combines different techniques in the same painting.* □ *You will learn various techniques for dealing with difficult customers.*

technology noun

1 the application of scientific knowledge for practical purposes, especially in industry: *advances in computer technology.* **2** machinery and equipment developed from such scientific knowledge: *The company has invested in the latest technology.*

Word family **technological** adjective of, relating to, or using technology: *the quickening pace of technological change.*

tempo noun

the rate or speed of motion or activity; pace: *They soon adapted to the slower tempo of life on the island.* □ *the tempo of life dictated by a heavy workload.*

Usage In music, *tempo* is the speed at which a passage of music is or should be played.

tenacious adjective

that does not give something up easily: *He paused, without releasing his tenacious grip.* □ *The party has kept its tenacious hold on power for more than twenty years.*

Usage **tenacity** or **determination**? *Determination* has a wider range of meaning than *tenacity*. People often show *determination* in the face of difficulty, danger, or suffering; it is often spoken of in the phrase *courage and determination.* People show *tenacity* in less important or serious situations that do not need courage, but do require people to keep trying if they are to succeed. **Usage** Words that combine with *tenacious* include *grip* and *hold* in both literal and figurative meanings, and *defence*. **Word family** *tenaciously* adverb: *Though seriously ill, he is still clinging tenaciously to life.* **tenacity** noun the determination to continue trying to do something: *They competed with skill and tenacity.*

tender *noun, verb*

noun a formal offer to carry out work or provide goods or a service for a particular price, in competition with other companies: *The local authority has invited tenders for the supply of school meals.* □ *Cleaning and laundry services have been put out to tender* (= companies have been asked to make offers to supply these services). □ *verb* **1** to offer goods or services as a tender: *Local firms were invited to tender for the building contracts.* **2** to offer or give something to someone: *He has tendered his resignation to the Prime Minister.*
Usage The verb *tender* is a more formal way of saying *offer* when you are talking about giving your resignation or apologies.

tentative *adjective*

1 not certain or fixed; provisional: *a tentative conclusion.* **2** done without confidence; hesitant: *He eventually tried a few tentative steps round his hospital room.*
Word family *tentatively* adverb: *The book is tentatively set for autumn publication.* **tentativeness** noun: *the tentativeness of this conclusion.*

test *noun, verb*

noun **1** a procedure intended to establish the quality, performance, or reliability of something, especially before it is put into widespread use: *No sparking was visible during the tests.* **2** an event or situation that shows how good, strong, etc. someone or something is: *This is the first serious test of the peace agreement.* □ *The local elections will be a good test of the government's popularity.* **3** a short written or spoken examination of a person's proficiency or knowledge: *a spelling test.* □ *verb* **1** to take measures to check the quality, performance, or reliability of something, especially before putting it into widespread use or practice: *This range has not*

been tested on animals. **2** to reveal how strong, able, etc. someone or something is: *Such behaviour would severely test any marriage.* **3** to give someone a short written or oral examination of their proficiency or knowledge; to judge or measure someone's proficiency or knowledge by means of such an examination: *All children are tested at eleven.*

thankful *adjective*

1 pleased and relieved: *They were thankful that the war was finally over.* □ *I was very thankful to be alive.* **2** expressing gratitude and relief: *an earnest and thankful prayer.*
Usage The word *thankfully* has been used for centuries to mean 'in a thankful manner': *She accepted the offer thankfully.* Since the 1960s it has also been used as a sentence adverb to mean 'fortunately': *Thankfully, we didn't have to wait.* Although this use has not attracted the same amount of attention as *hopefully*, it has been criticized for the same reasons. It is, however, far commoner now than the traditional use.
Word family *thankfully* adverb **1** used to express pleasure or relief at the situation or outcome that one is reporting; fortunately: *Thankfully, everything went smoothly.* **2** in a thankful manner: *She thankfully accepted the armchair she was offered.* **thankfulness** noun

theme *noun, verb*

noun the main idea in a talk, piece of writing, or work of art: *North American literature is the main theme of this year's festival.* □ *Several familiar themes emerged from the discussion.* □ *The stories are all variations on the theme of unhappy marriage.* □ *verb* to give a particular theme or setting to a leisure venue, event, etc.: *The amusement park will be themed as a Caribbean pirate stronghold.*
Usage In music, a *theme* is a prominent or frequently recurring melody or group of notes in a composition. The word *theme* is also used to refer to a setting given to a leisure venue or activity: *a family fun park with a western theme*, and to a restaurant or pub in which the décor and the food and drink served are intended to suggest a country, historical period, or culture: *an Irish theme pub.* □ *American themed restaurants.*
Word family *thematic* adjective: *a thematic study of the Bible.* **themed** adjective: *Independence Day was celebrated with special themed menus.*

theoretical *adjective*

1 concerned with the ideas and principles on which a subject is based rather than with practice or experiments: *We aim to provide you with both theoretical and practical knowledge of your subject.* □ *The emphasis of his lectures is on theoretical physics.* **2** that could possibly exist, happen, or be true, although this is unlikely: *It's a theoretical possibility.*

Usage The opposite of *theoretical* is *practical* or *applied*.

Word family theoretically *adverb*: *It is theoretically possible for him to overrule their decision, but highly unlikely.* □ *Theoretically, education is free in this country.*

thorough *adjective*

1 doing things very carefully and with great attention to detail: *He was determined to be thorough in his research.* **2** including everything and with great attention to detail: *You will need a thorough understanding of the subject.* □ *The police carried out a thorough investigation.*

Usage The word *thorough* is used especially to describe someone's knowledge or understanding or the way they carry out a task.

Word family thoroughly *adverb*: *The work had not been done very thoroughly.*

thoughtful *adjective*

1 absorbed in or involving thought: *brows drawn together in thoughtful consideration.* **2** showing careful consideration or attention: *Her work is thoughtful and provocative.* **3** showing consideration for the needs of other people: *He was attentive and thoughtful.*

Word family thoughtfully *adverb*: *answer/reply thoughtfully.* **thoughtfulness** *noun*

thought-provoking *adjective*

stimulating careful consideration or attention: *thought-provoking questions.* □ *a thought-provoking film.*

Word family thought-provokingly *adverb*

thrilling *adjective*

exciting and enjoyable: *Don't miss next week's thrilling episode.* □ *The game had a thrilling finale, with three goals scored in the last five minutes.* □ *a thrilling adventure.*

Usage thrilling, exciting, or **exhilarating**? See **exciting.**

Word family thrillingly *adverb*: *thrillingly subjective.*

thrive *verb*

to develop quickly and be successful; grow well and be strong, healthy, and happy: *He's clearly thriving in his new job.* □ *New businesses thrive in this area.* □ *These animals rarely thrive in captivity.* □ *She seems to thrive on stress* (= enjoy it).

Usage The word *thrive* can be used to talk about people, businesses, places, plants, or animals. It is used especially to talk about the conditions in which a person, animal, or plant can become strong, healthy, or happy. Words that combine with *thriving* in business contexts include *company, business, industry, trade, market, economy, centre, town,* and *port.*

Word family thriving *adjective* (of a business or area) economically strong and successful: *Twenty years ago London Road was a thriving commercial centre thronged with shoppers.*

tidy *adjective*

1 keeping things ordered and arranged in the right place, or liking to keep things like this: *I'm not a very tidy person.* □ *Even young children can be taught tidy habits.* **2** (of a place) arranged neatly and with everything in order: *Someone needs to keep the place tidy.* □ *The room was clean and tidy.*

Usage tidy, neat, or **orderly**? See **neat.**

Word family tidily *adverb*: *Tubes of paint were set out tidily.*

timely *adjective*

done or occurring at a favourable or useful time; opportune: *a timely warning.* □ *This has been a timely reminder.*

Usage timely, opportune, or **auspicious**? See **opportune.**

tone *noun, verb*

noun the general character and attitude of something such as a piece of writing or the atmosphere of an event: *The overall tone of the book is gently nostalgic.* □ *The article is moderate in tone and presented both sides of the case.* □ *She set the tone for the meeting with a firm statement of company policy.* □ *verb* (**tone down**) to make a speech or opinion less extreme or offensive: *The language of the article will have to be toned down for the mass market.*

trace *verb, noun*

verb **1** to find or discover by investigation: *Police are trying to trace a white van seen in the area.* **2** to find or describe the origin or development of: *Bob's book traces his flying career with the RAF.* **3** to give an outline of: *The article traces some of the connections between education, qualifications, and the labour market.* □ *noun* **1** a mark, object, or other indication of the existence or passing of something: *remove all traces of the old adhesive.* □ *The aircraft disappeared without trace.* **2** a very small quantity, especially one too small to be accurately measured: *His body contained traces of amphetamines.* **3** a slight indication or barely discernible hint of something: *just a trace of a smile.*

track record *noun*

all the past achievements, successes, or failures of a person or organization: *As a company we have a proven track record in catering.* □ *Britain has a poor track record in foreign-language teaching.* □ *He has an excellent track record as an author.*
Usage You should take care not to overuse this expression.

tradition *noun*

1 a long-established custom or belief that has been passed on: *Japan's unique cultural traditions.* **2** an artistic or literary method or style established by an artist, writer, or movement, and subsequently followed by others: *visionary works in the tradition of William Blake.* **3** the transmission of customs or beliefs from generation to generation, or the fact of being passed on in this way: *Members of different castes have by tradition been associated with specific occupations.*
Word family **traditional** *adjective* **1** existing in or as a part of a tradition; long established: *the traditional festivities of the church year.* **2** produced, done, or used in accordance with tradition: *a traditional fish soup.* **3** habitually done, used, or found: *the traditional drinks in the clubhouse.* **traditionally** *adverb*

train *verb*

1 to teach a person or animal the skills for a particular job or activity; to be taught these skills: *All members of the team have been trained in first aid.* □ *He trained as a teacher before becoming an actor.* □ *They train dogs to sniff out drugs.* **2** to prepare yourself for a

particular activity, especially a sport, by doing a lot of exercise; to prepare someone in this way: *We watched the athletes training for the Olympics.* □ *I train in the gym for two hours a day.* □ *He trains the Olympic team.*
Usage **train** or **coach**? See **coach**.
Usage The word *trainee* is usually used to talk about someone who is learning to do a job which requires a higher level of education than that required for an apprentice. In British English it is frequently used before another noun: *a trainee teacher/pilot/nurse/journalist.*
Word family **trainee** *noun* a person who is being taught how to do a particular job: *She joined the company as a management trainee.* **trainer** *noun* a person who trains someone in a particular job, skill, or sport: *Her trainer was on hand to give some advice.* □ *There was a shortage of teacher trainers* (= people who train teachers). □ *Only rich people can afford a personal trainer* (= someone who helps an individual to exercise and get fit). **training** *noun* the process of preparing to take part in a sport, especially a sports competition, by doing physical exercise: *Phillips is in serious training for the Olympics.* □ *She did six months' hard training before the marathon.*

tranquil *adjective*

quiet and peaceful in a way that makes you feel relaxed: *It is a tranquil place of quiet beauty.*
Usage In American English the word *tranquillity* is usually spelt *tranquility.*
Word family **tranquillity** *noun* the state of being without noise, violence, or anxiety: *It is the perfect place to relax in an atmosphere of peace and tranquillity.*

transferable *adjective*

(of skills) able to be used in different jobs: *Doing voluntary work meant I gained so many transferable skills, like teamwork and communication skills.*
Word family **transferability** *noun*

transparent *adjective*

1 easy to perceive or detect: *The residents will see through any transparent attempt to buy their votes.* □ *The meaning of the poem is by no means transparent.* **2** having thoughts, feelings, or motives that are easily perceived; open: *Parliament should render government transparent.* □ *You'd be no good at poker - you're too transparent.* **3** (of a material or article)

allowing light to pass through so that objects behind can be distinctly seen: *transparent blue water*. □ *fine transparent fabrics*.
Word family **transparency** noun: *the transparency of business transactions*. **transparently** adverb: *a transparently feeble argument*.

treasure *noun, verb*
noun a very valuable object: *She set out to look at the art treasures*. □ verb to value highly: *The island is treasured by walkers and conservationists*.
Word family **treasured** adjective: *His library was his most treasured possession*.

treat *verb*
1 to behave towards or deal with in a certain way: *She had been brutally treated*. □ *He treated her with courtesy*. 2 (**treat as**) to regard something as being of a specified nature with implications for your actions concerning it: *The names are being treated as classified information*. 3 to present or discuss a subject: *The lectures show a striking variation in the level at which subjects are treated*.
Word family **treatment** noun 1 a way of behaving towards someone or dealing with something: *equal treatment for women and men*. 2 the presentation or discussion of a subject: *her treatment of the topic*.

tremendous *adjective*
very great in amount, scale, or intensity: *Penny put in a tremendous amount of time*. □ *There was a tremendous explosion*.
Usage The word *tremendous* also means 'extremely good or impressive; excellent': *The crew did a tremendous job*.
Word family **tremendously** adverb: *tremendously exciting*.

trenchant *adjective*
vigorous or incisive in expression or style: *The White Paper makes trenchant criticisms of health authorities*.
Word family **trenchantly** adverb: *legitimize the war they had so trenchantly opposed*.

trend *noun*
1 a general direction in which something is developing or changing: *an upward trend in sales and profit margins*. □ *social trends*. □ *a growing trend towards earlier retirement*. 2 a fashion: *the latest trends in modern dance*.

Word family **trendsetter** noun a person who leads the way in fashion or ideas: *a trendsetter in technology*. **trendsetting** adjective: *trendsetting bars/shops/restaurants*. **trendy** adjective (*informal*) very fashionable or up to date in style or influence: *I enjoyed being able to go out and buy trendy clothes*.

triumph *noun, verb*
noun 1 a great success, victory, or achievement: *a garden built to celebrate Napoleon's many triumphs*. 2 the state of being victorious or successful: *The team returned home in triumph*. 3 joy or satisfaction resulting from a success or victory: '*Here it is!*' *Helen's voice rose in triumph*. 4 a highly successful example of something: *The marriage had been a triumph of togetherness*. □ verb 1 to achieve a victory; to be successful: *They had no chance of triumphing over the Nationalists*. 2 to rejoice or exult at a victory or success: *She stopped triumphing over his failure*.
Word family **triumphant** adjective 1 having won a battle or contest; successful or victorious: *two of their triumphant Cup team*. 2 feeling or expressing jubilation after having won a victory or mastered a difficulty: *He couldn't suppress a triumphant smile*. **triumphantly** adverb

trusted *adjective*
that a person or people feel they can rely on: *As time went on he became a trusted adviser to the king*. □ *the world's most trusted dictionaries*.
Word family **trustworthy** adjective that you can rely on to be good, honest, and sincere: *Women were seen as more trustworthy and harder-working*.

turning point *noun*
a time or event when an important change takes place, usually with the result that a situation improves: *The promotion marked a turning point in her career*. □ *reach a significant turning point*.

typify *verb*
to be a typical example of something; to be a typical feature of something: *These are clothes that typify the 1960s*. □ *There's a new style of politician, typified by the Prime Minister*.
Usage *typify* or *epitomize*? See **epitome**. See also **distinctive**.

Uu

ubiquitous *adjective*
seeming to be everywhere or in several places at the same time: *the ubiquitous mobile phone.* □ *His ubiquitous influence was felt by all the family.* □ *The ubiquitous portraits of the president usually showed him in military uniform.*
Usage You should take care when using this word as it sometimes has humorous overtones.

ultimate *adjective, noun*
adjective **1** being the best or most extreme example of its kind: *the ultimate accolade.* **2** basic or fundamental: *The ultimate constituents of anything that exists are atoms.* □ *noun* (**the ultimate**) the best achievable or imaginable of its kind: *the ultimate in decorative luxury.*

unanimous *adjective*
completely agreeing about something: *a unanimous vote/decision/verdict.*
Word family **unanimity** *noun*: *We won't all agree, but we need to achieve a degree of unanimity.* **unanimously** *adverb*: *The motion was passed unanimously.*

unbiased *adjective*
fair and not influenced by your own or someone else's opinions or wishes: *We'd like an unbiased opinion, if possible.*
Usage A variant spelling is *unbiassed.*

uncluttered *adjective*
not having or impeded by too many or any unnecessary objects, details, or elements: *The rooms were plain and uncluttered.* □ *The font has a simple uncluttered feel to it.*

uncontested *adjective*
without any opposition or argument: *He was officially elected mayor in an uncontested election.* □ *These claims have not gone uncontested* (= they have been contested).

underline *verb*
to emphasize or show that something is important: *The report underlines the importance of pre-school education.* □ *Her question only underlined how little she understood him.*
Usage A *report* or *statement* most often underlines a *fact*, *need*, or *point*. A person might *underline* their *determination* or *commitment* to do something.

underlying *adjective*
important in a situation but not always easily noticed or stated clearly: *The underlying assumption is that the amount of money available is limited.* □ *Unemployment may be an underlying cause of the rising crime rate.*
Usage Words that typically combine with *underlying* include *cause*, *assumption*, *reason*, *motive*, *trend*, *theme*, *problem*, *reality*, and *aim.*

underpin *verb*
to support, justify, or form the basis for: *The theme of honour underpins his two books.*
Word family **underpinning** *noun* a set of ideas, motives, or devices that justify or form the basis for something: *the theoretical underpinning for free-market economies.*

understand *verb*
1 to perceive the intended meaning of words, a language, or a speaker: *He didn't understand a word I said.* □ *He could usually make himself understood.* **2** to perceive the significance, explanation, or cause of: *She didn't really understand the situation.* **3** to be sympathetically or knowledgeably aware of the character or nature of: *Picasso understood colour.* □ *I understand how you feel.* **4** to interpret or view in a particular way: *As the term is usually understood, legislation refers to regulations and directives.* **5** to infer something from information received (often used as a polite formula in conversation): *As I understood it, she was flying back to the States*

tomorrow. **6** (often **be understood**) to assume to be the case; to take for granted: *He liked to make a bit on the side, that was understood.*
Word family **understandable** *adjective* **1** able to be understood: *Though his accent was strange, the words were perfectly understandable.* **2** to be expected; natural, reasonable, or forgivable: *Such fears are understandable.* □ *It is understandable that mistakes occur sometimes.* **understandably** *adverb*: *Understandably, Richard did not believe me.* **understanding** *noun* **1** the ability to understand something; comprehension: *foreign visitors with little understanding of English.* **2** the power of abstract thought; intellect: *a child of sufficient intelligence and understanding.* **3** an individual's perception or judgement of a situation: *My understanding was that he would try to find a new supplier.* **4** sympathetic awareness or tolerance: *a problem which needs to be handled with understanding.* **5** an informal or unspoken agreement or arrangement: *He and I have an understanding.* □ *He had only been allowed to come on the understanding that he would be on his best behaviour.* **understanding** *adjective* sympathetically aware of other people's feelings; tolerant and forgiving: *People expect their doctor to be understanding.*

understated *adjective*
presented or expressed in a subtle and effective way: *understated elegance.*
Word family **understatement** *noun* the presentation of something as being smaller or less good or important than it really is: *a master of English understatement.* □ *To say I am delighted is an understatement.*

undisputed *adjective*
that cannot be questioned or proved to be false; that everyone accepts or recognizes to be true: *She began by laying out the undisputed facts of the case.* □ *The film is an undisputed masterpiece of the 20th century.*

undoubted *adjective*
used to emphasize that something definitely exists or is true: *She has an undoubted talent as an organizer.* □ *The event was an undoubted success.*
Word family **undoubtedly** *adverb*: *There is undoubtedly a great deal of truth in what he says.*

unequivocal *adjective*
expressing your opinion or intention very clearly and firmly: *She gave a typically unequivocal answer.* □ *The reply was an unequivocal 'no'.*
Usage An *unequivocal* statement has only one clear or definite meaning and cannot be understood in more than one way.
Word family **unequivocally** *adverb*: *He stated unequivocally that he knew nothing about the document.*

unflagging *adjective*
tireless; persistent: *His apparently unflagging enthusiasm impressed her.* □ *an unflagging commitment to the ideals of peace.*
Word family **unflaggingly** *adverb*: *unflaggingly courteous/loyal/supportive.*

unflinching *adjective*
not showing fear or hesitation in the face of danger or difficulty: *He has shown unflinching determination throughout the campaign.*
Word family **unflinchingly** *adverb*: *glare unflinchingly.*

unforgettable *adjective*
impossible to forget; very memorable: *A visit to Morocco is a truly unforgettable experience.*
Word family **unforgettably** *adverb*: *have an unforgettably powerful feeling.*

unify *verb*
to join the parts of a country, region, or system so that they form a single unit or work together well; join the people of a country, region, or organization together so that they have the same aims and work together well: *What we need is a unified transport system.* □ *The new leader hopes to unify the party.*
Usage **unify** or **unite**? Both of these words can be used to talk about a group or area into which individuals are brought together: *to unify/unite the country/the party/Europe. Unite* but not *unify* can be used to talk about the individuals who are brought together: *to unite two political parties/the two Germanies/the people. Unify* not *unite* can be used to talk about joining together the parts of a system: *to unify the tax/transport system.*
Word family **unification** *noun*: *the unification of Germany.* **unifying** *adjective*: *a unifying factor/force/principle/theme.*

unique *adjective*
1 being the only one of its kind; belonging to or connected with only one particular person, place, or thing: *Every human being has a unique fingerprint that does not change over time.* □ *Each item has a unique 6-digit code.* □ *Her lawyer said the case was unique in French law.* □ *The pattern of stripes is unique to each individual animal.* **2** very special in a way that makes someone or something different from all other people or things of the same type: *The museum is of unique historical importance.* □ *I have had a unique opportunity to observe the problems faced by the police in this city.*
Usage Strictly speaking, since the main meaning of *unique* is 'being the only one of its kind', it is impossible to use adverbs with it that modify its meaning, such as *really* or *quite*. However, *unique* has a less precise sense in addition to its main meaning, 'very special or unusual': *a really unique opportunity.* Here, *unique* does not relate to an absolute state that cannot be modified, and so the use of *really* and similar adverbs is acceptable.
Word family **uniquely** adverb: *Some of the regulations apply uniquely to the 16–19 age group.* □ *He was a uniquely gifted teacher.*
uniqueness noun the quality in a person or thing of being the only one of their kind and different from anyone or anything else: *The author stresses the uniqueness of the individual.*

unite *verb*
to combine different qualities to form something new and complete; to join the parts of a country so that they form a single unit; to join people so that they have the same aims: *She unites keen business skills with a charming personality.* □ *His aim was to unite Italy.* □ *A special bond unites our two countries.* □ *The two countries united in 1887.*
Usage **unite** or **unify**? See **unify**.
Word family **unite** united adjective: *We need to become a united team.* □ *present a united front.*

unity *noun*
1 the state of being in agreement and working together; the state of being joined together as one: *European unity* □ *a plea for unity within the party.* **2** (in art etc.) the state of looking or being complete in a natural and pleasant way: *The design lacks unity.* **3** (*formal*) a single thing that may consist of a number of

different parts: *If society is to exist as a unity, its members must have shared values.*

universal *adjective*
done by or involving all the people in the world or in a particular group: *A representative assembly is a near universal feature of modern democracies.* □ *Agreement on this issue is almost universal.* □ *The party wanted to introduce a universal health care system.*
Word family **universally** adverb: *The document is now universally acknowledged as a forgery.*

unleash *verb*
to suddenly let a strong force, emotion, etc. be felt or have an effect; to release from a restraint: *The failure of the talks could unleash more fighting.* □ *The government's proposals unleashed a storm of protest in the press.* □ *The abundance of natural resources unleashed the country's creativity.*

unparalleled *adjective*
having no parallel or equal; exceptional: *The sudden rise in unemployment is unparalleled in the post-war period.* □ *an unparalleled opportunity to change society.*

unrepeatable *adjective*
not able to be done or made again: *an unrepeatable opportunity/event/offer/moment.*
Usage The word *unrepeatable* also means 'too offensive or shocking to be said again': *mutter a lot of unrepeatable words.*

unrivalled *adjective*
better than everyone or everything of the same type: *the television channel's coverage of foreign news is unrivalled.*
Usage In American English, this word is spelt *unrivaled.*

unspoilt *adjective*
(of countryside) beautiful because it has not been changed or built on: *It's a country of stunning landscape and unspoilt beaches.*

unusual *adjective*
1 remarkable or interesting because different from or better than others: *a man of unusual talent.* □ *The conference has generated an unusual degree of interest.* **2** not habitually or commonly occurring or done: *The government has taken the unusual step of calling home its ambassador.*

u

Word family *unusually* adverb: *Unusually for a city hotel, it is located near a lovely garden.* □ *an unusually talented designer.* *unusualness* noun

update *verb, noun*

verb **1** to make something more modern or up to date: *Security measures are continually updated and improved.* **2** to give someone the latest information about something: *The reporter promised to keep the viewers updated.* □ *noun* an act of bringing something or someone up to date; an updated version of something: *an update on recently published crime figures.*

Usage As a verb, the stress is on the second syllable: up-**dayt**; as a noun, the stress is on the first syllable: **up**-dayt.

Word family *updated* adjective: *an updated list of subscribers.*

upgrade *verb, noun*

verb to raise to a higher standard, in particular improve equipment or machinery by adding or replacing components: *to upgrade the facilities.* □ *noun* **1** an act of upgrading something. **2** an improved or more modern version of something, especially a piece of computing equipment.

Word family *upgraded* adjective: *upgraded software.*

uplifted *adjective*

feeling happier or more hopeful: *Although it is an emotional play, you leave the theatre feeling strangely uplifted.*

Word family *uplifting* adjective making you feel happier or more hopeful: *It's a gloriously funny, uplifting comedy.* □ *an uplifting tune.*

urgent *adjective*

needing to be dealt with immediately: *The situation calls for urgent action.* □ *The law is in urgent need of reform.*

Word family *urgency* noun: *This is a matter of some urgency.* □ *The attack added a new urgency to the peace talks.* *urgently* adverb: *New equipment is urgently needed.*

utopian *adjective, noun*

adjective modelled on or aiming for a state in which everything is perfect; idealistic: *utopian dreams/fantasies.* □ *The feminist ideology, framework, and utopian aspirations all have their origin in the writings of Marx and Engels.* □ *noun* an idealistic reformer.

Usage *Utopia* is an imagined place or state of things in which everything is perfect. The word was first used in the book *Utopia* (1516) by Sir Thomas More.

Word family *utopianism* noun: *youthful utopianism.*

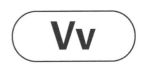

Vv

valid *adjective*
1 that is legally or officially acceptable: *a valid passport.* □ *a bus pass valid for one month.* □ *They have a valid claim to compensation.* **2** based on what is logical or true: *She had valid reasons for not supporting the proposals.* □ *The point you make is perfectly valid.* **3** (*computing*) that is accepted by the system: *a valid password.*
Word family validity *noun* **1** the state of being legally or officially acceptable: *The period of validity of the agreement has expired.* **2** the state of being logical and true: *We had doubts about the validity of their argument.* **validly** *adverb*: *The contract had been validly drawn up.*

validate *verb*
1 to prove that something is true: *to validate a theory.* **2** to make something legally valid: *to validate a contract.* **3** to state officially that something is useful and of an acceptable standard: *check that their courses have been validated by a reputable organization.*
Word family validation *noun*: *product validation.*

valuable *adjective*
1 very useful or important: *a valuable experience.* □ *The book provides valuable information on recent trends.* **2** worth a lot of money: *valuable antiques.* □ *Luckily, nothing valuable was stolen.* □ *The thieves took three pieces of valuable jewellery.*
Usage *Valuables* are things that are worth a lot of money, especially small personal things such as jewellery or cameras.

value *noun, verb*
noun **1** the amount of money that something is worth. **2** the importance or worth of something: *He realized the value of education.* **3** (**values**) beliefs about what is right and wrong and what is important: *moral values.* □ *a return to traditional values in education,* such as firm discipline. □ *The young have a completely different set of values and expectations.* □ *verb* **1** to estimate the value of something: *The property has been valued at over £2 million.* **2** to consider to be important or worthwhile: *She had come to value her privacy.*
Word family value-added *adjective* (of goods) having features added to a basic line or model for which the buyer is prepared to pay extra: *value-added digital technology.*

vantage point *noun*
a position from which you watch something; a point in time or a situation from which you consider something, especially the past: *The café was a good vantage point for watching the world go by.* □ *From the vantage point of the present, the war seems to have achieved nothing.*

varied *adjective*
of many different kinds; consisting of things of many different kinds: *The opportunities the job offers are many and varied.* □ *They stock a wide and varied selection of cheeses.* □ *a long and varied career.*

variety *noun*
1 several different types of a particular thing: *There is a wide variety of patterns to choose from.* □ *He resigned for a variety of reasons.* □ *This tool can be used in a variety of ways.* □ *I was impressed by the variety of dishes on offer.* **2** a type of a thing, for example a plant or language, that is different from the others in the same general group: *Apples come in a great many varieties.* □ *The variety of English that they speak is closer to American than British.* □ *They stock over 200 varieties of cheese.*
Usage *variety* or *range*? See **range**.

vehement *adjective*
showing strong feeling; forceful, passionate, or intense: *Her voice was low but vehement.* □ *vehement criticism.*

Usage The word *vehement* is often used in negative associations: *vehement opposition/denial/protest/criticism/attack*, but not always: *a vehement supporter/response*.

Word family **vehemence** noun: *surprised at the vehemence of the reaction*. **vehemently** adverb: *vehemently opposed to the attack*.

venture *noun, verb*

noun **1** a business enterprise involving considerable risk: *prospective business ventures*. **2** a risky or daring journey or undertaking: *pioneering ventures into little-known waters*. □ *verb* **1** to dare to do something or go somewhere that may be dangerous or unpleasant: *She ventured out into the blizzard*. **2** to dare to do or say something that may be considered audacious (often used as a polite expression of hesitation or apology): *May I venture to add a few comments?* □ *I ventured to write to her.* □ *He ventured the opinion that Smith was now dangerously insane.* **3** to expose to the risk of loss: *His fortune is ventured in an expedition over which he has no control.*

Word family **venture capital** noun capital invested in a project in which there is a substantial element of risk, typically a new or expanding business. **venture capitalist** noun

verify *verb*

to make sure or demonstrate that something is true, accurate, or justified: *His conclusions have been verified by later experiments.* □ *Can you verify that the guns are licensed?* Word family **verifiable** adjective: *That's just your opinion, not a verifiable fact.* **verifiably** adverb: *call upon the country to completely, irreversibly, and verifiably abandon its nuclear arms programme.* **verification** noun: *the verification of official documents.*

versatile *adjective*

1 (of a person) able to do many different things: *He's a versatile actor who has played a wide variety of parts.* **2** (of a thing) having many different uses: *Eggs are easy to cook and are an extremely versatile food.* Word family **versatility** noun: *the versatility of the Internet.*

veteran *noun, adjective*

noun a person who has had long experience in a particular field: *a veteran of the human-rights movement.* □ *adjective* having long experience in a particular field: *a veteran political reporter.*

Usage The word *veteran* is used to refer to a person who has had long experience of military service (*a veteran of two world wars*) or an ex-serviceman or -servicewoman.

Word family **veteran car** noun an old style or model of car, specifically one made before 1916, or (strictly) before 1905. Compare **vintage car**.

viable *adjective*

that can be done; that is likely to be successful and is therefore worth considering or supporting: *There is no viable alternative.* □ *If there was any delay then the rescue plan would cease to be viable.*

Usage A company, plan, or project that is *commercially/economically/financially viable* is capable of producing a profit.

Word family **viability** noun: *assess the viability of the business.* **viably** adverb: *achieve a viably sustainable social structure.*

vibrant *adjective*

1 full of life and excitement: *a vibrant cosmopolitan city.* □ *Thailand is at its most vibrant during the New Year celebrations.* **2** (of colours) bright and strong: *The room was decorated in vibrant blues and greens.*

Usage **vibrant** or **vivid**? Vivid emphasizes how bright a colour is; *vibrant* suggests a more lively and exciting colour or combination of colours.

Usage The word *vibrant* is often used in tourist literature to describe busy cities where there are many different types of people and commercial activities. It also suggests that there is a lot of activity at night, with bright lights and an exciting atmosphere.

Word family **vibrancy** noun: *the vibrancy of the city's restaurant scene.* **vibrantly** adverb: *vibrantly coloured hair.*

victory *noun*

success in a game, competition, election, argument, or war: *The team are celebrating a 3–2 victory over Poland.* □ *Labour swept to victory in the 1997 election.*

Usage A *moral victory* is a situation in which your ideas or principles are proved to be right and fair, even though you may not have succeeded as far as practical results are concerned: *In spite of the result, we felt we had won a moral victory.*

Word family **victorious** adjective having won a victory, for example in a battle, election, or sport; ending in victory: *The victorious army entered the city.* □ *Canada was victorious over Australia at the start of the World Championships.* **victoriously** *adverb*

vigilant *adjective*
keeping careful watch for possible danger or difficulties: *The burglar was spotted by vigilant neighbours.*
Word family **vigilance** *noun*: *Preventing medication errors requires constant vigilance.* □ *heighten/increase/maintain vigilance.* **vigilantly** *adverb*

vigorous *adjective*
(of a person or activity) showing great energy and determination: *They conducted a vigorous campaign against tax fraud.* □ *a vigorous opponent/supporter/campaigner.* □ *Take vigorous exercise for several hours a week.*
Word family **vigorously** *adverb*: *She shook her head vigorously.* □ *The accusation was vigorously denied.*

vintage *noun, adjective*
noun denoting something of high quality, especially something from the past or characteristic of the best period of a person's work: *a vintage Sherlock Holmes adventure.* □ *Tonight's concert is vintage Mozart.* □ *adjective* of, relating to, or denoting wine of high quality: *vintage claret.*
Usage The adjectival use of the word *vintage* derives from its meanings referring to wine, especially of a high quality: the year or place in which wine was produced and a wine made from the crop of a single specified district in a particular year.
Word family **vintage car** *noun* an old style or model of car, specifically one made between 1917 and 1930. Compare **veteran car.**

visible *adjective*
that can be seen; that is obvious enough to be noticed: *The house is clearly visible from the beach.* □ *Most stars are not visible to the naked eye.* □ *He showed no visible sign of emotion.*
Word family **visibly** *adverb*: *He was visibly shocked.*

vision *noun*
1 the ability to see: *within my field of vision.* **2** the ability to think about the future with imagination or wisdom: *The organization has lost its vision and direction.* □ *a leader with great vision.* **3** an experience of imagining

something, or of seeing someone or something in a dream or trance: *a prophetic vision.* □ *I had visions of us getting lost.*
Word family **visionary** *adjective* thinking about the future with imagination or wisdom: *a visionary leader.* **visionary** *noun* a person with imaginative and original ideas about the future: *The company needs visionaries to see opportunities.*

vista *noun*
1 a pleasing view: *There's a marvellous vista from the hotel balcony.* **2** an imagined future event or situation: *Vistas of freedom seemed to open ahead of him.*

visual *adjective, noun*
adjective relating to seeing or sight: *The child has visual defects.* □ *Many cheap car alarms have no visual indication that they are in operation.* □ *noun* a picture, piece of film, or display used to illustrate or accompany something.
Usage **visualize** or **imagine**? See **imagine.**
Word family **visualize** *verb* to form an image of someone or something in the mind: *Try to visualize yourself walking into the interview calmly and confidently.* **visually** *adverb*: *visually impaired.* □ *visually interesting.*

vital *adjective*
essential: *Bean sprouts contain many of the vitamins that are vital for health.* □ *Good financial accounts are vital to the success of any enterprise.* □ *It is vital that you keep accurate records when you are self-employed.* □ *The police play a vital role in our society.*
Usage **vital** or **essential**? There is no real difference in meaning between these words and they can be used with the same range of nouns and structures. However, there can be a slight difference in tone. *Vital* is often used when there is some anxiety felt about something, or a need to persuade someone that a fact or opinion is true, right, or important. *Essential* is used to state a fact or opinion with authority. *Vital* is less often used in negative statements: *It was vital to show that he was not afraid.*

vitality *noun*
(in a person, place, or work of art) energy and enthusiasm: *She is bursting with vitality and new ideas.* □ *The music has a wonderful freshness and vitality.* □ *The project will provide*

V

jobs and help to restore economic vitality to the region.

vivacious *adjective*

having a lively, attractive character or personality: *He had three pretty, vivacious daughters.* □ *the vivacious beauty of cyberspace.*
Usage When referring to people, the word *vivacious* usually describes a girl or woman.
Word family **vivaciously** adverb: *a vivaciously atmospheric watercolour.* **vivacity** noun: *He was charmed by her beauty and vivacity.*

vivid *adjective*

1 producing powerful feelings or strong, clear images in the mind: *Memories of that evening were still vivid.* □ *a vivid description.* 2 (of colours) intensely bright and strong: *His eyes were a vivid green.*
Usage **vivid** or **vibrant**? See **vibrant**.
Word family **vividly** adverb: *I can still vividly recall his words.* **vividness** noun: *the vividness of the imagery.*

vocation *noun*

1 a kind of work or way of life that you strongly believe is particularly suitable for you, especially one that involves helping other people; a belief in this: *Nursing is not just a job - it's a vocation.* □ *She seems to have a*

vocation for healing. 2 a person's employment or main occupation, especially regarded as particularly worthy and requiring great dedication: *her vocation as a poet.*
Word family **vocational** adjective 1 of or relating to an occupation or employment: *They supervised prisoners in vocational activities.* 2 (of education or training) directed at a particular occupation and its skills.

vogue *noun, adjective*

noun a fashion for something: *the vogue for child-centred education.* □ *Black is in vogue again this winter.* □ adjective popular; fashionable: *'Citizenship' was to be the government's vogue word.*
Word family **voguish** adjective: *the added cachet of a voguish name.*

voyage *noun*

a long journey, especially by sea or in space: *The spacecraft began its voyage to Mars.* □ *The Titanic sank on its maiden voyage* (= its first voyage)*.* □ *Writing a biography is a voyage of discovery.*
Usage In the phrase *bon voyage*, the word *voyage*, used to express good wishes to someone about to set off on a long journey, is pronounced voy-**ahzh**.

warrant *noun, verb*

noun **1** a document issued by a legal or government official authorizing the police or some other body to make an arrest, search premises, or carry out some other action relating to the administration of justice: *Magistrates issued a warrant for his arrest.* □ *an extradition warrant.* **2** a document that entitles the holder to receive goods, money, or services: *We'll issue you with a travel warrant.* **3** justification or authority for an action, belief, or feeling: *There is no warrant for this assumption.* □ *verb* **1** to justify or necessitate a certain course of action: *There is not enough new evidence to warrant a reference to the Court of Appeal.* **2** to officially affirm or guarantee: *The vendor warrants the accuracy of the report.*
Usage See also **guarantee**.
Word family **warranty** *noun* a written guarantee, issued to the purchaser of an article by its manufacturer, promising to repair or replace it if necessary within a specified period of time: *The car comes with a three-year warranty.*

watchful *adjective*

watching or observing someone or something closely; alert and vigilant: *They attended dances under the watchful eye of their father.*
Word family **watchfully** *adverb*: *stand watchfully by the door.* **watchfulness** *noun*

watershed *noun*

an event or period of time when an important change takes place: *The granting of the vote represented a watershed for the rights of women.*
Usage This is a figurative use of the word *watershed* meaning 'an area or ridge of land that separates waters flowing to different rivers, basins, or seas.'

wealth *noun*

a large amount of money and property that a person, organization, or country owns; the state of being rich: *She called for a redistribution of wealth and power in society.* □ *The purpose of industry is to create wealth.*
Word family **wealthy** *adjective* rich: *She comes from a very wealthy family.* □ *They live in a wealthy suburb of Chicago.* □ *He promised tax cuts for the wealthy* (= people who are wealthy).

weigh *verb*

1 to assess the nature or importance of, especially with a view to a decision or action: *The consequences of the move would need to be very carefully weighed.* **2** (**weigh against**) to compare the importance of one factor with that of another: *They need to weigh benefit against risk.* **3** to influence a decision or action; to be considered important: *The evidence weighed heavily against him.*

weight *noun, verb*

noun **1** the ability of someone or something to influence decisions or actions: *A recommendation by the committee will carry great weight.* **2** the importance attached to something: *Individuals differ in the weight they attach to various aspects of a job.* □ *verb* **1** to attach importance or value to: *Speaking, reading, and writing should be weighted equally in the assessment.* **2** (**be weighted**) to be planned or arranged so as to put a specified person, group, or factor in a position of advantage or disadvantage: *The balance of power is weighted in favour of the government.*
Usage In statistics, the word *weight* refers to a factor associated with one of a set of numerical quantities, used to represent its importance relative to the other members of the set.
Word family **weighting** *noun* **1** an allowance or adjustment made in order to take account of special circumstances or compensate for a

distorting factor. **2** an extra amount of wages or salary paid especially to allow for a higher cost of living in a particular area: *London weighting is payable.* **3** emphasis or priority: *they will give due weighting in quality as well as price.* **weighty** *adjective* **1** of great seriousness and importance: *He threw off all weighty considerations of state.* **2** having a great deal of influence on events or decisions.

welcoming *adjective*
pleased to welcome guests; generous and friendly to visitors: *He found the locals extremely welcoming.* □ *one of the most welcoming countries in the world.*

well disposed *adjective*
having a positive, sympathetic, or friendly attitude towards someone or something: *The company is well disposed to the idea of partnership.*
Usage When used before a noun, *well disposed* is hyphenated: *help from well-disposed friends.*

well founded *adjective*
(especially of a suspicion or belief) based on good evidence or reasons: *Their apprehensions were well founded.*
Usage When used before a noun, *well founded* is hyphenated: *well-founded fears.*

well known *adjective*
known widely or thoroughly: *a well-known television personality.* □ *His books are not well known.*
Usage When used before a noun, *well known* is hyphenated: *She's married to a well-known actor.*
Usage **well-known**, **celebrated**, **famous**, or **renowned**? See **celebrate**.

well reasoned *adjective*
supported by logic or good sense: *Her analysis was well reasoned.*
Usage When used before a noun, *well reasoned* is hyphenated: *clear and well-reasoned arguments.*

well researched *adjective*
being the result of a thorough systematic investigation: *His story lines are always well researched.*
Usage When used before a noun, *well researched* is hyphenated: *This is a well-researched and readable account.*

well written *adjective*
skilfully composed in a clear and elegant style: *The text book is comprehensive and well written.*
Usage When used before a noun, *well written* is hyphenated: *It is a thoroughly researched and well-written book.*

wholehearted *adjective*
complete and enthusiastic: *The plan was given wholehearted support.*
Word family **wholeheartedly** *adverb*: *I wholeheartedly agree with you.*
wholeheartedness *noun*: *the team spirit and wholeheartedness of this happy band of brothers.*

wide-ranging *adjective*
including or dealing with a large number of different subjects or areas: *The commission has been given wide-ranging powers.* □ *The activities stimulated a wide-ranging discussion.*
Usage Typical words that combine with *wide-ranging* are those relating to discussing things and those relating to change: *a wide-ranging debate/discussion/review.* □ *wide-ranging talks.* □ *wide-ranging reforms/changes/recommendations.*

widespread *adjective*
existing or happening over a large area or among many people: *The storm caused widespread damage.* □ *The decision met with widespread approval.* □ *The use of steroids was widespread in many sports.*

window *noun*
1 a means of observing and learning about something: *Television is a window on the world.* **2** an interval or opportunity for action: *The parliamentary recess offers a good window for a bid.*
Usage Some people object to the use of the phrase *window of opportunity*, meaning 'a favourable opportunity for doing something that must be seized immediately if it is not to be missed': *We now have a small window of opportunity in which to make our views known.*
Word family **window dressing** *noun* a skilful but superficial or misleading presentation of something, designed to create a favourable impression: *The government's effort has amounted to little more than window dressing.*

winning *adjective*
that wins or has won something, for example a race or competition: *Next week we will publish the winning entry in the short story competition.* □ *He scored the winning goal in the final.*
Word family **win-win** *adjective* referring to a situation in which each party benefits in some way: *We are aiming for a win-win situation.*

winsome *adjective*
attractive or appealing in appearance or character: *a winsome smile.* □ *a winsome personality.*
Word family **winsomely** *adverb*
winsomeness *noun*

wise *adjective*
1 (of people) able to make sensible decisions and give good advice because of the experience and knowledge that they have: *a wise old man.* □ *I'm older and wiser after ten years in the business.* **2** (of actions and behaviour) sensible; based on good judgement: *a wise decision.* □ *It was very wise to leave when you did.* □ *The wisest course of action is just to say nothing.* □ *I was grateful for her wise counsel.*
Word family **wisdom** *noun* **1** the ability to make sensible decisions and give good advice because of the experience and knowledge that you have: *a woman of great wisdom.* □ *words of wisdom.* **2** how sensible something is: *I question the wisdom of giving a child so much money.* **3** the knowledge that a society or culture has gained over a long period of time: *the collective wisdom of the Native American people.* □ *Conventional wisdom* (= the view that most people hold) *is that riots only ever happen in cities.* **wisely** *adverb*: *She nodded wisely.* □ *He wisely decided to tell the truth.*

world-class *adjective*
(of a person, thing, or activity) of or among the best in the world: *a world-class university.* □ *world-class athletes.*

W

Subject Index

Application letters
able
accomplish
accomplishment
accredited
accurate
achieve
active
adapt
admire
advance
advantage
advocate
affirm
aim
all-round
ambition
amenable
analyse
applicable
applied
apply
appoint
appreciate
approach
appropriate
apt
aptitude
arrange
artistic
aspire
assert
assertive
asset
assign
astute
audition
authentic
authoritative
authority
available
avid
aware
back
balance
basis
benefit
best
broaden
business
calibre
capable
capacity
certify
challenge
character
chief
choice

circumstance
claim
classify
clear
coach
coherent
cohort
colleague
combine
commend
commerce
commission
commit
communicate
competent
comprehensive
concise
condition
conducive
confident
confirm
conscientious
consider
consistent
consult
coordinate
creative
credential
dedicate
delegate
dependable
deserving
design
detail
determined
develop
devote
diligent
dynamic
effective
efficient
exact
experience
expert
fact
factor
factual
far-reaching
feasible
feat
feature
flair
flourish
fluent
focus
foresee
formative
forward-looking

foundation
framework
fresh
fruitful
fully-fledged
fundamental
generic
goal
highlight
honest
important
industrious
inform
initiative
integrity
intelligent
interpersonal
leader
leadership
major
methodical
meticulous
motivate
natural
opportune
organize
original
passionate
personality
portfolio
precise
presentation
professional
proficient
purpose
qualify
realm
recommend
recruit
relevant
reliable
renowned
represent
resourceful
responsible
rigorous
role
self-confident
self-motivated
self-starter
significant
skill
specialism
speciality
state
stature
steady
study

success
suitable
summary: *see*
  outline
support
technique
thorough
thrive
track record
train
transferable
underline
versatile
vocation

Attention, catching
abundant
acclaim
advice
advocate
affirm
alive
amaze
announce
apparent
appeal
applaud
approach
apt
ardent
arena
arrange
arrest
aspire
assert
assertive
asset
assure
astonish
astound
attention
attract
attractive
auspicious
authentic
authoritative
authority
available
avant-garde
aware
awe
back
basis
beautiful
beneficial
benefit
best
blend

Subject Index

significant
single-minded
skill
society
solve
sound
special
specific
specify
stage
stakeholder
state
stature
status
statutory
stimulus
strategy
strength
strong
substance
substantive
succeed
success
succinct
suitable
suite
supplement
supply
support
survey
sustain
synergy
system
tackle
tactic
talent
tangible
target
tender
test
thorough
thrive
timely
transferable
trend
turning point
unbiased
underline
underlying
underpin
undisputed
unique
unparalleled
urgent
venture
viable
vital
well disposed
well-known
well-reasoned
well-researched
well-written
wholehearted
wide-ranging
window

CVs
able
accomplish
accomplishment
accredited
accurate
achieve
active
adapt
admire
advance
advantage
adventure
advocate
affirm
aim
all-round
ambition
amenable
applicable
applied
apply
appoint
appreciate
approach
apt
aptitude
articulate
artistic
aspire
assert
asset
assiduous
astute
audition
authentic
authoritative
authority
available
avid
aware
balance
basic
benefit
best
broaden
business
calibre
capable
care
careful
certify
challenge
chief
choice
clear
clever
coach
cohort
colleague
combine
commerce
commit
communicate
competent

comprehensive
condition
confident
confirm
conscientious
consider
consistent
creative
credential
dedicate
delegate
dependable
determined
develop
devote
diligent
diplomatic
dynamic
efficient
enterprise
exact
excellent
experience
expert
facility
far-reaching
far-sighted
feasible
feat
flexible
flourish
fluent
focus
formative
forward-looking
framework
fresh
fruitful
fulfil
fully-fledged
fundamental
goal
health
incisive
independent
industrious
initiative
integrity
intelligent
interpersonal
leader
leadership
methodical
meticulous
natural
organize
outgoing
painstaking
personality
portfolio
precise
presentation
proactive
professional
proficient

qualify
range
recommend
relevant
reliable
represent
resourceful
responsible
rigorous
self-confident
self-motivated
self-starter
significant
skill
specialism
speciality
study
suitable
support
technique
thorough
track record
train
transferable
versatile
wide-ranging

Essays
accentuate
accessible
accurate
agree
amend
analogy
analyse
apparent
applicable
applied
apply
appreciate
approach
appropriate
apt
argue
aspect
assert
asset
associate
assume
authentic
authoritative
authority
axiom
back
balance
basic
basis
brief
careful
cause
central
centre
certain
chief
circumstance

well disposed
well-founded
well-known
well-reasoned
well-researched
well-written
wholehearted
wide-ranging
widespread
winsome
wise
world-class

Events, describing
abundant
accelerate
admire
anticipate
applicable
appropriate
arrange
ascertain
aspect
assure
avant-garde
award
balance
boom
bountiful
campaign
capacity
care
celebrate
character
chronicle
circumstance
classic
closure
commemorate
commentary
communicate
conducive
consider
contemporary
delight
dependable
descriptive
detail
discover
distinct
document
dramatic
emerge
encourage
enterprise
envision
evoke
exceptional
exciting
exhilarating
expressive
fact
factual
famous
fascinating
fashion

favour
feast
feature
fest
festival
fine
flavour
fluctuate
foil
foresee
forward-looking
foundation
fruitful
functional
galvanize
halcyon
harvest
herald
historic
idyllic
impact
implement
incomparable
individual
inescapable
inherent
interest
intrigue
landmark
leader
magnificent
memorable
modern
momentous
momentum
multi-purpose
notable
optimum
participate
phase
pleasurable
portrait
portray
precise
primary
purpose
remarkable
responsible
role
serendipity
showcase
significant
soothe
special
stage
state
stimulate
strategy
study
suitable
survey
thought-provoking
thrilling
tone
trace
turning point

typify
underlying
vantage point
voyage
watershed
well-known

Good qualities
able
accentuate
acclaim
accolade
accomplish
accomplishment
accredited
accurate
achieve
active
adapt
admire
advance
advantage
adventure
advocate
affinity
affirm
agree
alive
all-round
alternative
amaze
ambition
amenable
amend
amenity
analyse
animated
appeal
applaud
apply
appreciate
appropriate
approve
apt
aptitude
ardent
aroma
array
arrest
articulate
aspect
aspire
assertive
assess
asset
assiduous
assist
associate
assume
assure
astonish
astound
astute
atmosphere
attention
attract

attractive
audacious
augur
auspicious
authentic
authoritative
authority
avant-garde
avid
award
aware
awe
back
balance
beautiful
beneficial
benefit
best
blend
blessing
bliss
bloom
blossom
blue-chip
blueprint
boast
bold
bolster
bonus
boom
boost
bountiful
brave
breathtaking
bright
brilliant
broaden
budding
bullish
buoyant
business
calibre
calm
capable
capacity
captivate
care
careful
cascade
catalyst
celebrate
certain
challenge
champion
character
charisma
charm
cheerful
cherish
chief
choice
clarify
class
classic
clean
clear

politic
popular
positive
potential
practicable
practical
pragmatic
preferable
preference
premium
presentation
primacy
primary
priority
proactive
prodigious
professional
profound
progress
prominent
promise
promote
prompt
prospect
prospective
prosper
provoke
purpose
qualify
quintessential
radical
ramification
reality
realize
reason
receptive
recommend
refreshing
reinforce
relative
relevant
reliable
remarkable
renowned
represent
representative
reputable
reputation
resolute
resolve
resonance
resonate
responsive
reveal
revisit
revitalize
robust
satisfy
savour
self-motivated
seminal
sensitive
sentiment
serious
shrewd
significant

sincere
single-minded
solve
special
spectrum
stature
steadfast
stimulus
stoical
strength
striking
strong
substance
succeed
success
suitable
support
sustain
synergy
tactful
talent
tangible
tasteful
tenacious
thoughtful
thrive
tone
tradition
trenchant
trusted
ultimate
unbiased
underline
underlying
underpin
understand
undisputed
undoubted
unequivocal
unusual
uplifted
valid
validate
valuable
value
vehement
venture
vigilant
vigorous
vogue
watchful
well disposed
well-known
wholehearted
wide-ranging
winsome
wise

Places, describing
abundant
access
accessible
adventure
affinity
agenda
alive

ambition
amenity
appeal
aroma
aspect
associate
atmosphere
attract
attractive
aura
austere
autonomy
awe
base
bask
beautiful
bijou
blend
boast
bonus
bountiful
boutique
breathtaking
bright
buffer
calm
capacity
centre
centre
character
charm
cheerful
choice
clear
close
comfort
command
commemorate
community
compact
conducive
conspicuous
cosmopolitan
cosy
culture
delight
descriptive
detail
develop
discover
distinctive
distinguish
dramatic
elegant
enchant
enhance
ethnic
ethos
evoke
exciting
exclusive
exhilarating
explore
extraordinary
facelift
facility

famous
fascinating
fashion
favour
feature
festival
fine
flavour
flourish
focus
foil
fragrance
fresh
glory
grand
harmony
heart
heritage
hub
hygiene
ideal
identify
idyllic
image
imposing
impressive
indigenous
individual
interest
interface
intimate
intricate
majestic
memorable
milieu
modern
mosaic
multi-purpose
notable
observe
palpable
panorama
pastoral
picturesque
pioneer
plentiful
portrait
portray
prevalent
prominent
quality
quintessential
range
recognize
relaxed
remarkable
renowned
resonate
revitalize
revive
romance
sanctuary
scene
scent
secluded
select

self-contained
serene
showcase
significant
silhouette
smart
snug
splendid
stunning
suitable
symphony
tasteful
theme
tidy
trace
tradition
tranquil
treasure
unique
unspoilt
vantage point
varied
vibrant
visible
vista
vitality
vivacious
voyage
welcoming
well-known
widespread

Reports
able
abundant
accelerate
accentuate
accomplish
accomplishment
accurate
adjust
admire
advance
advantage
advice
advocate
affinity
affirm
agenda
agree
aim
alive
all-round
alter
ambition
analyse
announce
anticipate
apparent
applicable
applied
apply
approach
appropriate
apt

argue
arrange
ascertain
aspect
assert
assess
assiduous
associate
assume
authentic
authoritative
authority
authorization
authorize
autonomy
aware
back
balance
basic
basis
benchmark
beneficial
benefit
best
blueprint
bold
brief
broaden
bullish
buoyant
business
calculate
calibre
campaign
candid
capacity
careful
categorical
cater
cause
central
certain
character
choice
chronicle
circumstance
clarify
classify
clear
close
cocktail
code
coherent
combine
command
commend
comment
commentary
commerce
commission
commit
communicate
community
compare
compatible
compelling

complex
compliment
comprehensive
concise
conclude
concomitant
condition
conducive
confident
confirm
connect
connotation
consent
consequence
consider
consistent
consolidate
constructive
consult
contemporary
contour
contrast
coordinate
core
correlate
corroborate
cosmopolitan
cost-effective
creative
credible
criterion
critical
critique
crux
culture
debate
decisive
declare
definitive
dependable
design
detail
develop
dimension
discern
discover
discuss
display
distinct
distinctive
distinguish
diverse
document
dramatic
dynamic
effective
emerge
emphasis
empower
enhance
enjoy
enterprise
establish
ethnic
evaluate
exact

examine
exhaustive
expert
explain
facilitate
fact
factor
factual
fair
famous
far-reaching
far-sighted
fascinating
feasible
feature
fine
firm
flair
flexible
fluctuate
fluent
focus
formative
forum
forward-looking
foundation
framework
fresh
fruitful
fulfil
fulsome
functional
fundamental
generic
genre
germane
goal
guide
halcyon
harvest
heart
herald
highlight
high-profile
holistic
humane
identify
identity
illustrate
impact
impartial
impetus
implement
imply
important
improve
incentive
incisive
incomparable
incontrovertible
independent
in-depth
indispensable
indisputable
inescapable
inevitable

inexorable
influence
inform
inherent
initiative
innovation
insight
inspect
integrate
integrity
intensify
intention
interest
interpret
key
keynote
landmark
learning curve
legitimate
leverage
major
manage
mandatory
marginal
meaningful
measure
merge
methodical
milieu
minded
mobilize
model
moderate
modern
modest
modify
momentous
momentum
monitor
multifaceted
multi-purpose
mutual
negligible
notable
nucleus
objective
observe
operational
optimum
option
organize
outdo
outline
outstanding
overview
panorama
paradigm
parameter
participate
partner
pattern
permit
perspective
persuade
persuasive
phase

pinpoint
pivotal
plethora
poignant
pointed
popular
portfolio
portrait
portray
positive
potential
practicable
practical
praiseworthy
precise
predominant
preeminent
preferable
preference
preferred
premise
prerogative
presentation
prevalent
primacy
primary
prime
principal
priority
probity
productive
professional
profile
programme
progress
project
prominent
promote
prompt
propensity
prospective
provide
provision
prudent
purpose
quantify
radical
ramification
range
rapid
rational
realism
reality
realize
realm
reason
recognize
recommend
reinforce
relate
relative
relevant
reliable
remarkable
represent
representative

responsible
retain
reveal
review
revisit
rigorous
robust
role
safeguard
salient
sample
scope
scrupulous
scrutinize
seamless
secure
select
self-contained
selfless
self-motivated
seminal
serious
significant
simulate
society
solve
source
special
specialism
speciality
specific
specify
sphere
stabilize
stable
stage
stakeholder
standard
state
status
statutory
steady
stimulus
straightforward
strand
strategy
strength
strong
structure
study
substance
substantive
subtle
succeed
success
suitable
supplement
supply
survey
sustain
symbiosis
synthesis
system
tactic
target
task force

technique
technology
tenacious
tentative
test
theme
theoretical
thorough
thought-provoking
thrive
timely
tone
track record
transparent
treat
trenchant
trend
turning point
typify
unbiased
uncontested
underline
underlying
underpin
undisputed
undoubted
unequivocal
universal
unleash
unparalleled
update
urgent
valid
validate
varied
venture
verify
viable
vital
watershed
wealth
weigh
well disposed
well-founded
well-known
well-reasoned
well-researched
well-written
wide-ranging
widespread

Topics, discussing
accentuate
accessible
accomplishment
achieve
advance
advantage
advice
advocate
affinity
agree
aim
alive
all-round

analogy
analyse
announce
anticipate
appeal
applicable
approach
appropriate
approve
apt
arrange
ascertain
aspect
assert
assess
asset
associate
assume
assure
authentic
authoritative
authority
authorization
authorize
autonomy
avant-garde
aware
axiom
back
balance
basis
beneficial
benefit
best
blend
blueprint
bonus
broaden
campaign
candid
capacity
cascade
categorical
cater
cause
celebrate
central
certain
challenge
character
choice
chronicle
circumstance
clarify
classic
close
code
command
commend
comment
commentary
commission
communicate
compelling
complex
comprehensive

concise
conclude
condition
confirm
connect
consequence
consider
consistent
contrast
convince
correlate
corroborate
crux
decisive
declare
detail
develop
dimension
discern
discover
distinct
distinctive
distinguish
diverse
document
dramatic
dynamic
effective
empower
enhance
enthral
establish
evaluate
exact
examine
exhaustive
expert
explain
fact
factor
factual
fair
far-reaching
far-sighted
fascinating
favour
feasible
feast
feature
fine
firm
flexible
flourish
fluent
focus
foil
forum
forward-looking
foundation
framework
fresh
fruitful
functional
fundamental
generic
germane

goal
guide
hallmark
horizon
identify
illustrate
imply
important
improve
incisive
incomparable
in-depth
indispensable
individual
inescapable
inevitable
influence
inform
initiative
interest
interpret
key
learning curve
leverage
major
marginal
measure
memorable
modern
motif
multifaceted
multi-purpose
objective
organize
outline
overview
panorama
par excellence
parameter
participate
pattern
platform
pointed
positive
prevalent
primacy
priority
prominent
provoke
purpose
ramification
range
realize
realm
reason
relevant
reliable
remarkable
represent
representative
rigorous
safeguard
scope
self-contained
seminal
significant

simulate
smooth
solve
special
spectrum
sphere
spirit
state
stature
strand
strategy
strength
style
substance
subtle
suitable
survey
symbol
system
tackle
test
thorough
thrive
trenchant
typify
underlying
undoubted
unleash
vantage point
varied
variety
venture
wide-ranging
widespread

Products or services
abundant
accelerate
accessible
acclaim
accolade
accomplish
accomplishment
accredited
accurate
achieve
adapt
adjust
admire
advance
advantage
adventure
amaze
anticipate
appeal
apply
approach
apt
aroma
array
arrest
asset
associate
astonish
astound